Women

A CENTURY OF LIFESTYLE, FASHION, WORK AND PLAY

Maureen Hill

Photographs

ATLANTIC PUBLISHING

Introduction

The last 100 years has seen immense change socially, technologically, and in virtually every sphere of life — and one of the most significant of these has been in the role of women in society. Women have won many legal and political rights since 1900 when they had no vote, were classed with children in most employment law and could not divorce a husband for adultery, even though evidence of her adultery was sufficient grounds for a husband to divorce a wife.

Women: A Century of Lifestyle, Fashion, Work and Play chronicles the lives of ordinary women as well as those whose achievements made them famous, dealing with protests and campaigns along with timeless themes such as marriage and money, health and housing, hairstyles and hats.

For more than one hundred years the *Daily Mail* has featured a 'women's page' mirroring many aspects of the changes in women's lives. Accompanying the informative text, a selection of extracts and facsimile pieces from these newspaper pages offers a fascinating insight into the contemporary view of what might attract the attention of female readers — whether advice as to how to iron out wrinkles on the forehead, choosing the perfect billiard cue, how to whitewash a ceiling, the damaging effects of Valium or the perennial subject of advice on matters of the heart.

More than 500 photographs, ranging from rare images of the Suffragettes at the beginning of the 20th century, through women at war, the heady days of the sexual revolution in the swinging 60s, as well as those who play a starring role on the world stage today, illustrate the milestones in women's history, as well as the fads and fashions that formed a part of daily life.

Women: A Century of Lifestyle, Fashion, Work and Play charts all aspects of women's lives, from housework and hemlines to the fight for equal pay and opportunity.

CONTENTS

The Century Opens

Despite the fact that 1900 was the 61st year of Queen Victoria's reign, women in Britain and throughout her far-flung empire had benefited in only a small measure from having a woman in so prominent a position. In fact, the Victorian era had seen the cultivation and acceptance of a curious paradox about the nature of women. While society and science nurtured the beliefs that they were less intelligent and weaker both physically and emotionally than men, women were also revered and elevated for their sensitivity and feminine virtue. Women, or at least those of the middle- and upper-class, had to be protected and cosseted from the brutal realities of the world. Such beliefs, held by women as well as men, meant many of the iniquities and inequalities, such as the denial of voting rights, could be justified on the grounds either that women were incapable of understanding or that they would be tainted by the experience.

However, during the latter half of the nineteenth century there had grown a feminist movement in Britain, with women such as Sophia Jex Blake, Josephine Butler, Millicent Fawcett, Emmeline Pethick-Lawrence and many others. The cause of women's emancipation took much of its inspiration from the eighteenth-century thinker Mary Wollstonecraft. Her book *A Vindication of the Rights of Woman*, published in 1792, claimed women were equal to men and had caused much controversy.

By 1900 women had made some gains both legally and socially in that wives were no longer regarded as their husbands' property to the same extent as they had been in 1800. But many of the gains were offset by other judgements. In 1870 women lost the right to retain their British citizenship when they married a foreigner. And as late as 1899 a court ruled in a case brought to trial that a man could not be found guilty of raping his wife if she refused to have sex with him, even if he was suffering from a disease (presumably venereal disease) of which he was aware but she was not.

As the century opened, in every sphere of life – education, employment, marriage, finance, legal and political rights, inheritance, social status – women had a long way to go before they could be said to be equal to men.

LOOKING BACKWARDS.

Early Fashions Revived for Mourning.

The very simplest evening dresses for the home circle only, are now being made, and the dressmakers are mounting pin-spotted net upon silk for the purpose. Two illustrations of its efficacy are shown in this column. In one, beneath a soft cloud of black tulle, an embroidered white crêpe bolero and sleeves

A Simple and Effective Evening Gown.

in combination appear, and in the other all the trimming given the gown is gauging, with bunches of black and white violets on ribbon ends hanging from the décolletage.
Three-quarter length coats are truly elegant when well made and worn by the tall and graceful. The one sketched of crêpe cloth has an ermine collar and pair of cuffs upon it; it is lined with white satin and banded thrice across the front with black satin bars held by satin buttons. Military notions and ideas are being very much exploited in mourning modes. A picture in the last column shows handsome jet and silk cord frogs upon a little tightly-fitting bodice of the coat persuasion sharply pointed in front. White braid lace is very effective upon a background of black or grey chiffon or satin, with a vivid contrast of black satin ribbon, and as a sketch in our fourth column will prove, it can be applied to a house gown of black cloth with excellent results, or of grey, when grey becomes possible as a mourning fabric. Picture millinery is prevailing at present; it is so much more becoming than the toque when a complete mass of effective black is wanted.

Above: Lady Sarah Wilson, who became the first woman war correspondent when she sent dispatches back to the *Daily Mail* from South Africa during the Second Boer War.

Left above: A middle-class family pictured at home amongst the trappings of their wealth.

Left below: Ladies in their finery rest in the shade at Ascot races in 1907.

Opposite top left: Working class women shop at a market in south London.

Opposite top right: A group of young Edwardians at Scarborough. A day at the seaside once or twice a year was something many of the working class could afford.

Opposite: Piccadilly Circus in 1900.

Women at Work

In 1901 there were few opportunities for women to earn money and mostly theirs were poorly paid, low-status jobs. Even where a woman entered a profession, the very fact that she was female deprived her of the respect granted a male colleague. Although the 1901 Census revealed that there were 212 women doctors, two architects and a few women clerks and assistants in the legal, banking and insurance worlds, many professions were still closed to women. At the beginning of 1901, eighteen-year-old Margaret Hall had found a solicitor in Scotland willing to have her articled to him but was awaiting a High Court order granting her permission to sit for an entrance exam.

Of the three and a half million women in paid employment, 50 per cent were confined to jobs in domestic service. In certain areas of the country a tradition of female factory workers had developed and the textile industry alone employed more than half a million women who, despite being highly skilled, were paid low wages.

As purveyors of education the governesses of the nineteenth century remained, but more women were turning to teaching as a means of finding better rewards for their skills – although not rewards equal to those of a man in the same job.

Nursing had begun to attract 'respectable' women after the tireless efforts of Florence Nightingale and others and in 1901 there were 68,000 nurses in Britain.

In 1901, 29 per cent of the workforce were women and most were single. Only 10 per cent of married women worked outside the home. The convention was that a man should earn enough to keep his wife and family and, apart from a few areas such as textiles where a different tradition had developed, it was a source of shame for a wife to work outside the home. That is not to say that the woman at home led a life of leisure. For the servanted classes time did hang heavy on the hands of the women, but for the great majority of women life was a never-ending drudgery trying to feed and clean for, and give birth to, large families.

Legal Rights

During the second half of the nineteenth century women had been granted some rights in law, but many laws only emphasised the inequality of treatment of men and women. A man could divorce an adulterous wife but a woman could not divorce her husband just for adultery, she also had to prove cruelty, desertion, bigamy or incest. Custody of the children in any divorce or separation was invariably granted to the father, although laws in the nineteenth century had undermined the father's automatic right to custody. Once divorced a woman had few means of supporting herself. For most women at the beginning of the century, lack of money resulted in a dependence on men.

It was less than 20 years since the Married Women's Property Act gave wives the same rights as husbands over their own property but as few daughters inherited, few women, married or single, had property over which to have rights. The vast majority of women had no money and no right to any money. Unless they brought their own money and property to the marriage, everything legally belonged to the husband.

A husband was also legally responsible for any crimes his wife might commit in his presence. The assumption being that women only did, and were expected to do, their husbands' bidding and were incapable of autonomy of action when with them.

Left: Mrs Pankhurst being carried by a policeman from outside Buckingham Palace in the early years of the WSPU campaign.

Left: Millicent Fawcett pictured in 1928, shortly before she attended the House of Commons to hear the Royal Assent for the Bill to give women equal voting rights with men, more than 60 years after she had first become committed to the cause.

Right: Emmeline Pankhurst (centre) leads women in a suffrage demonstration.

Opposite: Women working in Early's blanket factory, Witney, Oxfordshire, 1897.

The Women's Social and Political Union

In 1897 Millicent Fawcett, sister of Elizabeth Garrett Anderson, one of the first women doctors, formed the National Union of Women's Suffrage Societies. This brought together under a national umbrella all the associations that had fought for votes for women. The various groups had achieved some successes in the last quarter of the nineteenth century, gaining the vote for women householders in local elections and the right for women to be elected to Boards of Guardians, the bodies which administered the Poor Laws. They had also agitated for, and won, a change to the London Government Act which barred married women from membership of the Metropolitan Borough Councils. The National Union of Women's Suffrage Societies campaigned, as had its individual member societies before it, for constitutional change, but despite the aforementioned limited successes no woman in Britain had the power to elect anyone to a legislative assembly. In fact, in 1903, the only women in the world with those rights were the those of New Zealand and Australia.

In 1903 a group of women in Manchester founded the Women's Social and Political Union (WSPU). Their leader was Mrs Emmeline Pankhurst, a long-time campaigner for female suffrage and a widowed mother of five. She had been elected a Poor Law Guardian in 1895, and said her experiences there convinced her to think of 'the vote in women's hands as not only a right but as a desperate necessity'. Mrs Pankhurst's and the WSPU's motto was 'Deeds, not Words' and they chose to follow a militant course, pestering politicians and seeking publicity for their campaign to gain voting rights for women.

WOMEN WHO HAVE FOUND NEW PROFESSIONS.

WHEN women set themselves to make incomes they do not invariably invade professions peopled by men; such as the medical, in which, as at Burnley the other day, they have met many rebuffs.

Shrewd enough are the cleverest among them to grasp the fact that a new calling when successfully engineered has more chances of becoming highly lucrative than an old one; hence of late there have been several prosperous callings invented by women workers.

One clever young lady, for instance, has discovered that there is a wide field in designing pottery, especially those knick-knacks that are known as "uglies." Miss Vulliamy, the lady-potter in question, not merely designs vases, tobacco-jars, and the like, but in common-sense fashion sells them at good prices. Her dainty little studio in Kensington is a splendid object-lesson in the go-ahead spirit which imbues the " new woman"—in the best sense of that ill-used term.

Her Majesty the Queen has shown her appreciation of Miss Vulliamy's art by purchasing a selection of her vases.

A lucrative employment for women with a love for travel is that of personally conducting sketching parties of girl students to all parts of England and the Continent.

In such centres of concentrated beauty as Sark and the other Channel Islands, Brittany, Italy, and Switzerland, these parties may frequently be met. Girl artists are proverbially feckless beings whose souls soar above the mundane; therefore the mana-geress of such bands must be a good commander, and able to plan routes and smooth away all the difficulties of travel. The pupils are personally conducted to the scene of their labours, and there, grouped in most picturesquely unstudied clusters, seated on portable camp-stools, their easels in front of them, and sheltered by large umbrellas, they paint each one her view of the subject before her. In the winter snow-sketching parties under the tutelage of a lady conductress are taken to Switzerland and elsewhere, and there temporary wind screens are erected to shield the painters.

So successful have these conducted art tours been that the originator is likely to have many imitators.

It required the innate instinct of a woman to see that a violet farm ought to pay, and pay well.

Until lately the south of France and the vicinity of Paris supplied the florists with violets, but lately ladies have taken to farming the lovely blossom, and particu-larly in Ireland, where the air is mild and moist, have found their enterprise prosper.

There is a violet farm at Cork, the property of Mrs. Egerton Coghill, where in a field sheltered from rude blasts there are acres of violets all a-growing and a-blowing. Mrs. Egerton Coghill affects principally the lovely Princess of Wales violet, the Czar, and Devoniensis.

The method of violet culture is simple. The "runners," of which 16,000 are required to cover one acre of ground, are purchased at prices ranging from about £3 10s. per 1,000 to £4, and are planted in the months of February and March. In the winter season, when there is a scarcity of violets, as much as 1s. 10d. is given in public auction for a nosegay of eight dozen blooms. But the supply is often much inferior to the demand, so the prospect looks promising for more cultivators.

There is now in London a German lady, Fräulein Wilke, who has founded a college for training girls to become tutors in physical exercise. Her pupils are all between the ages of eighteen and twenty-five. Each one of these healthy, graceful girls is learning to be a gymnastic professor on her own account. It is claimed that at present the demand for certificated exponents of the art-science of physical training is so great that salaries ranging from £100 and in exceptional cases to much higher sums are obtainable as soon as the pupil has qualified.

Repoussé work (embossing and ornamenting copper and silver in relief) has two great advantages. The artistic work is growing more and more popular, and the most delicate girl can undertake it.

1900s Postscripts

1900: The 1899 London Government Act was amended to allow married women to be members of Metropolitan Borough Councils. Initially the Act had excluded them.

March 1900: Women in Germany petitioned the Reichstag for the right to sit state examinations and attend university.

March 1900: The government in France limited the hours women and children were allowed to work to eleven. In Britain, too, employment legislation invariably placed women and children in the same category, as in the 1848 Factory Act which limited their working hours to ten per day and the 1842 Mines and Collieries Act which barred them from working underground.

May-Oct 1900: The second Olympic Games was held in Paris with women competing for the first time. They had been barred in 1896.

January 1901: The death of Queen Victoria.

May 1901: Norway enfranchised some women taxpayers for local elections.

July 1901: Charlotte Sterry won the Ladies' Championship at Wimbledon for the second year running. She was reigning Olympic Champion, having won at the 2nd Olympiad held in Paris in 1900.

Educating Girls

By the beginning of the twentieth century some strides had been made in education for women and girls. The 1870 Education Act provided for elementary education for both boys and girls and also allowed women to sit on the School Boards responsible for carrying out the provisions of the Act. However, while girls were taught the three Rs, the elementary school curriculum for girls also included cookery, hygiene, laundry work, sewing and infant care lessons. This was especially so after 1904 when a report on the poor state of the nation's health, revealed when trying to recruit soldiers to serve in the Second Boer War, blamed not poverty, poor housing, bad diet and lack of medical facilities but low standards of housewifery and mothering.

In 1900 there were a number of secondary schools for girls but even they devoted time to educating their pupils in domestic skills. Some, like the North London Collegiate School and Cheltenham Ladies' College, were for the daughters of the wealthy. Girls from the middle classes whose parents wished a secondary education for them would usually attend a Girls' Public Day School. These schools often offered scholarships to pupils whose parents could not afford the fees, but as books, uniforms and other items had to be paid for secondary education was out of reach for very many girls.

Attitudes to education for girls were changing, but while the idea was fading that an education would hamper a girl's chances of marriage, a new rationale had taken its place: elementary schools educated poor girls to be good wives, mothers and domestic servants, and secondary schools turned out more educated and accomplished wives for the rich and middle classes, or women who could earn a respectable living if they failed to marry. Many of the women providing the education fought this rationale but it was there nonetheless.

Higher or university education for women was rare – there were women's colleges at both Oxford and Cambridge but while the women could attend lectures they were not allowed to sit for degrees. The Scottish universities, London University and some of the English provincial universities did award degrees to women but there were very few female students.

There were arguments that women were not suited to higher education and indeed many of these arguments were exactly those used against the education of girls in earlier centuries – namely that education damaged their health, fertility and attractiveness to possible suitors. The *Daily Mail* in July 1904 reported on a paper delivered by an American doctor which claimed that the health of American women was endangered by higher education because excessive education took blood to the brain and away from other parts of the body which then became diseased. He also claimed that highly educated women had fewer and weaker children.

WHY WOMEN FAIL

To the Editor of the Daily Mail:
The great number of women who are now finding their way into professions formerly monopolised by men must not be taken as an indication that women have really made up their mind that a life of toil is the highest feminine idea.

At heart the majority of women detest all work other than that connected with the home, which to them is only a labour of love.

This latent desire for the sheltered ease of home life accounts, in my opinion as a woman, for the surprisingly small number of feminine successes in directions which demand originality of mind and sustained mental or physical effort.

BA (Lond.)
Daily Mail, 14 May 1903

Playtime Story
FOR THE LITTLE ONES.
No. 116.

APRIL 7.—Queen Victoria had quite a number of boys and girls of her own, and her eldest girl was known as the Princess Royal of England. She was awfully proud to have that title, and I do believe she thought herself the most important little girl in the world.

Like all her brothers and sisters, she had a little garden of her own, and one day she was putting in some plants when her mother, the Queen, came to watch her.

Now, what do you think? If the little Princess Royal had not on a pair of quite *new* kid gloves, to protect her hands from the dirt!

Her mother did not like that, of course, so she said, "When I was a little girl, I always did my gardening in old gloves."

"Yes, mother," replied the little girl, tossing her head proudly. "but you weren't born Princess Royal of England!"

Above left: Some of the girls' public schools echoing the philosophy of boys' public schools included rigorous exercise on the curriculum.

1900s Postscripts

February 1902: An Imperial Decree in China abolished the practice of binding the feet of female children, although the practice was to continue for some years.

May 1902: The government of Prussia, the principal region of Germany, denied women the right to form political associations, a ban which lasted until 1908 when the central German government, the Reichstag, lifted it.

October 1902: The *Daily Mail* reported a proposal that lady correspondents should indicate whether they are married or not, perhaps with an M if married and S if single after their name, so that any reply could be properly addressed.

October 1903: The Women's Social and Political Union is founded in Manchester by Emmeline Pankhurst, her daughters Christabel and Sylvia a small group of like-minded women.

December 1903: Marie Curie became the first woman to win a Nobel Prize when, together with her husband Pierre and Henri Becquerel, she was awarded the prize for Physics.

November 1904: A large increase in the numbers of people in receipt of poor relief was reported. In 1904 there were about 250,000 people in workhouses and more than 500,000 receiving aid without having to go into the workhouse. Women formed a very high percentage of those receiving poor relief.

Above : A church parade in Hyde Park, 1912.

Below: Folkestone 1910. Even when at the seaside there was no overlooking any breaches in propriety.

Right and below: Elaborate fashions on display in the Royal Enclosure, Ascot, in 1909. Ascot was one of the most exclusive events in the social calendar.

Men Hold the Purse Strings

On 8 August 1905 the *Daily Mail* carried an article quoting a report in the magazine *Good Housekeeping* that three out of four housewives must beg for money from their husbands. The *Mail* article pointed out that such a situation must obviously lead to marital difficulties and asked husbands to imagine how they would feel had they to beg for money from a relative.

While there were such pleas for understanding of women's financial position and for generous behaviour from men, there was no belief that a woman had any right to money from her husband. A husband was supposed to support his family and whatever money he chose to give his wife was the only money she had, unless she was one of the ten per cent of married women who earned money. The Married Women's Property Act of 1882 had given married women the same rights over their own property as single women, but if a woman saved money from the housekeeping money given to her by her husband it still legally belonged to him.

This meant that she could only spend money on things approved by her husband.

There was no entitlement to any allowance from the State and it was to be another 12 years before Eleanor Rathbone was to make her call for family allowances. Any support for poor families came from the Poor Laws, the administrators of which handed out money after a means test or forced the family into the workhouse.

The workhouse or Poor Law relief was frequently the only recourse for women with children whose husbands failed to support them. A man might be unemployed or squander his wages or simply desert his family. A report in 1909 found a 33 per cent increase in the desertion of wives and blamed it on higher living costs. It was possible for wives to sue for maintenance if they were deserted. However, a loophole which meant the husband did not have to pay maintenance when in jail was an option pursued by some.

Sportswomen

Throughout September 1902 the *Daily Mail* had carried a great deal of correspondence on the linked subjects of women, beauty, health, exercise and sport following an article by a Mr H. B. Marriot Watson. Mr Marriot Watson argued in his article that the increasing vogue for women to take exercise or play some sport would only create gaunt, flat-chested women who would be weak and prone to illness. Many letters totally refuted Mr Marriot Watson's idea and spoke of the benefits of exercise to women's health and beauty. Other correspondents clung to the notion that it was ladylike to be rather frail and claimed that a woman's feminine grace was damaged by sport, while one woman suggested that the only exercise a woman need take was to sweep the house from top to bottom each day.

In 1906 the Physical Director at Harvard University suggested that sports such as lacrosse, hockey and netball might be physically damaging to women and girls. Sport was more widely participated in by both sexes in the USA, although the curriculum of many British girls' secondary schools and colleges included sport. Elizabeth Garrett Anderson had suggested some form of exercise in girls' schools as an antidote to the objection that girls' health suffered from too much study.

However, many of the arguments against education for girls were transposed to women and sport. It was said sport would damage their health and, more crucially, damage their chances of having children, which in a country like Britain with an Empire to people and run would be a severe problem if it could be proved true. Even cycling was cited as dangerous, but whether that was because of the exertion involved or the unladylike clothing and posture required for riding is unclear.

Above: A day at the seaside, Hove, circa 1900 :

Left: British champion Dorothea Lambert Chambers won the Wimbledon Singles title seven times between 1903 and 1914 – while wearing stiff petticoats and a corset.

Below: A riding habit, with fashionable nipped-in waist, circa 1900.

NEW SPRING SALADS.
Dainty Recipes Worth Trying at Home.

AS every spring comes round the craving is a natural one for the wholesome salad, and now a day's vegetables, nuts, and fruit are combined in such unusual and amusing ways that they quite repay the study of the epicure.

The following recipes, which are new and original and culled from various sources, have been tried and pronounced excellent:—

TOMATO SURPRISE.

Cut in halves round, even tomatoes, but do not peel them. Scoop out the inside and fill with small dice of cucumber, well salted and mixed with mayonnaise. Make the tops even, spread with a coating of mayonnaise. Lay two anchovies crossed on top and serve on lettuce.

ROQUEFORT CHEESE SALAD.

Separate slightly a white head of lettuce that has been dried after it has been laid in ice water. Arrange among the leaves some bits of Roquefort cheese, using two tablespoonfuls to a head of lettuce. Surround the whole with watercress and pour over it French dressing. Serve wafers of thinnest toast with this. Asparagus, always excellent in salad, should be served very cold. It is good merely cooked and covered with a dressing, and is better in combination with cucumber.

RICE SALAD.

To two cupfuls of carefully boiled rice take one cupful of deep-red beets, finely chopped, and one cupful of chopped celery. Do not mix together until just before dressing, then combine with a French dressing and serve in cup form on blanched lettuce leaves.

them until they coil, instead of breaking. When tender, drain and stand in a bowl of cold water until ready to use, and then dry on a cloth. Cut into inch pieces, sprinkle with a French dressing and let stand about half an hour. Cut three hard-boiled eggs lengthwise into quarters. Wash and dry a head of escorol or lettuce and arrange it on a platter.

Heap on the macaroni and arrange the quartered eggs in a circle round the base. Pour over the French dressing and serve.

GRAPE FRUIT SALAD.

Good with duck and wild duck. Carefully cut out the quarters from a large grape fruit, and with a sharp knife or scissors remove all pith. Pour a French dressing over the fruit and the finest of chopped parsley.

CHEESE ICE SALAD.

Take one pint of cream cheese, mash until perfectly smooth. It is best to mash it through a fine sieve. Add one quart of rich cream; put into a freezer and freeze like any other ice.

Lay five lettuce leaves on individual plates. Put a small cheese ice the shape of a heart in the centre of a circle of leaves on each plate, and sprinkle all over with finely chopped walnut meats and a little pepper and salt.

Eat with thin brown bread and butter or slices of thin pumpernickel—i.e., German black bread.

TOMATO ICE SALAD.

Cook a quart of tomatoes soft; strain and season with salt, grated lemon peel, a little grated nutmeg and sugar and paprika. Freeze until firm, preferably in round apple-shaped moulds.

Put each ice in a crisp lettuce leaf, pour mayonnaise over, lastly some chopped olives, and serve at once.

Family Planning

In the 1900s the birth rate in Britain continued the fall begun in the late 1870s. In 1876 it was 36 per 1,000 of the population; in 1901, 28.6 per 1,000; and in 1905, 27.2 per 1,000.

In 1877 Annie Besant and Charles Bradlaugh were prosecuted for publishing 'obscene material'. The material in question was information on methods of birth control, which was priced to enable working-class women to purchase it. The middle classes had had access to this knowledge for a few years and their family sizes, when matched against the families of the poorer classes not infrequently numbering 12 or more, indicate that at the end of the nineteenth century they were putting that knowledge into practice. Fewer years spent pregnant and fewer children gave middle-class women time and energy to turn their attention to issues and pastimes outside the home, be it charities to help the poor, sport,

politics or the campaign for the emancipation of women. It is interesting to note that most of the suffragettes were middle-class women.

Methods of birth control available in 1907 were withdrawal, injections of alum and water, the vaginal sponge soaked in quinine, quinine pessaries, the sheath, and the Dutch cap which had been invented in Holland in the 1870s. Although it was against the law to disseminate information about birth control, some people did gain some knowledge. Many of these methods had been known throughout the world for centuries but in Britain few people had any idea of them before the last quarter of the nineteenth century. Prior to that, infanticide and abortion were the only real options in family limitation, and remained so for many poorer women.

A large family group assembled on the sand dunes, circa 1900.

1900s Postscripts

May 1905: As supporters of women's suffrage gathered outside Parliament, the Enfranchisement Bill proposed by Bamford Slack was 'talked out' without a vote.

October 1905: Christabel Pankhurst, oldest of Emmeline's five children, and Annie Kenney were the first suffragettes to be imprisoned when they refused to pay their fines imposed for assaulting a policeman at a political meeting.

November 1905: Universal suffrage was granted in Austria.

December 1905: Austrian Bertha von Suttner was awarded the Nobel Peace Prize.

February 1906: The *Daily Mail* published an article entitled 'Shall Women Have the Vote?' by a Dr Emil Reich. In his article he claimed women should not have the vote, not on the grounds of intelligence or fairness, grounds on which he admitted they did have a claim,

but on the grounds that women knew nothing of politics and if they had the vote, logically they would have to be able to be MPs, a role for which they were eminently unsuited. But Dr Reich did not believe that women should have to stick to the kitchen. He thought they should go into Civil Service jobs to free men, especially university-educated men, at home and in the Empire for the work which their mentality and character more suited them.

Opposite above left and upper centre: Proof that the idea of airbrushing images of women is not new. These images artificially exaggerate the effect of a corset to create the desired wasp-waist.

Opposite above right: Outfits were often accessorised with elaborately trimmed hats.

Opposite below left: A vest and drawers protect the delicate skin from the stiff whalebone corset.

Opposite below centre: Society ladies attend the Eton v Harrow cricket match at Lord's in 1906.

Opposite below right: Wealthy women 'dressed for dinner'. This evening dress emphasises the fashionable wasp waist and the curve of the hips and bust with the use of a corset, petticoats, lace and ruffles.

Above: A pretty parasol and wide-brimmed hat are protection against the sun at Ascot in 1913. The London Season ran from February to July and allowed wealthy women the opportunity to parade the clothes they had bought in Paris at places such as the Opera at Covent Garden, the Royal Drawing Rooms as well as at private balls – and, of course, the Royal Enclosure at Ascot.

Right: At the beginning of the decade, skirts trailed to the floor and although bustles had almost disappeared, clothes were still heavy and restrictive.

1900s Postscripts

April 1906: The Independent Labour Party called for female suffrage and Labour MP Keir Hardy had a motion in favour of votes for women 'talked out' in the House of Commons.

However the Labour Party's attitude to female enfranchisement was ambiguous. As there were a number of poorer male workers who still did not have the vote they felt that it was in some respects wrong to fight to enfranchise what they believed would be a group of mainly upper- and middle-class women.

June 1906: The results of a census in the USA showed that of 303 occupations, women worked in 300 of them, ranging from blacksmiths to architects, undertakers to journalists, barbers to house painters. The *Daily Mail* reported it under the title 'Queer Trades For Women'.

November 1906: Keir Hardy introduced another Bill for Female Suffrage which failed.

December 1906: Suffragettes in Holloway Prison refused to eat Christmas Dinner.

January 1907: The *Daily Mail* published a fulsome obituary of Josephine Butler, who had campaigned vigorously in the 1860s for the repeal of the Contagious Diseases Acts which meant that any woman in an army or naval town suspected of being a prostitute could be imprisoned and medically examined, forcibly if necessary, for signs of venereal disease. The

The Female Form

Much of the debate about 'athletic women' concerned how it would affect their physique. The flat chests and thinness said to result from the taking of exercise were frowned upon in Edwardian Britain. What was admired were full bosoms and bottoms and a certain plumpness which suggested that a woman was well nourished and consequently well provided for by the men of the family.

Clothing and fashion emphasised the bust and bottom. Corsets pulled in the waist, which accentuated the bosom, and the fashion for bustles made the bottom another focus of attention. Fashion further dictated a pale skin unaided by any form of cosmetics, which meant women had to shelter from the sun either by staying out of it or under parasols.

A pale skin, and the voluminous and heavy clothes and corsets which women from all walks of life wore, were in themselves a way of limiting women's lives. It was very difficult to move freely, let alone run, play games or take part in many outdoor activities in tight corsets, wearing clothes weighing more than ten times that of women's clothing today and having constantly to shade the face from the sun.

Even poorer women followed the general fashion trends although with perhaps only one or two outfits, nowhere near as many as a wealthy woman might have in her wardrobe. Rather in the way children dress dolls, women from the upper and middle classes, who had servants to run their homes, would spend their days changing from one outfit to another depending on the time of day, the season, the proposed activity and whether they were in the town or the country.

Above: An old-fashioned nosegay is the finishing touch to this Directoire costume – sometimes called an incroyable coat – with it's wide lapels.

Below right: Hair pieces were often used to create elaborate hairstyles, on top of which sat elaborately trimmed, wide-brimmed hats.

Above: Teacher Elsa Myres was expedient in restricting her activism to the school holidays. When her school was closed for a month in 1913 she smashed a window at the War Office and was subseqently imprisoned for a month. However, Myres was released just in time to return to work and her crime was not discovered by the school.

WHAT WOMEN WANT

Many people are still under the impression that we claim the vote for every woman, but this is not the case. On the contrary our demand is the essentially moderate one that women occupying a position and fulfilling the responsibilities equal to those of a male voter shall be placed on the roll of electors. Are married women to vote? is a frequent enquiry, to which our reply is that we do not expect to obtain votes for married women unless they happen to have a distinct qualification of their own. If the house is taken in the husband's name he will have the vote; if it is in the wife's name she will have the vote.

*Extracts from an article by
Christabel Pankhurst
Daily Mail, 13 June 1908*

Beauty's Secrets from a Beauty's Boudoir.

† Let your forehead remain immobile and calm, so avoid furrows on it. Try to express nothing by your forehead. Do that by means of speech. Try the following recipe handed down to us from our grandmother. Melt some white wax slowly. Then dip a cloth in it until it is thoroughly covered by the wax. Bind this cloth around the forehead on going to bed at night and it will iron out the wrinkles. Be careful to have the forehead smooth when you put the bandage on, or you may iron in the wrinkles.

† The hair should be thoroughly cleaned not oftener than twice a month but this does not mean that it should necessarily be washed. Blonde hair, which is delicate and inclined to break easily, should be wetted as little as possible. Wheareas the brunette may use water or a prepared shampoo. If you are blonde take the grease out with a powder.

† Be out in the fresh air, but keep the air from your face. Wear veils, use powder, and protect the skin with a layer of good cold cream.

† Do you ever cry? Being a woman, I suppose you do. It is a foolish practice for though it may relieve the pent up feelings, it inflames the lids and makes the eyes look heavy and dim.

† Nothing can be more disagreeable to a dainty woman than to have hands that are unbearably moist. Rub the palms of your hands several times a day with a bit of linen dipped in the following preparation: seventy parts of eau de cologne and fifteen of tincture of belladonna, and before putting on your gloves plunge your hands, just for an instant, into water mixed with allum.

Daily Mail, 1905

EVENING AND DAY-TIME MILLINERY.

A Charming Butterfly and Rose Head-dress.

The battle concerning the enormous hats with their wealth of plumage, worn by so many women in Paris at the theatres, is reaching a stage that is acute. In vain do the milliners hold before the eyes of the majority of their customers millinery models that will not obstruct the view of those who sit behind them at the play. There are still not a few who insist upon wearing ostrich feathers and aigrettes that prove almost a complete barrier to the view of the stage.

And yet there are head-dresses that are very becoming and that have been specially planned by the milliners for appearance at the theatres. One is made merely of tea-roses, which lightly rest upon the coiffure, decorated at the back with a very large black and white butterfly, fragile in appearance, thoroughly decorative, and altogether most charming. The wings of the pretty papillon are purposely bent downwards, so that while sufficient height is given to the head-dress to make it look smart, there is no chance of its distracting the eye of the theatre-goer or of proving a barrier to his enjoyment.

Another theatre head-dress is simply made of a rosette of mole-coloured velvet with a long grey ostrich feather arranged at the back of it, not with tantalising height, but so as to embrace the hair and look compact and neat.

Such head-dresses as these are in vogue in London for restaurant wear, the consensus of opinion being in favour of small millinery rather than of large models for such occasions.

The cachepeigne is largely to blame as an obstructionist, and when aided and abetted by lofty plumage the barrier to sight becomes complete. Yet for the street there is undoubted smartness in such a millinery model as the one depicted in the last column, which is made of buttercup yellow straw, and is trimmed by means of a wreath of little fruits, including apples, cherries, and mulberries, at which a couple of millinery birds, with spiked wings, apparently peck.

Less ornate, and happily much less extraordinary, than the hats and turbans made for their seniors, summer millinery for girls is, all the same, very charming and fresh in appearance.

Suffragettes

In the years following its foundation in 1903, the Women's Social and Political Union had succeeded in bringing the cause of women's enfranchisement much publicity. Newspapers debated the issue and published articles on both sides of the argument. The *Daily Mail* appears to have been somewhat ambiguous on the matter, believing that female enfranchisement would come but that women were not quite ready for it.

WSPU supporters believed the time was right for women to have the vote and organised mass rallies throughout the country as well as protests at the Houses of Parliament and directed at individual political figures. When the police tried to break up their meetings the women refused to move. Many who felt they had been roughly handled by the police found themselves in court charged with assaulting the police. A policy of refusing to pay fines imposed by the courts led to the imprisonment of Christabel Pankhurst and Annie Kenney in 1905. Many more women were to follow them and soon after the first suffragettes were imprisoned some began to refuse food.

Panicked by the thought of a suffragette dying on hunger strike and in an effort to assert authority, the government sanctioned the practice of forcible feeding. 1909 was the year in which the policy of force feeding suffragettes on hunger strike really came to the attention of the public, with Keir Hardy asking questions in the House of Commons.

The following year in 1910 there was a public outcry against the policy when it was revealed that Lady Constance Lytton who suffered from heart disease had been force fed. Upper-class women were given preferential treatment in prison on health grounds. Lady Lytton knew this and dressed as a seamstress to lead a demonstration through Liverpool. When arrested she gave her name as Jane Wharton. She was imprisoned, went on hunger strike and was force fed without a compulsory heart test being carried out. When she vomited while being force fed the prison doctor hit her. As a result of her treatment in prison she was permanently injured and suffered a degree of paralysis for the rest of her life.

Above: Christabel Pankhurst strikes a pose.

Left: A woman chained to the railings outside Downing Street – a popular suffragette tactic as it meant they could not be removed bodily from the scene of a protest.

Above: Unlike most members of the WSPU, Mary Kenney came from a working-class background. It was while employed as a cotton mill worker in Oldham that Kenney heard Christabel Pankhurst speak and subsequently became involved in the suffrage movement.

1900s Postscripts

January 1907 (*continued*): theory was that men could thus be protected from 'unclean women'. There was no censure of unclean men, and that men used prostitutes was an accepted fact of life. Josephine Butler's campaign brought prostitution and all the attendant moral and social issues into the public eye.

May 1907: The Finnish parliament met following elections in March at which women had the vote. It was also the first parliament in the world to have female MPs.

November 1907: Florence Nightingale, aged 87, was awarded the Order of Merit.

1908: Hoover introduced their first vacuum cleaner, although the cost meant that it could only be afforded by the wealthy for use by their servants.

May 1908: Following the passing of the Qualification of Women Act in 1907, which enabled women to stand for county and borough councils and to be elected Mayor, Elizabeth Garrett Anderson became Britain's first woman Mayor in her home town of Aldeburgh.

June 1908: The largest suffragette rally to date, when 200,000 women and men gathered in Hyde Park. Trains were chartered to bring suffragettes from all over Britain to London.

September 1908: The *Daily Mail* quoted Mr Herbert Elvin of the National Union of Clerks who said, 'The undercutting by women clerks is a grave evil.' In 1908 male clerks earning between 32s and £3 were being replaced by women being paid between £1 and 30s.

June 1909: The first British performance of the opera *The Wreckers* by composer and suffragette Ethel Smyth.

Girl Guides

Lord Baden-Powell had founded the Boy Scouts in 1907. His experiences during the siege of Mafeking had determined him, once back in Britain, to begin a movement for boys which would teach outdoor skills such as tracking and firemaking as well as first aid and lifesaving techniques. The Boy Scout movement would above all aim to promote good citizenship, discipline and a sense of duty. There was never any intention that there be a parallel movement for girls. However, there grew a demand from girls, attracted by the adventure they sensed in scouting, for a similar association.

The girls' demands were finally met in 1910 when Lord Baden-Powell and his sister Agnes, who became the Association's leader, formed the Girl Guides. The aim of the Girl Guides was to encourage obedience, health and resourcefulness. Girl Guides, like their brothers in the Scouts, learned first aid, but most of the outdoor skills taught to the boys were replaced by indoor skills. Badges, such as the Little House Badge, were awarded for domestic skills such as sewing, cleaning and cooking. For many years the adventurous camps of the Boy Scouts were limited to day events for Girl Guides.

Above: One of the first Girl Guide Troops. In 1914 a junior section of Guides was formed for eight to ten-year-olds. Initially called Rosebuds, they were later renamed Brownies. It was not until 1987 that Rainbow Guides were formed.

Left: A London troop returning home from a day camp in Buckinghamshire.

GAMES FOR GIRLS.
PRACTISING GOLF.

THE world of sportswomen, taking to golf as an outlet for the active spirit born of the war, is discovering that there is something in the game which did not appear previously to exist.

There was an interesting article in this journal last week concerning the difficulties of girl beginners on the links. It pointed out that these enthusiastic novices, finding the pastime less easy than they had imagined it, were apt to retire crestfallen and embarrassed when they realised that, owing to their failure to propel the ball with reasonable accuracy round the course, they were hindering other players.

There can be no doubt that too many novices still approach golf in the frame of mind of the irresponsible individual whose motto is, "Here's a ball; let's hit it."

But on the links there is a correct way of hitting the ball, and it is because the girl beginner who has had no instruction thinks that any way will do that she brings so much harassment to herself—and to other people.

SOLO PRACTICE.

For a month, or even more, the best way for the beginner is not to play a match at all. She will be much more profitably employed practising shots in a quiet corner of the course.

An hour's teaching by a competent professional is worth a thousand hours of self-guided efforts. But, assuming that the professional is not always available, there are certain points which may be laid down for the direction of recruits to the game.

Left: Mrs McNair competes in the English Ladies' Golf Championship in 1913. The Ladies Club (later the Ladies' Putting Club) at St Andrews, is the oldest women's golf club in Britain and was founded in 1867. Many more clubs followed, including Westward Ho! in Devon, Musselburgh, Wimbledon, and, in 1873, Carnoustie. Women's competitive golf was given a boost by the formation of the Ladies' Golf Union and the inaugural Ladies' Championship in 1893. In the United States, Shinnecock Hills Club on Long Island opened its doors to women in 1891 and by 1895 the first US Women's Amateur Championship was held at the Meadow Brook Club in Hempstead, NY.

"The Men We Love and the Men We Marry."

Romantic Ideals and Their Disillusion

Loving a Husband into being what He Should Be.

I HEARD a woman respond to the toast, "The men we love and the men we marry." She began like this: "The men we love and the men we marry are no more alike than the lives we live and the lives we dream." There is here a strong commentary upon the evil of dreaming, which is certainly one of the great mistakes of womankind.

We have no right to "dream." Life is before us full of beauty, full of suffering, full of joy, full of sorrow—if we are not big enough to cope with it we must not lay the blame upon the other fellow.

True, the other fellow may be in a sense "to blame," but the deficiency of a fellow mortal, even though that fellow mortal be our nearest and dearest, is never a valid excuse for our failing too.

Often that which a man has to offer to the girl he marries is only "love"; and the girl declares that she will be satisfied with it, then discovers that love was not like she had imagined it, and that life has cheated her into a bad bargain.

THE SIGN OF LOVE.

It would be very well for girls if they were taught from infancy something about their real station in life, what they may expect, what they have a right to hope for, and that in marriage they take up a profession for which they need a special training.

I know a number of women who are merciless in their demands upon the men they have married—and then, too, I know a lot of men who are merciless in their demands upon their wives; it is, perhaps, about evenly divided.

But let us take the case of a woman who is suffering through thinking wrongly about the man she has married. Maybe she is a little ashamed of him. Many women are ashamed of their husbands. This is a pretty good sign that they love them.

There is a great humiliation in seeing the object of one's affection fall short of one's ideal.

THE HARD STRUGGLE.

If a woman is going to live with a man at all she might as well be the wife of whatever he is. You are called to be the wife of the man you married, not the wife of the man you thought you married when youth and the little god had somewhat blinded your eyes.

No tare ever grew faster in a field of good grain than does the thought, once admitted, that maybe after all we do not love the man we married. There is a sort of literary twang to such a thought that tickles the fancy and seems to chime with the last novel we read. Here indeed is food for thought: Pernicious thought, that should at once be banished in favour of plans for winter bazaars or children's wardrobes, or the work that lies nearest. Of course you love the poor fellow though he spoke unkindly to you, though he seemed selfish with his money and unreasonable in his demand upon your strength. Life is a hard struggle. You may not know just how hard—for woman's life is sheltered when she has a "man," even if only poorly, and she may not know when he is staggering under his load.

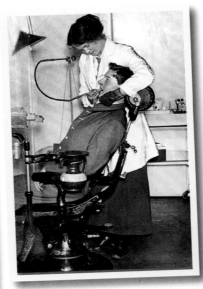

Right: Elizabeth Garrett Anderson and Emmeline Pankhurst (right) lead a suffragette delegation to Parliament in 1911. In 1865 Garrett Anderson's persistence was rewarded and she obtained a Licentiate in Medicine and Surgery from the Society of Apothecaries. Initially her qualification was not recognised by the British Medical Register but in1872 she founded the New Hospital for Women in London (later renamed after her) and in 1876 an act was passed permitting women to enter the medical professions.

Top: The shortage of doctors during the war meant greater responsibility for medical students like these women at the Royal Free Hospital in north London, which was the first in Britain to admit female students in 1877.

The medical register listed 25 female doctors in 1881. This number grew rapidly – with 930 in 1911 and 2,100 in 1921 – although census data from those years seems to indicate that around one third of these women were not practising.

Above right: Marie Curie. At the beginning of 1911 the Académie des Sciences in Paris voted to admit Jean Becquerel rather than have a woman member. The woman proposed for membership of the Académie was Marie Curie, who ironically became the first person ever to win a second Nobel Prize when she received the award for Chemistry in Stockholm in December of the same year.

Above: A female dentist at work during World War One.

'Now it is to stem this gigantic evil,' said the Bishop, 'that I summon the forces of the Church today. The Roman Church, all honour to it, has never wavered in condemning such practices [birth control] as a sin, and it would ill become the Church of England to condemn less clearly the practice which, if it continued, must eat away the life blood of our country. Let teaching be given in suitable ways and at suitable times on the responsibility which married life entails, on the glory of motherhood and the growing selfishness which first thinks of creature comforts, of social pleasures, and then of the primary duties and joys of life.'

Daily Mail, 1 December 1911

Militant Suffragettes

Despite the fact that the Women's Social and Political Union had gained much publicity for the cause of female suffrage, votes for women, even the limited franchise the WSPU demanded, were in reality no nearer by the end of the decade than they had been in 1903. In 1911 the male franchise had been extended, which meant that virtually every man in Britain over the age of 21 had a vote. This measure had been passed by the Liberal government which was still split over the issue of votes for women, Prime Minister Asquith being anti female suffrage. In the all-male House of Commons there was also a majority against female enfranchisement. In the face of this political opposition, the WSPU embarked on a far more radical route to achieve their objective.

In 1912, despite the fact that the Labour Party Conference committed the Party to votes for women, the WSPU broke their affiliations with Labour and all other similar organisations. The WSPU had decided on a course of militant action. With the aim of pushing insurance companies to pressure the government into accepting the WSPU's demands, they began a window-smashing campaign. Armed with stones and hammers, suffragettes, in groups and individually, smashed windows in shops, post offices, labour exchanges and other government buildings. Damage was also caused to well-known paintings and works of art.

Throughout 1912, 1913 and into 1914 suffragette tactics became increasingly violent with arson and bomb attacks on pillar boxes, churches and the homes of politicians. Mercifully no one was badly injured in any of these attacks and indeed that was not the intention of the suffragettes, who only aimed to damage property and gain attention for their cause. In April 1913 Mrs Pankhurst was sentenced to three years in jail for a bomb explosion at Lloyd George's newly built golf villa.

By the end of 1912 the WSPU was virtually an underground organisation as police raids on their offices forced the decision to move their headquarters to Paris, where they remained until the outbreak of the Great War in 1914 brought a dramatic turnaround in their policies

The results of this increased militancy are difficult to judge, but the 1912 Women's Enfranchisement Bill was defeated by 14 votes on its second reading in March 1912, and the government withdrew, it claimed on technical grounds, its own Franchise Bill in January 1913, which was what largely provoked the bombings and arson attacks. A number of men both inside and outside Parliament, who had perhaps not been wholly committed to the idea of female suffrage, found the militancy and violence a good excuse, or perhaps were genuinely horrified by what they saw, and withdrew their support. But the militant campaign did keep the issue of votes for women at the forefront of the public imagination and the political agenda.

Far left: Lady Barclay and the Honourable Edith Fitzgerald are seen in conversation with two policemen outside Buckingham Palace as they attempt to deliver a letter from Mrs Pankhurst to the King.

Above: A crowd of suffragettes who took part in a window-breaking raid wait for Bow Street Police Court to open in 1912.

Left: Emmeline Pankhurst and her daughter Christabel in prison dress in 1914.

Above right: Women attend a rally presided over by Mrs Fawcett in 1913. Millicent Fawcett was a 'suffragist', believing that the vote should be won by constitutional means rather than violent protests.

Right: Police hold back crowds gathered to see suffragettes at the Monument in London.

Left: Christabel (left) and Emmeline Pankhurst.

Below: Fellow suffragettes watch over the coffin of Emily Davison outside Victoria Railway Station. Davison died of injuries sustained at the Epsom Derby in 1913 after she stepped in front of the King's horse.

1910s Postscripts

July 1910: Chancellor of the Exchequer Lloyd George said reform of the House of Lords would have to take priority over women's suffrage. The power of the House of Lords to veto any legislation passed by the Liberal government was creating a constitutional crisis.

November 1910: 'Black Friday' the 18th, when 119 suffragettes were arrested attempting to rush the House of Commons. The following day Home Secretary Winston Churchill ordered that charges against 100 women be dropped. Mrs Mary Clarke, sister of Emmeline Pankhurst, and Cecilia Wolseley Haig both died as a result of 'Black Friday'.

December 1910: By the end of 1910 the first woman had qualified as a chartered accountant and another had qualified as a banker.

March 1911: Norway's first woman MP, Anna Rogstadt, took her seat in Parliament. Women did not have an equal franchise with men but there were women voters and women could stand for Parliament.

November 1911: In Britain more than 200 women were arrested following angry demonstrations when Parliament voted to extend the male franchise. Hopes had been high that PM Herbert Asquith might accept some limited female franchise.

November 1912: The Royal Commission on Divorce recommended that the grounds for men and women seeking divorce should be the same, also suggesting that divorce be made easier to obtain.

'Cat and Mouse'

Since the case of Lady Constance Lytton had come to attention in 1910, there had been much public disgust at the practice of force feeding hunger-striking suffragettes. The government had been severely censured both at home and abroad with allegations of torture being levelled, particularly at Prime Minister Asquith. With increased suffragette militancy bringing greater numbers of hunger-striking women into jail, public pressure on the government grew and it responded by passing the 'Cat and Mouse' Bill.

This bill allowed for prisoners to be given temporary release from jail on the authority of the Home Secretary if he felt that their health was in danger. This meant that hunger-striking suffragettes were no longer force fed. A hunger striker was allowed to become very weak, and then was released subject to various bail-style conditions. When she was well enough she was simply re-arrested and continued to serve her sentence. A single prisoner could be released and re-arrested many times before her sentence was completed. It was likened to a cat playing with a mouse, with the cat always winning in the end, hence the name 'Cat and Mouse' Act. This absolved the government from the charge of torturing women and to a large extent satisfied the public's anxieties over the treatment of suffragettes in prison.

TORTURING WOMEN IN PRISON

VOTE AGAINST THE GOVERNMENT

Left: A WSPU poster highlighting the damaging effects of force feeding.

Below: British suffragette Flora Drummond is arrested in Hyde Park in April 1914. Nicknamed The General, Drummond was imprisoned nine times for her activism in the Women's Suffrage Movement.

Left: Lady Rochdale speaking at the mass rally of women's suffrage campaigners in Hyde Park in 1913. Societies from 17 cities all over Britain marched to London to promote their cause in a non-violent way.

Bottom left: Women gather outside the War Office in 1914, one of them holding onto a very practical-looking pushchair.

Women in the Home

In 1914 almost half of the 15 million women in Britain were either married or widowed and at home looking after children. One and a half million single women were also involved in looking after homes and families. When a mother died, most commonly in childbirth, it was often the case that the eldest girl or girls had to take over responsibility for the upbringing of younger brothers and sisters and the running of the house. Many of these girls missed out on the chance of marriage if they then found themselves looking after fathers or other elderly relatives. A further one and a half million women were employed in 'keeping home' as domestic servants. Of the remaining four and a half million women, some were employed outside the home, but often in family businesses, a few were students, others were retired and others were living off private means.

Although things were beginning to change, for the vast majority of women 'home' was their world. Most women did not have time for outside interests, all their time was consumed feeding and caring for their family. Even relatively wealthy women, who had servants to work for them, tied themselves to the home in the belief that it was their duty to 'manage' the running of the household. They might spend some time in charity work and other 'womanly pursuits' such as music, sewing and visiting friends, but generally it was not expected that any woman, whatever her class, would be interested in anything outside the home.

Right: An article from the *Daily Mail* in 1919 gives women detailed instructions on how to whitewash a ceiling, perhaps an indication that the war had changed expectations about the sort of jobs women could take on.

Below and below right: Poster parades, expecially outside the homes and workplaces of politicians, were a popular suffragette tactic.

HOUSE DECORATION.
HOW TO WHITEWASH A CEILING.

DESPAIR enters into the heart of the housewife, for the ceiling of the kitchen is sadly dirty, she sees no prospect of securing the services of a professional whitewasher. There is no help for it—she must whitewash it herself! It sounds a difficult undertaking, but if it is set about in the right way it is comparatively simple. In order to be able to spread the whitewash evenly, it is as well to practise on the ceiling of the scullery or a small bedroom before attempting that of a larger room.

First of all, prepare the room and gather together the necessary materials and plant. Either short trestles or two pairs of steps and a plank strong enough to bear a person's weight are required; two pails, two sponges, and a distemper brush. The sponges can be made by filling a bag of Turkish towelling with broken pieces of sponge. If the towelling wears out a fresh piece can be put over the old one.

EMPTY THE ROOM.

Take all the pictures, ornaments, and furniture that can be moved out of the room, cover any heavy furniture with dust sheets, and leave as much space as possible for moving the scaffold quickly from place to place.

If the ceiling alone is to be distempered and the walls untouched, the latter must be protected. Fix, with drawing pins, sheets of newspaper on the walls as close to the ceiling as possible; the lower part may be covered with old sheets.

Should there be any splashes on the paper when the whitewashing is finished rub them off gently with a little dough, and remove as soon as possible any spots that may have fallen on the paint.

Before beginning to distemper the ceiling the old distemper must be washed off. Place the scaffold, which is made by laying a plank on the trestles or steps, in position and dip the distemper brush in a pail of water. Mount the scaffold and wet the ceiling to remove the old coating of distemper. Clean as much as possible with the brush and finish with the sponge. Let the brush be fairly dry when rubbing near the edges of the wall-paper and the sponge pressed to as sharp a point as possible. If there are any bad cracks in the ceiling clear the distemper out of them with an old knife and fill them with cement. Wet the cracks or bad places; then press the cement in well.

A SIMPLE PREPARATION.

A simple preparation for whitewashing a ceiling can now be bought quite inexpensively at any oil shop, and does away with the first coating of size, which would otherwise be necessary. It is mixed according to the directions with cold water. Make ready a quantity of this preparation in a pail. It is better to prepare too much than too little, and the surplus can be always utilised to whiten the inside of a cupboard or larder. Before beginning, close the doors and windows of the room in order to keep the surface of the ceiling as wet as possible when working. It is best to work towards the light, although when a room is not square it is sometimes advisable to take the narrowest width of a ceiling.

Work from one end of the ceiling to the other and try to keep the edge wet, or when the ceiling is dry the marks where the brush overlapped will show.

The whitewash must be applied quickly, to avoid the edges drying, and care must be taken not to miss any part, as the ceiling cannot be retouched afterwards without showing. When the whole ceiling is finished open the windows and doors to allow it to dry quickly.

M. W.

1910s Postscripts

1912: The *Daily Mail* published a Leader supporting the minority report produced by the Royal Commission which, while accepting that grounds for divorce should be equal for both parties, refuted the idea of easier divorce, claiming that there was no public demand.

January 1913: The first sickness and maternity payments were made under the new National Insurance Act. The Act had been passed in 1911 but had to be amended in 1912 because the original terms did not allow for illness as a result of pregnancy or childbirth for women workers under the scheme. Even amended the Act did very little for most women. True, it guaranteed the family of an insured worker an income if he was off sick, but while her husband had access to free or assisted medical care, a wife and her children did not. There was not even medical care during pregnancy and childbirth.

June 1913: Emily Davison, an active member of the WSPU, died as a result of injuries sustained when she stepped out in front of the King's horse in the Derby to draw attention to the cause of female suffrage. Her death was to become one of the symbols of the suffragette movement.

June 1913: Emily Dawson was appointed the first woman magistrate in Britain.

June 1913: The Norwegian Parliament granted women equal electoral rights to men.

Women at War

Throughout history and its many wars women had been involved to varying degrees with 'front line action'. The camp followers and Service wives of the Napoleonic wars had, like many women before them, tended the wounded, removed the dead from the battlefield and helped feed and care for the active soldiers. During wars in the nineteenth century women had been moved further back from the front line as the army organised more of its own provisioning and medical care.

The First World War saw a new departure in the role women played at war. Initially the Women's Legion was formed in 1915 and women were engaged as auxiliaries to the men's Services, but in 1917 women's corps were formed – the Women's Army Auxiliary Corps (WAAC); the Women's Reserve Naval Service (WRNS or Wrens); and the Women's Reserve Air Force (WRAF). The Women's Land Army was also established to help with food production. There was never any conscription for women in the First World War and all the women in the Services were volunteers. Their job was principally to free men for the fighting. Women staffed the administration of the war both at home in Britain and nearer the front in continental Europe. When hostilities ended, the temporary nature of the women's corps, inherent in their titles – 'reserve' and 'auxiliary' – was underlined by their disbandment.

The women closest to the front line, on some occasions even working among the men in the trenches, were the various corps and groups of nurses. The British War Office turned down the offer of help from groups such as the First Aid Nursing Yeomanry and Dr Elsie Inglis and the Scottish Women's Hospital units, who went instead to work with the other Allied Armies at the fronts. There were nurses working for the British Military and these came from a variety of sources – the Voluntary Aid Detachments (VADs); the Territorial Force Nursing Service; Queen Alexandra's Military and Naval Nursing Services. The War Office deployed some of these nurses abroad and others to care for the wounded when they returned home to Britain. The War Office also changed its rules about women doctors and in 1915 did employ them but only as civilians; they refused to give women doctors commissions.

Many of the women who joined these volunteer corps were middle class, and had led sheltered lives, protected from many of what were considered to be the more unpleasant aspects of life. For them the war took them out of their close circle of family and friends, introduced them to men and women from other countries, classes and backgrounds and gave them a degree of freedom and independence unimagined only a few years earlier.

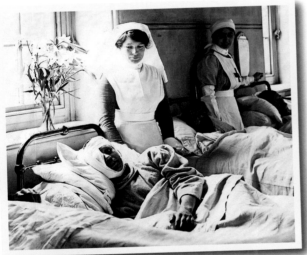

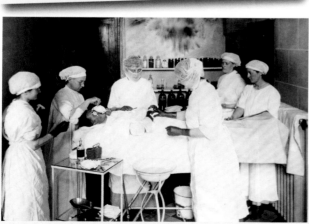

Above left and opposite bottom left: At the outbreak of war the Queen Alexandra's Imperial Military Nursing Service, founded in 1902, was the main trained corps of military nurses. During the four years of the war it grew from 300 to over 10,000 nurses. Nurses were required to work on the battlefields and in convalescent hospitals at home .

Above right: Recruits to the WRAF play their part in the war effort.

Far left: Initially female doctors were only welcomed by the French authorities (these Scottish doctors are working in Royaumont). This changed in 1915 when the Endell Street Military Hospital was set up in London.

Left: A British nurse in Serbia.

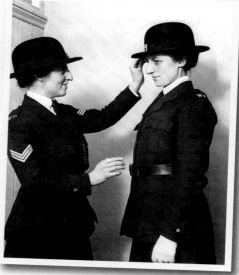

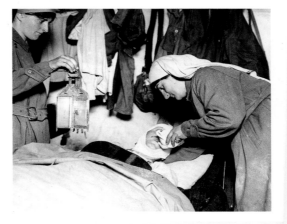

Top left: The Women's Legion Army Service Corps on their way to France in 1919.

Top right: Two of 300 constables recruited to 'guard women workers and prevent carelessness' try on their uniforms.

Above left: London County Council began recruiting female ambulance crews in 1917.

Above right: Families prepare for the separation as soldiers return to the Front.

Far right: Edith Cavell worked as a nurse in German-occupied Belgium where she helped soldiers from both sides. In 1915 she was shot by a German firing squad for helping allied soldiers to escape across the border into the Netherlands.

1910s Postscripts

October 1913: The 'Cat and Mouse' Act was enacted. This allowed the government to temporarily discharge women prisoners who were hunger striking for the vote–until they were fit enough to be imprisoned again.

1914: Iceland awarded women the franchise.

August 1914: The outbreak of the First World War put on hold all claims and possibilities of women's suffrage. The WSPU suspended their campaign, changed the name of the campaign paper from *The Suffragette* to *Britannia* and pledged full support to the

government and the war effort. Some of the WSPU's supporters believed this to be a betrayal of the cause and left to join the pacifist movement. Sylvia Pankhurst was one of the supporters to leave. A rift had already opened between Sylvia and her mother. Sylvia and her East London Women's Federation had split in early 1914 from the WSPU, basically on the issue of the WSPU cutting its ties with the Labour Party.

1915: Women in Denmark were given the vote.

March 1915: The government appealed to women to register for war work at their local Labour Exchange.

September 1916: US President Wilson, attending a women's suffrage rally, pledged to give women the vote.

October 1916: Ethyl Byrne and Margaret Sanger opened the first birth-control clinic in the USA. They were later arrested and convicted for running the clinic.

Top: 'Land Girls' helped maintain domestic food production to sustain the war effort, freeing up British agricultural workers for armed service.

Above: Women pulp paper in Purfleet on the Thames and tar-spray the roads in Westminster in 1918.

Above right: Blowing an Osram lamp.

Right: Women took over jobs in the printing industry.

Working for the War Effort

While thousands of women volunteered to join the Military and Nursing Services, thousands more women were working in war industries and taking over men's jobs to free more recruits for the fighting. Four hundred thousand women left domestic service and more than 750,000 entered paid employment for the first time in response to calls for workers to help the war effort.

Despite the hostility of employers and the male-dominated trade unions, women were willing to take on any job. Many middle-class women took up positions in offices of the Civil Service, businesses, banks, insurance companies and other institutions, drove ambulances and joined the newly formed women's police patrols. Working-class women took on a wide variety of jobs in industry – from munitions workers, wearing special clothing and with every item of metal removed to reduce the chance of a spark when handling highly explosive substances like cordite or TNT which turned the workers yellow, to non-munitions factory workers making anything from light bulbs to paper.

Women also took on a vast selection of semi-industrial and service jobs which previously only men had been thought capable of and allowed to do. It was not unusual to see women road-sweepers, postal workers, railway porters and ticket collectors, window cleaners, even road mending teams. The newspapers were full of pictures and reports of the newest area of work to be colonised by women. One of the most popular of these types of job was as a bus or tram conductress after the government allowed women to apply for licences as conductresses in October 1915. In some areas outside London women were also allowed to drive buses and in February 1917 the government gave permission for women to become taxi drivers.

All these jobs, however, were for the duration of the war only and when the 'boys' came home women found themselves out of work. All the temporary legislation and bending of the trade union rules were revoked and, as the title of the 1918 Restoration of Pre-War Practices Act suggests, things were back to how they had been in 1914. But for the women who had taken up paid work or volunteered to run canteens, administer war charities, collect salvage or supervise welfare schemes, life could not be exactly as it had been in 1914. They had experienced earning their own money and had the knowledge that they could achieve what they never would have dreamt of before the war.

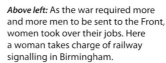

Above left: As the war required more and more men to be sent to the Front, women took over their jobs. Here a woman takes charge of railway signalling in Birmingham.

Above centre: Two women arrive for their shift on the London Underground. Although women worked as guards, mechanics and ticket collectors they weren't allowed to become drivers. The first woman to qualify as a London Underground train driver was Hannah Dadds, in 1978

Above right: The postman is replaced by the postwoman.

Left: A female railway porter pulls a luggage trolley.

Far right: Lady with a lamp – operating a cinema 'lantern' at a north London picture palace.

The Benefits of Marriage!

In 1918 the position of some six million women in society changed. Married women over the age of 30, who were also either householders or the wife of a local government elector, were given the vote in national elections.

Women's performance during the war was to be rewarded with this limited franchise. Even Herbert Asquith, a long time opponent of female suffrage, had changed his mind in the face of the evidence of women's abilities and the knowledge that Britain might well have not been able to win, or would have won only at great cost, the war against Germany had women not left their homes and staffed factories, services and offices throughout the country.

However, the advantage of a married woman over 30 being able to vote was counterbalanced by the fact that married women, even in wartime, were in most cases not allowed to have a job. Virtually every profession and public institution demanded that women leave their employment once married. Even when there was no hard and fast rule it was expected that a wife would give up her position to take care first of her husband and home and then any children they might have.

Above: A church parade in Hyde Park in 1912. By the second decade of the century, women's clothing, even for formal occasions, was beginning to be less restrictive, allowing a greater freedom to enjoy physical activity.

Opposite: Women packing Rowntree's chocolate in the factory in York, 1910.

MARRIED WOMEN NOT WANTED

'Women, and particularly married women, have risen so well to so many big occasions during the past few years – so many wives have prevented wreck and ruin by slipping into their husbands' business shoes when they have had to put on khaki – that it is surely time for it to be recognised generally that matrimony does not necessarily kill a woman's natural ability and that there is no sane reason why she should be deterred from keeping or taking a job just because she is married.

Extract from an article by H.M.K.N.,
Daily Mail, 17 September 1917

The Chances of Marriage.

WHERE THEY ARE BEST AND WORST. TOWNS AND COUNTIES WHERE MEN ARE MORE NUMEROUS THAN WOMEN.

If marriage is every woman's chief ambition the Census Returns now being issued must be very doleful reading. Probably very few women will care to examine these millions and millions of figures, and yet they contain matter of great feminine interest, for they tell exactly where a woman has the greatest chances of getting married, and where, on the other hand, the chances are more strongly in favour of her dying unmarried. The first important fact we come across is that every year women are increasing in number in proportion to men. At present there are 1,069 females of all ages to each 1,000 men.

WOMEN SCARCER IN SMALLER TOWNS

Then the distribution of the sexes throughout the country is very unequal. Women seem more dissatisfied than men with country life. They flock to the large towns, and especially to what may be called the pleasure towns.

In the smaller towns, say from two to ten thousand in population, a woman's prospect of marriage should be very good, for in these the sexes are fairly even in numbers. In many of the smaller towns there is an acutal scarcity of women and this is especially the case in the mining districts.

But in London, Manchester and Birmingham and all the large cities, women are so numerous relatively to men that tens of thousands of them have no chance of finding husbands. While in such places as Bath, Brighton and Bournemouth etc the excess of women is enormous.

It is not practical to give the very long list of all the places where women are in excess, and where they are in equal or small numbers than men. But the following facts form a useful guide.

In the best of these, for each 1,000 who can find husbands there is an excess of 100 women for whom there are none:

Sussex (East)	1,256	females to 1,000 males		
Cardiganshire	1,224	"	" 1,000	"
Surrey	1.166	"	" 1,000	"
Cornwall	1,164	"	" 1,000	"
Somerset	1,153	"	" 1,000	"
Middlesex	1,144	"	" 1,000	"
Gloucestershire ..	1,142	"	" 1,000	"
Isle of Wight	1,130	"	" 1,000	"
London	1,127	"	" 1,000	"
Sussex (West)	1,117	"	" 1,000	"
Westmorland	1,112	"	" 1,000	"
Carnarvonshire ...	1,106	"	" 1,000	"
Devonshire	1,102	"	" 1,000	"
Worcestershire ...	1,101	"	" 1,000	"
Cheshire	1,100	"	" 1,000	"

In many counties however, there is a shortage of women. The following is a list of these counties:

Monmouthshire	903	Females to 1,000 males		
Glamorganshire	925	"	" 1,000	"
Brecknockshire	952	"	" 1,000	"
Rutlandshire	973	"	" 1,000	"
Isle of Ely	980	"	" 1,000	"
Durham County	986	"	" 1,000	"
Radnorshire	992	"	" 1,000	"
Derbyshire	993	"	" 1,000	"

Equal Pay for Equal Work

A 1906 survey by Edward Cadbury showed that the great majority of women believed that it was right that they should receive lower wages than men. In 1906 the average man's wage in industry was 30 shillings, while women textile workers, who with a long tradition of trade unionism were among the best-paid women workers, earned on average 18s 8d. Most other women in industry earned between 9s and 10s.

There had been agitation for better pay and conditions in the few industries where women had a strong showing in the workforce, but this campaigning was not for pay equal to that of men in the same industry and it was seldom organised. Women had been excluded from most trade unions during the nineteenth century and when they were allowed to become union members they found that rather than fighting for equal pay for their few women members the unions sought only to promote the interests of their male membership.

During the First World War government, employers and trade unions all made many promises of equal pay for women. These promises were seldom honoured, although after strikes on the trains and buses the unions negotiated deals with the employers which ensured equal pay for women workers. The war brought equal pay to the fore as an issue – up until the conflict there were many occupations which had been seen as 'men's jobs', no one would ever have considered that these jobs could be done, let alone done equally well, by women. Necessity, during wartime, proved to women themselves that they were capable, and they began to press for equal pay.

1910s Postscripts

November 1916: Jeanette Rankin from Montana became the first woman member of the US Congress.

1917: After the Revolution, women in Russia were enfranchised on equal terms with men.

1917: The Family Endowment Council was established by Eleanor Rathbone to campaign for family allowances.

1918: The Maternal and Child Welfare Act was passed enabling local authorities to provide services such as welfare clinics and health visitors.

1918: Dr Janet Campbell reported to the War Cabinet Committee that women's health had improved due to better nutrition than in the pre-war years. Probably the extra money women earned and the setting up of workplace canteens aided this improvement in women's diets.

January 1918: Rosa Luxemburg was murdered by members of the State Police in Germany. A communist and believer in women's equality, Luxemburg, 'Red Rosa', had spent most of the war in prison for her agitation against the fighting, and post war had led a communist uprising in Berlin with Karl Liebknecht.

July 1918: Marie Stopes published her controversial book *Married Love*, which suggested that sex could and should be a pleasure for both men and women. As a sex instruction book *Married Love* became a bestseller overnight.

February 1918: The Representation of the People Act was passed, allowing women over the age of 30 who met a property qualification to vote. The Act extended the vote to all men over 21, regardless of property ownership.

November 1918: The House of Commons passed the Parliamentary Qualification of

The Handicap of Sport.

CHARM *versus* GAMES—
A WOMAN WHO FOUND HERSELF UNPOPULAR.

I HAVE made a great discovery. I feel as proud as though I had come across the horn of a unicorn or stumbled upon the nest of a dodo. For in the pages of a daily paper I have found a man who owns to liking the masculine girl. He writes in praise of her collars and ties, he admires her sensible shoes and her rough tweeds with their large " poacher " pockets; further, he says he should consider himself lucky to marry so sporting a damsel.

Frankly, I did not know such a man existed. He is a greater "find," I am sure, than the egg of a dodo. True it is that once upon a time—years ago, alas!—I set out from a finishing school equipped with tailor-mades, sport hats, shooting boots, and a covert coat. And I joined a tennis club and a cricket club and a golf club, and " took up " fencing and swimming and hunting. And I married and " lived happily ever after."

Inherited Charm.

But truth compels me to own that there was an element of luck about the affair, that I got my share of romance in spite not because of my athletic feats.

I fancy my husband was attracted by the exceedingly feminine glances which I have inherited from an Early Victorian mother,

and not by the muscle which I had developed by my own efforts. I do not fancy he married me because I can bowl overhand, keen as he is on the national game.

For the average man delights in a woman who contrasts vividly to himself. The better he is at games the less he values her prowess at them. Six foot three and broad in proportion, brown as a berry and strong as a bull, his ideal is a tiny pink and white thing with dimples and a lisp.

A Liking for Frills.

" Throw away those beastly collars—and what on earth made you buy those blouse things that look like one of my shirts? I like frilly things, with lots of lace." So said my husband, surveying the garments which I thought would specially please him because they were neat and business-like, and therefore seemed suitable for a country honeymoon.

I have learnt wisdom since then. Nowadays, if I must needs don a short, thick skirt for a country walk, my blouse keeps its frills; if my hat has to be close-fitting because I am going to motor it still has an alluring air about it. I give up my games and my love of out-of-door life for no man; but it is not by them that I expect to fascinate.

Because he adores me in silks and satins my husband tolerates me in sporting

Top left: A young woman enjoys a splash in the shallows in 1914. Before the turn of the century women took to the water in full dress and bloomers. By the outbreak of the war, these had given way to more practical all-in-one beach suits down to the knee, with hats to protect the hair.

Above left: A portrait of the gold-medal-winning British women's 4 x 100 metres freestyle swimming team, taken during the 1912 Olympic Games in Stockholm, Sweden. This was the first Olympic Games to hold swimming events for women. However, of the 2,408 competitors taking part in the 14 sports included in the Games, only 48 were women.

Top left: In 1919 Suzanne Lenglen won Wimbledon and amazed the crowd with her short and sleeveless tennis dress.

From Paris.

One of the smart and easily made tunics now so fashionable in Paris. This model is of Egyptian blue fringed with blue and with a rose embroidered in crimson, green and dull gold threads.

1910s Postscripts

November 1918 (continued): Women Act to allow women over the age of 27 to stand as Parliamentary candidates. Seventeen women stood for election.

October 1918: A women's employment committee at the Ministry of Reconstruction suggested there would be many new jobs post war for women as midwives, home helps, health visitors, nursery helpers, child welfare workers, women police and probation officers – all jobs as carers.

December 1918: The first General Election in which women could vote and stand as candidates took place on the 28th. Of the

1,600 candidates, only 17 were women and only one was elected. She was Constance Markiewicz, who stood for Sinn Fein in the constituency of Dublin, St Patrick's and refused to take her seat in the House of Commons.

1919: Italian women were allowed to become barristers and solicitors, but not to sit as judges.

September 1919: By the end of September all women conductresses on London omnibuses were replaced by returned soldiers and given a certificate, but no offers of jobs, in appreciation of their work.

November 1919: Nancy Astor won the by-election caused when her husband was raised to the peerage and had to give up his parliamentary seat. On 1 December she became the first woman to sit in the House of Commons.

November 1919: Women in France voted for the first time in a general election. As in Britain, it was not on a franchise equal to men. French women had to wait another 25 years for an equal franchise.

Women in Public Life

'A person shall not be disqualified by sex or marriage from the exercise of any public function, or from being appointed to or holding any civil or judicial post, or from entering or assuming or carrying on any civil profession or vocation, or from admission to any incorporated society.' So opened the Sex Disqualification (Removal) Bill which became law in 1919. However, many spheres of life were not covered by the Act. The Church, the Stock Exchange and the House of Lords were some of the areas outside the scope of the Act. There were other areas of life which although covered by the Act did not see any wholesale changes. For example, one clause said that university rules and statutes could not exclude women from being admitted to membership of the university. Oxford University acted quickly and changed its rules in1920, but it was not until after the Second World War that Cambridge allowed women to sit for degrees.

The Sex Disqualification (Removal) Act did, however, mean that women had a greater chance of pursuing a career or taking jobs that had previously been barred to them. The legal profession was one of the areas opened to women and on 30 December, one week after the Bill became law, Helena Normanton was admitted to Lincoln's Inn as the first woman student at the Bar. Women could also become judges, magistrates and Justices of the Peace, and gradually over the next few years women began to fill these posts in lower courts, although it was to be another 46 years before the appointment of the first woman High Court judge. For women as citizens, the Act was also important as it allowed them to sit on juries in the criminal courts.

The Civil Service came under the aegis of the Act but it also allowed the Service to organise its own rules for entry. Women were barred from some positions including overseas postings with the Foreign Office, obliged to resign on marriage and in most cases received lower pay than men. These conditions lasted, in the case of the marriage bar and overseas postings, until 1946. Equal pay, to which the Civil Service committed itself in 1921, did not arrive fully until the Equal Pay Act came into force in 1976, although a partial victory was won in 1955.

Right: Queen Mary visits the British Hospital for Mothers and Babies in Samuel Street, Woolwich, in 1917 and *(below)* greeting recipients of the Victoria Cross in the garden of Buckingham Palace after the war.

Above: Christabel Pankhurst, Women's Party candidate for Smethwick in the 1918 general election, pictured with two of her supporters – a soldier and a sailor.

Left: Nancy Astor after her election to parliament as Conservative member for Plymouth Sutton in 1919. Astor was elected in place of her husband, when he succeeded to the peerage, and held the seat until she retired in June 1945.

THE FIRST WOMAN TO SIT IN THE COMMONS

In this country our women have proved under the stern test of war that they can face the grim facts of life without flinching; and the gifts of intellect, energy and courage which they displayed in such varied directions have won them the confidence of the public. So much so we anticipate a large increase in the number of women Members, where there is so much legislative work for which they are peculiarly qualified waiting for them to do.

Extract from a Leader, Daily Mail, 2 December 1919

The Nineteenth Amendment to the US Constitution

In Britain men like John Stuart Mill, who attempted to gain the vote for women in 1867 by introducing an amendment to the voting Reform Act by substituting the word 'person' for 'man', fought to change the inequalities in the position of women. In the USA, the cause of female emancipation was hampered to an extent by the anti-slavery movement. While some abolitionists linked the causes of women and slaves, most channelled their energy into defeating the more obviously iniquitous and cruel practice of slavery.

Susan Anthony, who was to become a figurehead of the American women's movement in the nineteenth century, came from an anti-slavery background. Her father had been a strong campaigner for the abolition of slavery. Susan Anthony too became involved in the abolitionist movement while campaigning against alcohol on the slave plantations. In the 1850s, when she was in her thirties, she turned her attention to the cause of women's rights. In the early years of the twentieth century she founded the International Women's Suffrage Alliance which gave support and encouragement to women like Emmeline Pankhurst.

Women's rights campaigners in the USA had been fighting, and continued to fight throughout the nineteenth and early twentieth centuries, for a female franchise state by state. In 1869 Wyoming was the first state to enfranchise women and by the beginning of the First World War several other states, mainly in the western USA, had given women the vote.

Susan Anthony, however, had always insisted upon a federal amendment to the constitution rather than working for changes to the franchise state by state. In 1912, six years after her death, two women, Alice Paul and Lucy Burns, broke from the National American Suffrage Association whose policy was to fight to enfranchise women on a state by state basis. With first-hand experience of the militant suffragette movement in Britain, they formed the Congressional Union, later the National Women's Party, to campaign, as Susan Anthony had done, for a federal amendment to the constitution.

In August 1920 the 19th (Women's Suffrage) Amendment became part of the constitution of the USA, prohibiting any US citizen being denied the right to vote on the basis of sex.

Above: Christabel Pankhurst, who founded the WSPU with her mother and sisters, pictured in 1921. In 1905 she and fellow campaigner Annie Kenney were the first women to be arrested in the suffrage campaign.

Above: The battle continues: a suffragist is escorted by two policemen in 1921. Legislation in 1918 which only allowed women over the age of 30 who met a property qualification to vote meant that 60 per cent of women were still not eliglible to vote.

HOUSEHOLD ECONOMIES THAT COUNT.

"MY housekeeping expenses are much higher now than they were during war-time, yet our menus are much the same and prices are supposed to have gone down." So a harassed housewife as she sighed over her weekly "books."

UNCONSCIOUS SLACKING.

And many a housewife is confronted by the same problem. The reason is not really far to seek. It is simply that, the war being over, almost unconsciously little economies of the past are being dropped. Now that it is no longer so difficult to obtain certain commodities, we have grown imperceptibly slacker and we have become so accustomed to high prices that our standard of values has gradually changed.

For instance, we use perhaps more firewood than hitherto and have dropped lighting the fires with folded newspapers; also, we no longer bank the kitchen fire with rubbish folded in damp paper and wet slack when the day's cooking is done. Neither do we continue to sift the ashes and use them for cleaning saucepans and steels—instead we employ expensive cleaning materials. We are not so careful with the scraps; we perhaps do not bother to utilise the washed peelings and trimmings of vegetables for stock; we throw away stale pieces of bread as well as small portions of "left-over" dishes instead of transforming the latter into dainty little savouries. Also, we have grown careless about clarifying fat and utilising ends of soap by making them into soap jelly with which to wash kitchen rubbers.

Small economies may be tiresome, but they count in the long run. The Scotch truly say, "Mony a mickle mak's a muckle."

1920s Postscripts

May 1920: Women professors at Oxford were given equal status to their male colleagues.

October 1920: At Oxford the first 100 women were admitted to study for degrees.

1921: Helena Normanton became the first woman barrister at the English Bar.

January 1921: The first women undertook jury service in a Divorce Court.

July 1921: A survey showed that of the eight million women in paid employment in the USA, 87 per cent were in teaching or secretarial work.

August 1921: Official figures showed there were two million more women in Britain than men; 1,096 women to every 1,000 men, whereas the ratio had been 1,068: 1,000 in 1911.

1922: Rose Witcop, a socialist and women's rights campaigner, was prosecuted and found guilty of producing an obscene work when she published US birth control pioneer Margaret Sanger's *Family Limitation*.

February 1922: Marie Curie was elected to the French Académie des Sciences.

Mother's Clinic

In March 1921 Marie Stopes opened her Mothers' Clinic in Holloway, the first birth-control clinic in Britain. Stopes was a palaeobotanist who became the first woman lecturer at Manchester University. Despite her education and learning she was, like many women of her day, ignorant about sex. After five years of marriage she set about trying to find out why she had not become pregnant and discovered that in fact the marriage was unconsummated. She then read everything she could in English, French and German on the subject of sex and in 1918 published her book *Married Love* which suggested that both men and women had a right to enjoy sex. She also saw that sex was difficult for women to enjoy when they were continually faced with the possibility of pregnancy.

In setting up her Mothers' Clinic Stopes was not only trying to remove the fear of unwanted pregnancy from the women who attended her clinic, she had another and less altruistic motive. There was a belief at the time that unless the lower classes could be encouraged to practice birth control the stock of the nation and the race would be diminished, watered down by the unchecked reproduction of the mentally and physically less fit members of society. The middle and upper classses had been limiting the size of their families for several decades by this time but working-class families of ten or more were not unusual. Eugenics were not at the time as reviled as they were to become after Hitler's attempts to create a master race in the 1930s and 1940s. Nevertheless, there was a strong working-class feeling against birth control because it was an idea promoted by eugenicists and so seen as a way of keeping the masses in their place.

However, women did come to the Mothers' Clinic for advice and help. The main method of birth control offered to them was the cap. The efforts of the Mothers' Clinic and other clinics set up by people such as Dr Helena Wright and Norman Hare were hampered by both the law and popular prejudices. Any printed material about contraception was deemed by law to be obscene, so the dissemination of information about birth control was difficult. Many people, mainly men, feared that contraception would give women too much freedom, making them less willing to follow the route of marriage, home and family.

Left: Wives of unemployed miners in Royston, near Barnsley, return home with packages of seasonable fare provided by a charity in 1928.

ONLY CHILDREN.
Are They Robbed of Childhood?

THERE is one great danger which confronts mothers of only children—the danger of robbing the little ones of their most precious possession—the gift of childhood.

Children may be robbed either physically, mentally, or morally of childhood. Some poor mites are deprived in all three ways, but naturally a mother never robs her precious bairn on purpose—she simply errs through ignorance or lack of thought.

MISTAKEN KINDNESS.

We all know the mother who robs her boy of childhood—physically. She feeds him like his father and then wonders why he is never well. She keeps him up late at night, takes him into crowded and unhealthy places, and always dresses him unsuitably.

The child who is robbed mentally generally has a lonely mother. She makes a companion and a confidant of him—treating him always like a "grown up." Consequently the lovely little childish mind is overburdened and overdeveloped. The boy constantly says smart things and is considered "clever and advanced."

But what is cleverness compared with the whole world of childish wonders that are lost to him—the delicious frankness, the charming simplicity, the sweet innocence that once driven out can never come back?

Lastly comes the mother who robs her child morally. Thinking she is making him happy, she always indulges him. She never checks his faults, never teaches him control, but brings him up to behave as if everybody and everything were simply created for his selfish pleasure. Unless such a child is soon removed from this well-meaning but dangerous influence, he will eventually become one of the world's wasters.

IN LARGE FAMILIES.

The mother of many does not often rob her children. She has learnt how to look after them properly physically; she does not rob them mentally because they lead their own nursery life in each other's company; and she brings them up to be unselfish and self-controlled because otherwise the home life would be impossible.

But it may often mean much denial for the mother of one to see that her child *always* has plenty of fresh air, sound sleep, simple food, and the constant companionship of other children for which he naturally craves. Her reward will be the lasting health and happiness of her little one, while she will find that other mothers will give her helping hints and a helping hand. For there is a bond between mothers that few ignore.

1920s Postscripts

May 1922: Parliament passed the Separation and Maintenance Orders Bill which ensured that maintenance to a wife and family would be continued even if the husband was in jail. Previously, for some men, jail for non-payment of maintenance was seen as an alternative to paying up.

August 1922: Following the first Congress of the International Federation of Feminine Athletes, a one-day Olympiad for women athletes was held in Paris. Great Britain won with 50 points; USA came second with 31 points and France third with 29.

September 1922: The US Congress passed a bill giving women equal naturalisation and citizenship rights with men.

October1922: Mrs W. H. Felton of Georgia became the first woman Senator in the USA.

1923: The Matrimonial Causes Act made grounds for divorce the same for both sexes.

February 1923: A bill was passed making married women responsible for any crimes they committed in their husbands' presence. Previously husbands were deemed responsible for offences their wives might commit in their presence on the assumption that the wife was coerced by her husband into acting criminally.

Divorce on Equal Terms

The 1923 Matrimonial Causes Act granted women the right to divorce their husbands on the same grounds as men could divorce their wives. Eleven years before, in 1912, the Royal Commission on Divorce had recommended that the grounds for divorce should be equal for women and men. The Commission and finally the 1923 Act were the result of pressure against the inequality of the 1857 Matrimonial Causes Act.

Before 1857 divorce could only be granted through a Private Act of Parliament, the expense of which meant that it was a recourse only for the very few. The 1857 Act allowed divorce through the law courts but the grounds for divorce were not the same for men and women. A man could divorce his wife for adultery but a woman had to prove not only adultery on her husband's part but also bigamy, desertion, incest or cruelty.

The 1923 Act still relied on proving the adultery of the other partner – so divorce was still regarded as unacceptable to most people as in order to be divorced you had to have been involved in some way in an immoral act. If neither partner was guilty of adultery but the marriage had broken down and they wanted to divorce, one of the partners would have to furnish evidence of adultery, even if it meant fabricating that evidence.

At the time of the Royal Commission on Divorce fewer than one in 500 marriages ended in divorce. Divorce was only the remedy of the desperate. Divorcees, whether the 'innocent' party or not, were shunned by society, and indeed barred from the Royal Enclosure at Ascot.

Top: Lady Elizabeth Bowes-Lyon leaves her home in April 1923 for Westminster Abbey, where she was to marry the Duke of York, second son of King George V.

Left: Three-times-married actress Mary Pickford was known as America's Sweetheart in the 1920s. Making her first appearance in a movie at the age of 17 in 1909, Pickford wasted little time before becoming a producer on her own films. In 1919 she was a co-founder of the film studio United Artists along with Charlie Chaplin, director D. W. Griffith and her second husband Douglas Fairbanks – thus becoming the most powerful woman in Hollywood for many years.

Below: Alfred Hitchcock and Alma Reville on their wedding day outside the Brompton Oratory, London, in 1926.

Business Girls

For many working-class women who were not needed to help in the family home it had long been accepted that they would take a job, mainly as domestic servants, before they married and had a home of their own. Only a few middle- and upper-class women ever did paid work before the First World War but by the 1920s there was a growing number of women, 'business girls', working as clerks in a variety of businesses and institutions.

Women proved willing and able to use typewriters, which were becoming an increasingly common piece of office equipment. However, the fact that employers were able to pay women less than the male clerks was probably more of a reason than their skills for the increasing number of women clerks. This lower pay for women led to a great deal of ill-feeling on the part of the male clerks and, instead of fighting for equal or better pay for women, the clerks' unions decried women for taking men's jobs.

Outside business, there was an increasing number of women in professional jobs such as medicine, nursing and teaching and the first women had been called to the Bar. However, the number of women qualified or aspiring to be doctors, lawyers, accountants or aiming to follow a high-level career in business or the Civil Service was infinitesimal in relation to the number of men in those areas. A report in the *Daily Mail* in 1924 revealed that there were 25 women acting as, or qualified as, barristers; eight women qualified or admitted as solicitors; 30 women trying to qualify as accountants; a few women working as auctioneers; and a slowly increasing number of women as analytical chemists. The fact that, in most jobs, there was a stark choice between marriage and a career severely limited women's horizons.

BUSINESS GIRLS AND COLD WEATHER.

"WHAT a miserable, raw morning!" exclaimed Marion as she came into the office. "How I dislike the winter! I suppose I shall get my usual crop of chilblains and be thoroughly unhappy until spring comes again."

There are many business girls who really suffer in winter weather and are quite unable either to work efficiently or to look their best when a severe spell of cold or wet is in progress.

A Doctor's Advice.

The advice recently given by a woman doctor to a business girl of this type may be of assistance to others.

"Get up in good time every morning," advised the doctor, "have a brisk sponge down in hot water, followed by vigorous friction with a rough towel, and one or two simple Swedish exercises. Dress quickly and eat a good warming breakfast at leisure. Then walk part of the way at least to the office so that you arrive in a glow of healthy exercise."

The doctor was also very emphatic about suitable winter clothing for business girls. Rubber-soled brogue shoes, warm stockings, a reliable mackintosh for wet weather, a warm winter coat, and pure wool "undies" she regarded as essentials, with the additional recom- mendation of woollen gauntlet gloves for girls who suffer from chilblains.

The doctor, in addition, condemned the habit of the "tea and cake" luncheon. She suggested cheese sandwiches and a cup of cocoa; a bowl of good soup followed by a steam pudding, or scrambled egg and a glass of malted milk, as nourishing yet inexpensive luncheon menus. The business girl cannot hope to keep fit in winter time if she does not eat a sufficiency of sustaining food.

Proof Against Chill.

The problem of how to keep warm during office hours has been successfully solved by a business girl who used to suffer from constant chills and chilblains. She kept her hands warm by wearing deep cuffs knitted in rabbit wool. She wore double brown paper socks in her shoes with some dry mustard sprinkled between the layers, to prevent her feet from becoming chilled.

The business girl needs a brisk walk during her luncheon hour, so as to get the blood well circulating through the body again between her spells of sedentary work. Moreover, she would find great benefit to her health in winter time if she joined a hard court tennis or a Badminton club for regular exercise.

Top Left: Taking dictation in 1922.

Top right: Workers in the wrapping department of the Mackintosh's toffee factory, Halifax, in 1930.

Above: Mrs Vernet, Britain's first female bookmaker, who became a partner in Ladbrokes in 1918, at work in Tattersall's ring at Epsom races in 1920.

Women and Wireless.

By N. W. Fraser.

ALTHOUGH women are deeply interested in wireless and form the majority of this country's listeners-in, it must be admitted that their contributions to wireless progress have so far been unimportant. This at least appears to be true of the inventive, scientific, and engineering sides, and the Wireless Exhibition, held last week at the Royal Horticultural Hall, did not reveal any discoveries or improvements due to feminine research and ingenuity.

Opening for Lecturers.

Many women are finding careers of one kind or another in wireless as entertainers, accompanists, speakers, and lecturers. There are openings as lecturers for women possessed of expert knowledge of matters of particular interest to their sex. The field, however, is somewhat restricted by the fact that women's voices are generally inferior to men's for broadcasting purposes, although, as a broadcasting official pointed out recently, this may be the fault of the microphone, not of women's vocal organs.

Working for the microphone, however, is usually a temporary and part-time occupation. Apart from clerical work women hold whole-time posts as chief organisers and organisers under the British Broadcasting Company, but at present there are practically no vacancies.

MOCKING AT MARRIAGE

To the Editor of the Daily Mail:

Women are now taking the place of men in almost every sphere and like the nouveaux riches their new interests are intoxicating them and they have not found their true perspective. But the one thing they did stand for – finely and simply – the honour and sanctity of home, has been trodden down more ruthlessly by them than by men.

May Atkinson
Extract from letter to the Daily Mail,
23 November 1922

1920s Postscripts

March 1923: The actress Sarah Bernhardt died. She had gained a degree of freedom as an actress that she would never have achieved had she not gone on the stage. She earned enough money of her own to buy a theatre which she named after herself.

April 1923: The Académie Française, an association of 40 French scholars and writers, admitted its first woman member, Mme Alfred Mortier.

June 1923: Mussolini approved a bill to give Italian women the vote in local elections.

January 1924: The first Winter Olympics were held at Chamonix – but women were only allowed to compete in figure-skating events.

February 1924: A bill to give all women the vote at 21 was given a second reading, but it was never to become law.

November 1924: Stanley Baldwin, soon to be Prime Minister, stated in an election campaign speech: 'The discrimination between men and women contained in the present franchise cannot be permanent.'

1925: The Widows, Orphans and Old Age Pensions Contributory Act was passed giving widows a pension of 10 shillings a week from January 1926.

Dying to Give Birth

Three thousand women died in childbirth in 1924. To give birth to a child was four times more dangerous than for a man to work down a mine, the most dangerous job of the period. Countless other women were disabled or damaged by the process of giving birth or from the infections which spread through the increasingly commonly used maternity wards.

Following concern at the poor state of health of the nation's male population and the high infant mortality rates which deprived the state of fit soldiers during the Boer War at the turn of the century, efforts were made to cut the infant death rate. In 1900, for every thousand babies registered alive there were 154 which were stillborn or died soon after birth. By 1919, when the Maternal and Child Welfare Act came into force and the Ministry of Health was set up, the infant mortality rate had been cut by 42 per cent to 89 deaths per thousand live births. In the same period of time the reduction in the maternal death rate was less than 25 per cent.

It was again a war which prompted the government into action to try to improve women's health generally and reduce the cost, in terms of death and disablement, of childbirth. The need for women workers in wartime showed that women's health, and that of working-class women in particular, was in a poor state. The Maternal and Child Welfare Act was passed partly in response to these findings and partly because a proportion of women were now voters. Prior to 1919 there was no statutory requirement to provide education, supervision or medical care for a woman during pregnancy or childbirth.

The Act, however, made few inroads into maternal mortality – in 1929 the number of women dying in childbirth was 2,787. Ironically, one important reason for the failure to reduce these figures was the increasing tendency to encourage women to have their babies in hospital. Although the reason for more hospital births was because of the appallingly unhygienic state of housing, for many mothers the risk of infection and puerperal fever was much higher in hospital as it would spread from one mother to the next unless rigorous disinfection procedures were followed. The fact that obstetrics and gynaecology were looked down upon even by the medical profession itself meant there was a serious shortage of doctors with any training or experience in these areas, which further hampered efforts to reduce the maternal mortality rate.

Above left: Marie Stopes with her son Harry in 1924. Born in 1880, Stopes studied as a paleobotanist in London and Munich and later Manchester, where she became the first female member of the science faculty at the university. Her first book *Married Love*, published in 1918, was condemned by churches, the medical establishment and the press but it had sold 750,000 copies by 1931. A second book, *Wise Parenthood*, on the subject of contraception, followed in 1918.

In 1921 Stopes opened a family planning clinic in north London, the first in the country, offering a free service to married women. In 1925, the clinic moved to central London and more opened across the country.

By 1930, other family planning organisations had been set up and they joined forces with Stopes to form the National Birth Control Council (later the Family Planning Association).

Above right: The Duchess of York (later Queen Elizabeth, the Queen Mother) pictured meeting the latest arrival at Hitchin Hospital, Hertfordshire, in 1929. Before World War Two most babies were born at home, with hospital births only becoming a majority during the war. By 1975 the number of home births had fallen below five per cent, and has remained around this level ever since.

Left: Queen Mary pictured on a visit to Deptford Babies' Camp, south London.

Custody of the Children

In 1839 an Infant Custody Act was passed which for the first time gave mothers some rights of custody over their children under the age of seven. The courts could grant custody to the mother if the Lord Chancellor agreed and only if the woman was judged to be of good character. Despite these restrictions it was a major step forward and almost entirely due to the efforts of one woman.

Early in the nineteenth century, Caroline Norton's alcoholic husband deserted her and took their three sons with him, denying his wife access to the children. She had no recourse to the courts as the law said that the father alone had rights over his children.

Norton fought to have the law changed even though by the time the changes were introduced one child was dead and the others were too old for her to benefit.

A further law in 1886 again eroded some of the automatic rights of fathers to custody of their children. The Act stated that the welfare of the children should be taken into consideration when deciding on custody. It also allowed for a mother to become a child's sole guardian or to be joint guardian with a partner of the father's choice if the father died.

It was not until 1925 when the Guardianship of Infants Act was passed that the law gave fathers and mothers equal rights over their children. So, for example, a minor who wished to marry would require the consent of both parents when they were living together. When the parents were separated or divorced, consent went with custody and mothers were entitled to be considered equally with fathers for custody.

Top: Children with their teacher using a sewing machine – circa 1920. Isaac Singer popularised the modern sewing machine in the 1850s and soon commercial sewing patterns were widely available. However, the rapid growth of the ready-made garment industry in the 1920s and 1930s changed attitudes and the popularity of home dressmaking diminished.

Above: Miss Margery Springman a volunteer worker at St John's Wood Health Society's Day Nursery, taking her charges to play in Regent's Park in 1920. Note the number of children to be supervised by one adult!

THE SUBJECTION OF MEN

...though we may doubt if at any date married women were really treated as slaves or chattels by the British husband.

Since then a whole host of Acts of Parliament has removed woman's real or fancied disabilities, she has obtained the vote, and she is shortly to receive it on the same terms as men, which means that as she preponderates in numbers she will gradually dominate the electorate. Women have the right to sit in the House of Commons. They can practise at the Bar, and as solicitors, as doctors, as surgeons. They may act as Justices of the Peace. They can take university degrees at most of our universities, including Oxford, though not yet at Cambridge. What is more they appear to be dominating certain of the English Universities...

If there are disabilities in marriage today they attach to the mere male. The unfortunate husband can be sued if his wife is guilty of slander, libel or assault. He has to pay the penalty, and according to an excellent legal authority, it is doubtful whether he has any remedy against his wife's property. Divorce is now to be obtained by either sex on identical grounds. The subjection of women has certainly passed for ever, and it seems almost as if the subjection of men might be beginning.

Extracts from a Daily Mail Leader,
17 June 1924

The Care of Children's Clothes.
Some Hints Mothers will Appreciate.

THE cost of clothing three or four children nowadays is not a light one, but garments of all descriptions can be made to last longer and look fresher if care is bestowed on them by mother or nurse.

BOOTS AND SHOES.

A little castor oil should be warmed and rubbed into children's school boots before they are worn. This oil not only softens the leather and prevents it from cracking but it will keep out the wet. Boots so treated will not blacken very well for a few days, but when the oil has sunk in they will take a good polish. An excellent plan to make the soles of boots or shoes wear longer is to give them a coat of clear copal varnish, and this should be quite dry before the boots are worn.

Children often return from school with straw hats soaked with rain: if the ribbon is not discoloured it should be removed at once and wound round a bottle until dry, when it will look like new. The hat itself should be placed flat on a table and books with covers of little consequence placed round the brim to keep it in shape.

Some children fidget with the buttons of their coats until one gets lost, and an odd button cannot well replace it; and to save buying a new set the other buttons could be covered with a piece of good velveteen to match the material of the coat—only a tiny length will be needed—and an odd button could be used to replace the lost one

All socks and stockings worn by children will last longer if they are darned lightly at the heels and toes when bought, and to prevent ladders being started by suspenders the hose should be stretched out to their fullest extent and machine stitched with the same coloured cotton round the leg just below where the suspenders will grip.

The fingers of children's gloves are so small they often shrink and curl after being washed unless they are pulled into shape, or have glove stretchers placed in them, and they should not be dried too near the fire.

WHEN DAMP.

Children should be taught to hang up their clothes as soon as they remove them; it is crumpled and creased garments that look so shabby, and damp clothes should have special attention in this direction, as the creases are doubly pronounced if allowed to dry in their folds.

39

Far left: Woking Ladies play Hythe Ladies during the hockey festival at Folkstone in 1927.

Left: Golfers at the Women's Open Golf Championships at Hunstanton in 1928.

Below left: A tug of war between women wearing knickerbockers at Sudbury in 1921.

Below: Start of the Women's 800 metres race at the 1928 Olympic Games in Amsterdam, won by Frau Lina Radke of Germany.

RADIOGRAPH SILHOUETTES

Slimness More to be Desired than Sunburn – Wispy Women who Keep on the Fashionable Side of Nine Stone – A Standard Outline for all Nationalities – Deauville.

Like a radiograph is the silhouette of the lovely women and girls now in Deauville. Their flimsy, exquisitely made frocks seem to contain only a shadow of a human form. How they have managed so entirely to standardise themselves is a mystery, for they are all outlined in the same pattern: French, English, Italian, Spanish, whatever the race, they all conform to the tyranny of fashion. And fashion absolutely refuses to countenance any plump, round contours.

Daily Mail, 20 August 1926

MILLINERY CONTRASTS.
Small and Wide Brims.

THE best of the new hats run to extremes; they are either very small or very large. The cloche outline remains practically the same, but the narrow brim is given a coquettish twist that suggests something quite new without doing away with a popular favourite.

This coming summer 1880 hats are going to be immensely popular. They will be worn with fitted coat-dresses and with tube-frocks. These hats have very high crowns and very narrow brims —the latter curled up at the sides.

From Paris.

1920s Postscripts

January 1925: After her election in November 1924 as Governor of Texas 'Ma' Miriam Ferguson was sworn in as the first woman State Governor in the USA.

March 1925: Universal suffrage was granted to men in Japan.

1926: The Legitimacy Act was passed, making a child legitimate if its parents married after its birth. Previously an illegitimate child was illegitimate for life – its status could not be changed. But the Act did not allow for children born as a result of adultery to be legitimised.

May 1926: Women in India became eligible to stand for election to public office.

1926: The General Strike began and many women volunteered to help run essential services.

August 1926: Gertrude Ederle, a 19-year-old Bronze Medal winner in the 1924 Paris Olympics, became the first woman to swim the English Channel. Her time of 14 hours 31 minutes was two hours faster than the previous record set by a man.

1927: The birthrate in Britain was the lowest on record with a ratio of 85 births to every 100 deaths.

The Changing Shape of Women

By the mid-1920s women were wearing clothes undreamt of less than 20 years before. The period 1910 to 1919 had been very mixed years in terms of women's dress. The First World War saw many women in uniforms and other sorts of functional clothing. After the war there were some frills as a reaction to the severity of the war fashions but the general trend was for simpler, freer, more functional dress.

The war was not the only reason for this change. Women, mainly those of the upper and middle classes, were beginning to do more outside the confines of running the home, taking part in sports, some even having jobs. This busier lifestyle needed clothing to suit. Less use was made of corsets, and skirts became shorter as outfits became less fussy and heavy to wear. By 1919 clothes were much shorter and softer and the bust and bottom much flatter.

However, the greatest revolution in women's dress was yet to come. The 1920s saw a rapid acceleration of the earlier trends. By 1927 women's clothing was almost tubular, hiding any trace of female shape. Slimming became popular to achieve the desired pencil-like silhouette. The bust, bottom, even the waist disappeared under dresses and suits cut to eliminate them and hemlines reached mid-calf to knee length.

The clothing of the 1920s was not the only way in which women's looks changed dramatically. Images of women drawn from popular Hollywood films made cosmetics more acceptable and there was a growing fashion for suntans and sunbathing. Hairstyles changed too. In 1919 most women had long hair which they wore up in some form or other, but by the end of the 1920s short hair was more the norm. Shorter hairstyles such as the 'bob', the Eton crop and the 'shingle' were popular because they took less time to look after. They were also in a sense emancipating. Many men objected strongly to their wives and daughters having their hair cut.

The fashions of the 1920s reflected a growing sense of women's desire to be freer and to compete with men, so much so that in many respects the fashions denied women's femininity. And although most of the fashions were for middle and upper class women the hairstyles, shorter skirts and freer, more functional styles of clothing permeated all levels of society, revolutionising the way women felt they could dress.

Above: A wrap-coat with a Ballet Russe influence. After the 1917 Revolution, Russian émigrés fled to Paris and found work using their skills in embroidery and appliqué at fashion houses such as Patou and Chanel.

Left: The height of fashion in 1926. Hems just below the knee, dropped waists, bar shoes and short hair all allowed women to move around more freely.

Right: A coat in blue velour with squirrel-fur trim, 1925.

Far right: Towards the end of the 1920s 'pyjama suits', like this one in pink crêpe de Chine with a silver fur-trimmed coat, were all the rage in high society.

Women and the Trade Unions

In 1926 there were around three million women working in industry. For men industry was the most strongly unionised area of the economy, but for women the unions brought little advantage. Only in the textile industry, which had a long tradition of unionised women workers, did the trade unions offer any support to women. Most other trade unions discriminated against women, many even banning them from membership. Mary McArthur had founded the National Federation of Women Workers in 1906 to fight for better pay and conditions for women workers, but inevitably men's unions within particular industries were far stronger and better organised.

Pay was the issue which most affected the unions' treatment of women workers. There was also an underlying feeling that women should be at home. That it was legal, and in fact accepted, that women would be paid less than men drove the unions and their male leaders to fight, not for equal pay for women, but to exclude women from as many jobs as they could. They campaigned for restrictions on women's working hours, often classing them in the same category as children. This was not just in Britain but throughout the world – in 1919 the USA brought in legislation banning women and 'young persons' from night work.

Arthur Pugh, President of the TUC in 1926, estimated that of the five and three-quarter million women in work only one-sixth were in a trade union. The attitude of male trade unionists was responsible in large part for this, but many women were in jobs which were difficult to unionise. As unemployment began to bite, domestic service, still one of the main sources of work for women, was the only area of the economy to show an increase in workers. But it was difficult to organise domestic workers who often depended upon their employers for accommodation and food as well as wages, were based on widely scattered sites and had little time or opportunity to meet each other.

Women workers suffered greatly during the rising unemployment of the 1920s and 1930s. Many had been pushed out of their jobs at the end or soon after the end of the war in order to give work to returning soldiers – an agreement negotiated between employers, unions and government. The postwar economy failed to produce work for the many women seeking employment. And despite the fact that women were cheaper labour than men, when jobs were cut women were often the first to go in the belief that men as breadwinners should have any remaining employment.

Above left: Female engine-drivers, in light shoes, turn their hands to shovelling coal on a steam engine while a male colleague looks on during the General Strike in 1926.

Left: A woman engine-driver in cloth cap and high-heeled shoes fixes a lamp on her steam train during the General Strike.

Above: The *Daily Mail* reported that the increased patronage of football matches by women spectators was a marked feature of the 1920–21 English season. Five women are seen in this section of the crowd at Arsenal's gound, Highbury.

GIRL TO BE IN BY 10
Magistrate Agrees with Father's Rule

A girl aged 20 complained to the Willesden magistrate Dr Lloyd Williams yesterday that her father had taken away her latchkey. He did not approve of her going to dances and insisted on her being home by 10 p.m.

Dr Williams: I think he is right. What business has a girl like you to stay out after 10 p.m.? That is quite late enough, and you must obey your father.

Daily Mail, 8 January 1929

Higher Education for Women

In 1921, 1,000 women gathered in the Sheldonian Theatre at Oxford to be awarded their degrees. Many of these women had sat and passed the university degree exams years before but had had no formal recognition of their achievements because Oxford University refused to award degrees to women.

The 1919 Sex Disqualification (Removal) Act prompted Oxford to allow women to sit for full degrees in 1920, hence the retrospective award ceremony. However, the university statutes limited the number of places available for women students to one for every six male students. Cambridge University held out against awarding degrees to women until after World War Two. Even among the non-Oxbridge universities where women had long been accepted they were not admitted in equal numbers to men.

The limited places awarded to women led to a distinct dichotomy in the way girls were treated in schools. Vera Brittain in her book *Lady into Woman* suggests that in many secondary and private girls' schools much time was wasted teaching girls of average and lesser ability 'accomplishments' rather than giving them a real education. The more able pupils, especially in the public school system, were rigorously schooled for examinations at the expense of developing social skills and personal confidence.

However, for many girls in the 1920s and beyond, the ability to attend school was often limited by the expectation that they would help out in the home. Girls' education was still seen as something which could be sacrificed for this or if there were boys to be educated when money was short. Few girls, especially those in the working classes, ever had the opportunity to progress beyond the elementary school to gain a secondary education and fewer still had access to higher education.

SUCCESS IN GAMES:

A common error made by girls when taking up a sport in which they are quite inexperienced is to choose a heavy implement in the belief that it will enable them to hit with greater power.

It sometimes happens that the weight stamped on racquets, billiard cues, and so on, is not always accurate. In any case balance is far more important than nominal or actual weight, though a woman should not chose a lawn tennis racquet which exceeds 14oz. – many experts would say 13.5oz., or even less – and a billiard cue not more than 15oz. Hockey sticks vary in weight with the player's position. A range of from 18oz. to 22oz. or 23oz. should suffice.

Instinctive Judgement.

Closely allied with the balance is the 'feel' of the implement. Do not be in a hurry to make your choice. Keep on trying different samples until you pick up one that somehow or other you feel is the right one for you. In nine cases out of ten, this instinctive judgement will prove correct, but there is a tenth case. Out of a dozen, or, for that matter, fifty bats, racquets, clubs, identical in make and dimensions, perhaps only one will have a 'soul'. Instinct will generally detect that invaluable quality, but sometimes it takes actual play to reveal its presence or absence.

Top left: Some of the 1,000 women awarded degrees at Oxford in 1921. These women passed their degree exams in the first 20 years of the century, but because the university would not allow women to graduate they had never had formal recognition of their achievement.

Above left: Children of bargemen attend school at the Boatmen's Institute in Brentford, London, 1921.

Above: Girls study in the late 1920s.

1920s Postscripts

February 1927: Revisions to the Book of Common Prayer, including the dropping of the word 'obey' for women, were proposed. However, the House of Commons rejected the changes and none of the revisions were made.

1928: The Equal Franchise Act extended the vote to all women over the age of 21.

1928: Radclyffe Hall's novel *The Well of Loneliness* was withdrawn after advice from the Home Secretary and much public controversy over its content. The novel deals with a lesbian relationship which was something unimagined, let alone talked about, by the majority of people in 1928.

May 1928: A Leader in the *Daily Mail* asked for support for a manifesto published by the New Health Society which called for an improvement in the services to the 750,000 women giving birth annually, of whom only 50,000 had access to a bed in a maternity hospital and who were served by only 800 antenatal clinics nationally. There was also a plea to cut the maternal death rate.

Equal Franchise

Ten years after the first instalment of the vote for women, the second was delivered. Women at last had the vote on the same terms as men. Everyone over the age of 21, regardless of their marital status, could vote. The Equal Franchise Bill was dubbed 'The Flapper's Vote' and enfranchised six million more women. Flapper had come to mean almost any fashionable young woman, but it was originally a pejorative term for women who adopted new fashions and conventions and were seen as loose-living; it was derived from a German slang word for prostitute.

There were several reasons why it took ten years to secure votes for women on the same terms as men. First, the women's organisations which had been so vociferous before the war had lost much of their momentum as a result of the four-year conflict, and the fact that half the female adult population were given the vote in 1918 made it more difficult to argue a case of gross injustice.

Second, as many young women found opportunities to do things such as work outside the home, take part in sports and go out to social occasions unchaperoned, the fact that they had no political power seemed less urgent than if they had not had these new freedoms.

The fear on the part of men which existed before the first enfranchisement of women was the third and perhaps most overwhelming reason for the delay in bringing in an equal franchise. Men, and particularly those in Parliament, had feared that women would vote en masse for a woman's party, changing for ever the status quo and profile of the British political system. Ten years of women voting had shown that women distributed their votes fairly evenly among the existing political parties. While some men continued to argue that because there were more women than men giving women the vote was undemocratic and unfair on men, Parliament conceded that women should have the franchise on the same terms as men.

There had been benefits to women in the ten years since they had first been given the vote and had been able to become MPs. Between 1918 and 1928 16 Acts of Parliament which directly affected the status, health or rights of women had been passed. In the 18 years prior to that only four such Acts had become law. The vote had brought power to make changes, albeit limited, to women's lives.

Above left: One woman to another – a snapshot of two female canvassers interviewing a woman in Dover in 1921.

Above right: Emmeline Pankhurst's coffin leaves the church in June 1928 with nine of her old associates acting as pall bearers.

Far Left: A poster parade in support of the Equal Franchise Bill in 1928.

Left: A worker for Dame Helen Gwynne-Vaughan, Conservative candidate for North Camberwell, addressing an open-air meeting in October 1924.

Opposite left: The eight women MPs returned in the 1923 General Election: (L-R) Dorothea Jewson; Susan Lawrence; Lady Astor; Mrs Wintringham; the Duchess of Atholl; Mrs Hilton Philipson; Lady Terrington; Margaret Bondfield.

1920s

MASS CANVASSING. Election Time Work for Women.

"**N**UMBERS of women who come to offer their services during the election say they would like to canvass, but that they are too nervous to attempt. the work," said a girl who is assisting a woman candidate in one of the constituencies.

"We explain to them that canvassing need not be a *dreadful* ordeal—as they express it—but still a large number declared they could not set out and 'tackle' electors. We have overcome their difficulties by mass canvassing. This is what we do.

"Union is Strength."

"During the day we go in a party—as many as ten or even twenty of us—some in a car, some on foot, arranging to meet in a street in a poor part of the district, choosing the neighbourhood where a properly organised meeting is to be held in the evening. One of the party is an experienced canvasser, but the rest, for the most part, are making their first acquaintance with election work. We reach the appointed place, and when the whole of the party is together we ring a hand-bell. All the canvassers scatter and go to the various doors in the street and knock while the bell is ringing, and tell the women who open the doors that a short meeting is going to be held then and there, and request them to come to listen.

"Sometimes we get quite a chilly reception for the first few minutes—not even a dog barks at us!—but gradually a window is flung up over there, a door, which was first shut against us, is slowly opened. One by one, attracted by our enthusiastic clatter, women approach the car. We no longer speak to the empty air. We have an audience, which quickly grows bigger and bigger. Men returning to their dinner or tea stop to listen. Our crowd numbers more than fifty.

"In our speech we touch upon points which the candidate for this constituency will deal with in his or her programme.

An Earnest Discussion.

"Enthusiasm is catching. An inexperienced canvasser, emboldened by the interest shown among the audience, engages in an earnest discussion with a voter. Another girl does the same. On the way back several of our helpers recount how they 'found their tongues.'

"Again and again, after such an outing, a girl will tell me that she believes she is a born canvasser; in fact, she is eager to go out after that by herself. The 'bogey' which she has conjured up has disappeared. She has seen enough to gain confidence and has learnt that the *human touch* is the canvasser's surest asset to success."

Above: Miss Margaret Bondfield, the first woman Cabinet Minister, photographed at No. 10 Downing Street after returning from Windsor where she had an audience with the King in June 1929.

Below: The good looks of a large percentage of the women students at Oxford was commented on in the student magazine, *The Isis.*

'A woman of 30 may serve on a jury, she may be a doctor of medicine, she may decide on a question of life and death where an operation may take place, but there are people who say she is not fit to vote. That is rather difficult to defend in public.'

Stanley Baldwin addressing 2,000 women union delegates at the Albert Hall, as quoted in the Daily Mail, 28 May 1927

1920s Postscripts

June 1928: On the day the Equal Franchise Bill received its final reading in Parliament, the funeral cortège of Emmeline Pankhurst travelled through the spectator-lined streets of Westminster from the church of St John's, Smith Square, where her body had been lying in state, to Brompton Cemetery.

1929: Following an enquiry and criticism by the League of Nations, the age of marriage in Britain was raised from 12 for girls and 14 for boys to 16 for both sexes.

1929: Obstetrics and gynaecology gained 'respectability' with the formation of the British College of Obstetricians and Gynaecologists by William Blair-Bell and William Fletcher Shaw.

1929: Women were granted the right to sit in the Canadian Senate, Canada's second legislative chamber.

May 1929: The first General Election in which women had an equal franchise returned 13 women MPs.

May 1929: Dr Linda Gage Roth published a report on the health during pregnancy and childbirth of over 1,000 graduates from Smith College, one of the USA's most prestigious colleges. Dr Roth found that those among the women who took exercise suffered fewer complications than those who did not, contrary to the prevalent view that sport damaged women's ability to bear children.

June 1929: Labour Prime Minister Ramsay MacDonald named Margaret Bondfield as Minister of Labour. She was the first woman member of a British Cabinet.

October 1929: The Stock Market on New York's Wall Street suffered the Great Crash and markets in London and around the world fell, plunging the world into the Great Depression.

Competing with Men

In May 1930 Amy Johnson flew solo to Australia. She set off from the airfield at Croydon for the trip which was to take her 19 days in her tiny Gypsy Moth biplane. She became a heroine of the period, fêted by the press, even having a song, 'Amy, Wonderful Amy', to sing her praises. This flight was the first of many record-breaking attempts and achievements by Amy Johnson. The following year she flew from Britain to Japan via Siberia and in 1936 set a new record for the flight from London to Cape Town.

Amy Johnson was only one of a group of women aviators of the 1920s and '30s. She, and later also Beryl Markham, were the darlings of the British public because they were home grown but there were other women pilots throughout the world. In 1928 the American Amelia Earhart became the first woman to fly the Atlantic. She went on to fly solo across the Pacific in 1935. Attempting, in 1937, to be the first person to fly solo round the world, Amelia Earhart disappeared and no trace has ever been found of her or her plane.

Women aviators were perhaps the most obvious sign of women's achievements in areas of life where men dominated or where women were thought incapable of competing, but there were others. Gertrude Ederle had swum the Channel in 1926. She was the first woman ever to do so and cut two hours off the previous record set by a man. M. E. Foster won the King's Prize for shooting at Bisley in 1930. These were sports where women were competing against men and there was very much a feeling at the time that women had to prove themselves in a male environment if they were to be taken seriously.

Indeed, much of men's arguments against women in the past had been that women had not the capacity mentally, physically or emotionally to take on, let alone succeed, in a vast field of activities outside the home. Many women throughout the 1930s worked hard in many spheres of life to dispel some of these ideas, achieving many 'firsts' for women, and broadening the horizons for many women to come.

Above: Amy Johnson with her Gypsy Moth and *(opposite right)* American Amelia Earhart.

Below: American swimmer Gertrude Ederle (right) shakes hands with fellow swimmer Lillian Cannon. Ederle won three medals in the 1924 Olympic Games and in1926 became the first woman to swim the English Channel, which she crossed in 14 hr and 31 min, breaking the previous men's record.

WOMEN'S BRAINS ARE SMALLER-
Not their Intellect

'Women have smaller brains than men, but do not run away with the idea that they are less intelligent,' said Professor Cyril Burt in a lecture at Kingsway Hall, Kingsway, last night.

He was speaking on 'The Psychologist's Measurement of Intelligence', and he declared that the size of the brain had nothing to do with the efficiency of the mind.

Daily Mail, 30 January 1934

Left: The scene in Trafalgar Square in 1930 when aviator Amy Johnson passed through the cheering crowds on the way to a luncheon in her honour.

Right: The district maternity nurse in north Devon pictured on a new motorcycle given to help her cover her 200 square miles of territory.

The Morality of Birth Control

Throughout the 1920s the birth rate continued to fall, partly through the pioneer work of the few family planning clinics, although growing economic hardship and crisis was probably a greater reason for fewer babies being born. The 'great debate' about the forecasted chronic under-population of Britain by the end of the century due to the falling birth rate also brought information to many women ignorant of the facts, and the idea that it was possible to control the number of children born.

Few women avoided conception by the use of contraceptive devices; for most, withdrawal was the only method of avoiding pregnancy that was available or known to them. Illegal induced abortion was the other way to limit family size. These abortions were mainly self-administered with a variety of instruments, or by taking any of a whole host of 'special pills', many of which contained dangerous chemicals such as lead or other abortifacients, home-made mixtures of chemicals, herbal concoctions, or strong laxatives.

The fact that the Churches condemned artificial birth control only served to make those women or men who used contraceptive devices feel immoral. Even if they could justify their actions to themselves, society would not accept their reasons. The women who attended clinics run by Marie Stopes, Helena Wright and others had to be either very strongwilled or else desperate.

In 1930 came a revolutionary encyclical letter on the subject of birth control from the Archbishop of Canterbury, Cosmo Lang. The letter followed much debate within the Church of England and stated that, 'if there is good moral reason why the way of abstinence should not be followed, we cannot condemn the use of scientific methods, which are thoughtfully and conscientiously adopted.' This was not a wholehearted approval of contraception, especially as the letter went on to urge restrictions on its sale and advertising, and condemned most severely birth control for selfish gain and convenience. Nonetheless, this limited acceptance by the state Church in England paved the way for a far more tolerant public attitude towards contraception, so that by 1939, when the various clinics throughout the country came together as the Family Planning Association with the slogan 'Children by Choice, not Chance', the subject was almost respectable.

Within six months of the Anglican Church giving limited approval to artificial birth control, the Roman Catholic Church had reaffirmed its opposition to the practice. A papal encyclical issued in January of 1931 clearly condemned any attempts to prevent conception artificially.

Above: All-round athlete 'Babe' Didrikson. After winning medals in three disciplines at the 1932 Olympics, she toured with basketball and baseball teams before becoming a championship-winning golfer.

Left: Jane Addams – campaigner for human rights and winner of the Nobel Peace Prize.

1930s Postscripts

1930: Welfare Centres were allowed to give birth-control advice to married women.

1930: Mary Bagot Stack founded the Women's League of Health and Beauty to teach fitness through exercise and provide education on diet and hygiene.

1931: The results of the census showed that, including teachers and nurses, professional women outnumbered professional men by 389,359 to 356,762.

The census also showed that 200,000 more women were in domestic service than in 1921,

mainly as a result of the Depression and the fact that there was no other work available.

December 1931: American sociologist Jane Addams was awarded the Nobel Peace Prize. She had devoted her life to campaigning for the poor, women's rights and racial equality and had spoken out against the USA becoming involved in the First World War.

February 1932: The French government resigned after the Senate rejected plans to extend the female franchise.

May 1932: Amelia Earhart became the first person to fly the Atlantic twice, after which she said, 'I don't think it much matters who flies the Atlantic, men or women – it's all the same.'

August 1932: At the Los Angeles Olympics, Mildred 'Babe' Didrikson won three medals, gold in javelin and 80m hurdles and silver in the high jump – she was only allowed to enter three events. She is the only person ever to have won medals for running, jumping and throwing in one Olympic Games.

Nursery Education

The 1918 Fisher Education Act which raised the school-leaving age to 14, had also recommended the setting up of nursery schools for children under the age of five. This idea had perhaps been rooted in the fact that during the First World War a limited number of nurseries had been established to allow women with children to work. Although most closed at the end of the war, the prospect of economic growth ahead and an increased need for women workers would have necessitated greater nursery provision. The economy never in fact boomed but became depressed, so there was no pressure from employers or women themselves for more nursery places – the pressure was on women through the 1920s and '30s to stay at home.

By 1932 there were only 52 state nurseries, catering for only a tiny proportion of pre-school children. Not only had the economic situation made the establishment of nurseries or the adoption of existing nurseries difficult, but the 1919 Maternity and Child Welfare Act had transferred responsibility to the newly created Department of Health. The Health Department laid down far more rigorous standards for nurseries than the Education Department and subsequently few nurseries could match the requirements.

There was little public outcry at this low provision of nursery places. Many jobs operated a marriage bar so most women would be at home and expected to look after their children. Many other married women found their workplace bringing in marriage bars in the 1930s or felt under intolerable pressure to resign as male unemployment grew. And just as society had encouraged women to go out to work during the war, it now told women that the best place for them, and if they were mothers the only place for them, was at home with their family. Further, in order to make the role of mother a coveted one, it had to be seen as a job that only the mother could do and so home and not a nursery was said to be the best place for the child.

CHILDREN & THE NURSERY—
Sister Cooper, S.R.N.

*H*OW *to prevent a baby from turning on his face when sleeping.* F. I. B.
Harrow.
Provide a chaff pillow, and, until the habit is overcome, use webbing shoulder straps. Make sure feeding is correct, as to lie on the face sometimes indicates indigestion.

When is baby's 10 p.m. feed discontinued? (Mrs.) B.
Eccles.
This feed is decreased at 10 months and discontinued by the first birthday, though some babies progress well on four feeds a day earlier than this.

Approximate hours of sleep required by children between 6 and 15 years. ANXIOUS.
Leamington.
A child of six years needs 12 hours, nine years 11 hours, twelve years 10½ hours, fifteen years 9 hours.

I have difficulty in controlling my daughter at times ; she seems to need a good old-fashioned spanking!
Herts. JOHN BLUNT.
There are two opinions on the "spanking" question. I myself feel that there are other more satisfactory ways of maintaining discipline. To smack does not encourage self-control or independence, or enable the child to act rightly when there is no one to smack her. You are representing yourself as one who inflicts pain, not one who understands the activities and interests of a child. Remember the force of example, and do not fix your standard too high for the child's age.

Directions for making a sheath for protruding ears. (Mrs.) E.
Catford.
Choose a wide mesh net and have a band in front, passing over the top of baby's head, down over the ears, and fastening under his chin. The cap should be worn only at night.

Above: A home economics teacher at Durham Hill School holds a cookery class for a group of young girls in 1930.

Below: Children are served school meals in the 1930s.

*Y*OUTH should be the training time for life, but many parents forget this. They see the baby of to-day rather than the man of to-morrow, and, spoiling their baby, they spoil his future too, and leave him badly handicapped in the race for life itself. As he grows up they rob him of his greatest asset, a knowledge of how to live and how to get the most out of living.

A "Good Mother"

As soon as it was possible, my son was encouraged to do things for himself. It is the lazy parent who chooses to do everything for the child, believing that she is never sparing herself and being "such a good mother." It is maddening to watch a little boy's dilatory efforts to cope with the first knotty problems of dressing, but it should be dealt with.

Children can bath and dress many years before we allow them to do so.

I made my child buy his own sweets before he could talk properly, and he went alone, never attempting to cross dangerous roads or brave traffic heedlessly.

Early in life he learnt to appreciate honesty in adults. I never cheated and he knew it. Even a babe respects truth and has a right to demand it. All young creatures need one person at least in their world on whom they can rely for sincere judgment.

1930s Postscripts

1933: The British Nationality and Status of Aliens Act allowed women who married non-British nationals to keep their British nationality, but only in those cases where they did not acquire their husbands' nationality (previously in such cases they would have effectively been stateless).

1933: The Federal government and several large employers in the USA decided they would no longer employ married women. During the Depression married women workers were seen as a primary reason for the massive unemployment throughout the world.

1933: Various women's groups formed a Women's Health Committee to investigate the state of women's health and campaign for improvements in provision, especially for married women who had no right to free medical treatment under their husbands' insurance schemes.

July 1934: Briton Dorothy Round won the women's singles and the mixed doubles finals at the first Wimbledon Championship in which women were permitted to wear shorts.

September 1934: Evangeline Booth became the first woman General in the Salvation Army.

December 1934: As part of a general 'Westernization' of the country, women in Turkey were given the vote.

Although it was largely men who were involved in fighting, women were also affected by rise of Fascism and the subsequent conflict.

Above: Female inmates of Belsen pictured just after the liberation of the camp.

Below left: Refugees flee from the Germans' December 1944 offensive in the Ardennes, France.

Below centre: The people of Naples greet the Allies.

Right: Local girls dressed in traditional costume in the newly 'freed' Sudeten areas give German troops a warm welcome.

Below right: The women of Berlin work in chain gangs to clear rubble from bombsites in 1945.

Women in Fascist States

Between the two World Wars much of European political thinking was affected by Fascism. The two most obvious examples were Mussolini's Italy and Hitler's Germany but Spain, Portugal, Austria and most of the countries of Eastern Europe all had governments with affiliations to Fascism.

Fascism organised a nationalistic and militaristic society on authoritarian lines in a strict hierarchy. In Hitler's Germany it was the Jews who were at the bottom of the hierarchy, indeed excluded from it altogether. But women lost a great deal in Germany when the Nazis came to power in 1933. Unlike Italy where women had made few strides before Mussolini came to power, Germany had been the home of a strong women's movement from the mid-nineteenth century.

The Reichstag that convened in November 1933 was dominated by Nazis and devoid of women and Jews. This was despite the fact that women in Germany had had the vote since 1918 and up to 1933 there had been between 30 and 40 women in each of the post-war Parliaments. The Nazi party had no women candidates and even discussed rescinding women's suffrage.

Women in Germany consciously or unconsciously found themselves turning back into 'Hausfraus' in response to political pressure, propaganda and laws passed to encourage the idea that a woman's place was in the home. Marriage and child-bearing were encouraged; unemployed fathers had priority over single men in job applications; taxes were cut so that the larger the family, the less tax paid; posters, radio and magazines all put forward the ideal of the perfect Aryan family with father out at work serving the Reich and mother doing likewise by staying at home to look after a growing family.

Women who did work outside the home found that their jobs were taken over by men. This happened in industry and the professions, and women found that there were only jobs for them where the Reich needed them because men did not want to do the work. So, for example, women doctors lost their jobs but not nurses. Even with the outbreak of war the position of women did not improve. There was no need for them in the economy as there was in the Allied Countries because Germany used 'guest' workers from Occupied Europe to keep the country running. Ironically the women of the Occupied Countries found that much of the burden of providing for their children, organising resistance and keeping the country viable fell on them.

Slimming

'A woman can never be too thin or too rich,' was a famous saying of the 1930s, often attributed to Wallis Simpson, later the Duchess of Windsor. Whoever first said it, the sentiment expressed clearly the fashion and aspirations of the time. The Depression meant that money was in short supply for a good number of people, especially the growing numbers of working-class unemployed. Hollywood, with its lavish lifestyle and its vast output of films, was becoming an important source for images of women and many fashions had their origins there.

The fashions of the 1930s were, despite the economic climate, many and quite varied. Trousers and shorts for women became acceptable as casual wear. Bathing costumes, including two-pieces, became more recognizably modern. These casual clothes, together with the fashionable silhouettes of day and evening dresses, all demanded slimness, especially around the hips.

Slimming became a serious business for many women, and newspapers and magazines, together with a whole host of gadgets, all promised advice and results. Exercise was seen as a way of becoming slimmer and was a popular pastime in the form of golf, tennis and the like for the wealthy, while organisations like the League of Health and Beauty catered

to a wide range of women who participated in exercise classes. Dieting, too, was important to maintain the right figure, rather an irony in countries like Britain and the USA where many people barely had enough to eat because of the economic situation.

Around 1934 the shape of women's clothing began to change so that by the end of the 1930s the bustless, bottomless, waistless silhouette of the '20s had disappeared altogether. What replaced it was a more shapely outline, padded shoulders or puffed sleeves emphasizing the classic hourglass shape of the Victorian era. But the outline was slimmer than that of the Victorian women and dieting and exercise were usually necessary to maintain this shape.

Following the fashion trends in the 1930s was still mainly for the reasonably well off. There was more fashionable mass-produced and consequently cheaper clothing available but the economic situation meant that working-class women often struggled to buy anything at all, let alone something fashionable, to wear. They had to be content to dream about the looks they saw in films or magazines and newspapers and hope to be able to afford a scarf, belt, fabric trim or hat to enable them to look a little more 'glamorous'.

Treat Your Sun-tan Tactfully!

JOAN BERINGER

THIS tanning and bleaching business must be an annual source of mystery to the masculine mind.

Women, while the short holiday season lasts, do all they can to look like bronze statues. In a few days after their return home they will rush to their favourite beauty parlour for bleaching treatment.

Unreasonable, I admit. But then women *are* like that. My only objection comes when I hear women demand to have their complexions changed in the shortest possible time.

For it is dangerous, especially to a sensitive skin, to bleach too quickly. Bleaching must be done by degrees.

That Cream-and-Roses Look

Ideally one would put oneself in the hands of a beauty specialist and take a course of six to twelve treatments. This is outside the reach of the majority of us.

But a bleaching course can be given at home with perfect success, provided we restrain our impatience to return to cream and roses and use our bleaching preparations with due care.

TRAVEL LIGHT

Swim Suits

This year the quickly drying, silky telescopic swim suits are going to be a help, but for those who swim every day, I still think two swim suits a minimum.

One play suit is a must; and, if it is backless, so much the better, because you do your sunbathing in it. Then when you want to take a cocktail on the terrace, or a quick look-see round the town, you put over it a matching, do-up-down-the-front frock *Et voila*.

Since you are abroad, there is no reason why you cannot be a bit oh-la-la about your beach clothes. If your body can take it, indulge in a brightly printed cotton bras-and-pants sunbather. You are sure to see plenty of women whose bodies cannot take it.

Over this wear a skirt that ties round the waist, then flies open. Or, *à la Heim*, a backless affair, starting with a sari top cut in one with the bodice part, then a wide corseletted belt, then a wide reach-the-ground skirt buttoning down front.

minute, and the next so cold you wonder if you've really come to Greenland.

You will probably live and die in your swim, play, and sunning suits, plus-shorts, culottes, and slacks. But it is nice to have a frock or two by you. One might be of the dirndl type, which, this year, is at the peak of its popularity. Very pretty it is, too, in gay, printed, crease - resisting cotton, with a square-necked top, a full gathered skirt.

Two evening dresses should be enough, one a frothy thing in lace, net, tulle, one a printed crêpe with a matching bolero which would go over the frou-frou dress too.

It all depends. If you want to shake 'em in the casino you'll probably need three or four dresses.

Hat boxes take, of course, a hat for every outfit. My idea of a holiday is no hat except a large flat one for the first sunbathing days, and the hat I travel in.

I can keep serene hair all day long with a little girl ribbon, rather wide, tying on top in a big bow, the rest of the hair tucked quietly into an invisible hair net which really is invisible.

Shoe Sense

Coloured handkerchiefs tying beneath the chin, peasant style, are inclined to make the chin ache. Tie them mammy style instead. It is newer. Best of all, let the hair loose to the wind and sun. Sure, it will take out your curls, but it gives your hair new life, new vitality.

Nothing benefits from a holiday more than the feet. They are unrestricted, happier than at any time in the year. A pair of the new unbelievably comfortable wedge-heeled type for travelling and odd expeditioning, one pair of heelless or flat-heeled fabric beach shoes, one pair of rather dressier linen or canvas shoes to wear with your dresses, and you are all set up.

You will travel in a suit, I suppose, and big coat. A shirt-type dress and blazer is an even better idea. Both come in on any holiday far oftener than a suit does.

BON VOYAGE.

Top left: As swimming and sunbathing grew in popularity, swimsuits became more streamlined and exposed more of the body to the sun. Belts were not just for decoration – they helped stop the suit sagging when it was wet.

Above left: Part of a record crowd of 3,000 guests at the British Embassy garden party in Paris in 1933.

Top right: Members of the Women's League of Health and Beauty, wearing their uniform of a white sleeveless shirt and black shorts, rehearse for a display in 1934.

Above right: A slimming machine.

Opposite top left: Models sporting beach fashions and a tan in 1935. It is said that it was Coco Chanel who made having a suntan fashionable.

Opposite top right: Epsom Races 1935. Elegant, slim fitting suits and dresses were a feature of the 1930s style.

Opposite below: Ready for Ascot in 1934: a group women pictured wearing creations by Reville which used fabrics and patterns designed to emphasise femininity.

Left: Practical advice from 1938:
TRAVEL in a short-sleeved, square-shouldered grey flannel dress, belted the at waist, with white pique behind the high curving neckline, and a chalk striped tan fitted cardigan jacket, which will go over practically any other dress.
Top coat is a plumb -line-straight navy camel, unbelted, with patch pockets, a high neck. The hat is grey felt with a tan petersham band; shoes are white and tan, with wedge heel.

Married Women at Work

As the Depression deepened and unemployment grew during the 1930s following the Wall Street Crash of October 1929, married women workers found their position increasingly difficult. The unemployed, men whose jobs were threatened and single women who had to support themselves, saw married women who worked as a threat for a variety of reasons. Unemployed men and men whose firms were in difficult financial positions saw all women as a threat in the job market as the average woman's wage in industry was only 40 per cent of the average man's wage.

There was rarely any understanding that wives may have needed to work and no sympathy at all for wives who worked because they wanted to. Married women who worked were seen as greedy, working for pin money to buy luxuries for themselves when they already had a husband to support them. Single women earning their living often shared this view of working wives. Life was difficult for a single woman with no one to support her. While married women who were widowed became eligible for a pension, most single women in employment worked for years with no chance of a pension. Domestic service, a huge employer of single women in the 1930s, was not covered by unemployment benefit. An unmarried woman's only chance of providing for herself was to hang on to her job.

This, and the general public feeling against working wives, explains why often women themselves voted for, indeed insisted upon, marriage bars being imposed in many jobs. In 1930 women in the Civil Service had voted

in favour of just such a ban. And the policy of excluding married women from work continued throughout the 1930s. In June 1935 the London and Home Counties Joint Electric Authority adopted a recommendation that women employees who married should be required to resign. The following month after a fierce debate the London County Council decided to remove the bar imposed in 1923 on married women doctors and teachers but this was a rare case and often where no rule existed there was a de facto ban on working wives.

In Britain there was a long tradition of women giving up their jobs on marriage but the idea grew even in countries where no such rules had existed. In 1933 the Federal government and many large employers in the USA brought in a marriage bar. And in the Fascist states of Europe the exclusion policy went even further, banning all women from most jobs.

Above: 'Girls' operating census machinery at the Ministry of Health in London in 1932.

Far left: Students take their work seriously at St Helen's Ladies' College of Science and Logic in 1932.

Left: When Sir Isaac Pitman founded a school in 1870 where students could qualify as shorthand writers, only men were eligible to apply. By the 1930s the role of secretary was largely a female domain.

Below left: Parisian seamstresses at the studio of designer Mainbocher work on Wallis Simpson's trousseau in 1937.

Dorothy Evans of the British National Association of Women Civil Servants speaking at the opening (of the Conference of the International Federation of Business and Professional Women) said, 'We do not want to be "women chemists", "women artists", "women teachers", we are chemists, artists or teachers. The argument that men must be paid more because of family responsibilities is not to be taken seriously. Arguments against the adoption of equal pay have never been sound, we women in the Civil Service are undaunted by our government's attitude. We intend to return to the attack.'

Daily Mail, 29 July 1936

Divorce Made Easier

In December of 1936 King Edward VII abdicated in order to marry the divorcee Mrs Wallis Simpson after it had been made clear by both the Church and government that they would not sanction the marriage of the King to a divorced woman.

Only weeks before the King's abdication speech, MP and writer A.P. Herbert had introduced a Bill to widen the grounds for divorce. The 1923 Matrimonial Causes Act, while granting women equal grounds for divorce, still relied on proving adultery by one of the partners. A.P. Herbert said of the 1923 Act, 'People are encouraged to choose between two abominations – adultery or perjury.'

Ironically Herbert's Bill had the support of much of the same Church and State that had condemned the King's proposed marriage and the Act was finally passed in July 1937. The new Matrimonial Causes Act extended the grounds for divorce to enable either party to sue for divorce for cruelty or desertion after three years and for insanity after five years of marriage. This took some of the stigma out of divorce as it was not necessarily the result of an immoral act, although the Church continued to refuse to bless any remarriages.

Although divorce became a little easier to obtain with A. P. Herbert's Act it was still a drastic option for most women. As a divorce court judge warned wives in the same month the Bill was passed, they should not expect a third of their husband's earnings on divorce. He said there was no rule, as was commonly thought, that they were entitled to such a portion and that second marriages had to be taken into account. Divorce, then as now, brought financial problems to both parties but women, and especially women with children, fared worst of all.

Above: On 3 June 1937 twice-divorced Wallis Simpson married the Duke of Windsor at the Chateau du Candé in France. The bride wore a gown designed by Mainbocher in her signature pale blue colour with a blue straw hat trimmed with pale blue tulle.

Below left: Women in France were still fighting for equal franchise and using many of the same tactics as the pre-war suffragettes in Britain.

Below right: The Duke and Duchess in 1939.

> I am getting married soon, and as my fiancé's amusements and mine are so dissimilar I am wondering how we can meet each other more in our leisure. He always wants to be doing something, trying out gadgets and experimenting with wireless sets. He likes clubs, the cinema, playing cricket and golf.
>
> Can you suggest how I can make him enjoy sitting by the fire sometimes with a book? He says this does not appeal to him at all.
>
> A. K.
>
> BUT that's a tall order, isn't it? Making someone enjoy something! How would you feel if he pushed the works of a clock into your hands and said, "Now, just you enjoy mending that"?
>
> To you, reading is necessary as one of your interests, but, to be honest, lots of people get through life very well without being very keen on reading. Many people who prefer action when they are young do arrive at reading later on in life. They usually begin by reading about their own hobbies.
>
> So don't try to turn him into a sit-by-the-fire person. Let his home be for him a place where he can follow his interests happily. Then you will build up shared interests, and perhaps even come to take an active interest in those which are now dissimilar.

1930s Postscripts

July 1935: At a National Conference on Maternity and Child Welfare, Minister of Health Sir Kingsley Wood called Britain's failure to cut the maternal mortality figures 'a great blot on the good health record of the nation'.

September 1935: Women workers in Mexico were given the vote.

December 1935: Irène Joliot-Curie, daughter of Marie and Pierre Curie, was awarded the Nobel Prize for Chemistry, together with her husband Jean-Frédéric Joliot-Curie.

1936: The Soviet Union, which had legalised abortion on demand after the Revolution, changed its laws to make abortion less easy to obtain and aimed to give more support to mothers with large families, mainly as a result of the high death and injury rate caused by abortions. Many of these abortions had been carried out in poor medical conditions and by unqualified staff.

February 1936: The artist Dame Laura Knight became the first woman to be appointed to the Royal Academy.

May 1936: Jasmine Bligh and Elizabeth Cowell joined the BBC as the first women television announcers but old prejudices remained, expressed in comments such as these by a letter writer to the *Daily Mail* in November: 'When women read prose or poetry in a radio broadcast their voices lack character and emotion.

'What is there more to be desired than the voice of a man?'

HOUSEHOLD HINTS A.B.C.

ADHESIVE PASTE can be made for emergency use from a cold boiled potato. Rub it on to paper and it will make it stick quite well. This is excellent for fixing a dado or bordering of wallpaper that has become loose.

* * *

BRUSHES AND BROOMS will last longer and do their work better if they are washed every six weeks in a solution of two table-spoonfuls of household ammonia in half a gallon of water. Let the bristles stand in the solution for half an hour, then rinse thoroughly and dry in a cool place, away from the fire.

* * *

CREAM will whip more easily if the white of an egg is added to it. The addition of a few drops of glycerine often hastens the process, and for sweet dishes a little powdered sugar can be added. Stand in a draught, if possible, and use an egg whip.

* * *

EBONY ORNAMENTS for the dressing-table frequently become dis-coloured, but they can be revived by judicious applications of Indian ink. Apply the ink with a soft brush, leave to dry, then smooth with finest glass-paper. Apply the ink a second time, and, when dry, rub in a small quantity of linseed oil, using a little beeswax for a final polish.

* * *

FRUIT CAKES of the rich variety rise more evenly if, after the mixture is put into the baking tin, it is pressed into a slight hollow in the centre. If the cake is to be iced afterwards this often saves cutting the top off to make it even—a wasteful method which makes the cake liable to become dry.

* * *

HANDS should be rubbed over with damp soap, particularly round the finger-nails, before gardening or house work. Allow the soap to dry before setting to work. By this method the dirt will not become ingrained and will wash off easily.

* * *

Top right and middle right: Reading or knitting, often while listening to the radio, were popular ways to spend the evening. In 1936 the BBC had opened the world's first regular high-definition television service broadcast from Alexandra Palace but it wasn't until the 1950s that there was a mass audience for television.

Top left: A woman cooks on a modern gas oven and hob combination.

Above left: A roadside picnic in Cheshire, 1933.

Right: An advert dating from May 1937 illustrates summer 'ensembles' which are 'cool, smart and slenderising'.

MISSES WHO WANT TO BE MRS

Mrs Pethick Lawrence, one of the leaders of the Suffragist movement, wants to know why single women should be obliged to broadcast the fact by calling themselves 'Miss'.

Speaking at a luncheon of the Women's Freedom League in London yesterday, she said it had always been her dream that women should not have to be divided into 'Mrs' and 'Miss' when there was no indication of whether a man was married or unmarried.

Daily Mail, 10 June 1937

Women as Homemakers

In 1936 most women's sole job was that of homemaker. The woman at home was defined in census information as unoccupied. This was despite the fact that for most women, without any servants or labour-saving devices, a life looking after a home and family was still one of unremitting toil.

All washing was done by hand, often in water boiled specially for the job because there was no hot running water. There were no easy-care fabrics to lighten the load and in 1930 only a third of homes, rising to two-thirds by 1939, had electricity so that even ironing was a time-consuming process involving the heating of irons on an open fire or cooker before using them.

Cooking, too, took a great deal of time. Food had to be bought regularly, usually daily, because without refrigeration there was no way to keep it for longer. A lack of convenience foods and the fact that many homes, a third even by 1939, still had ranges, which had to be prepared and fuelled before cooking could begin, added to the demands on women's time.

Even though Hoover had marketed the first vacuum cleaner in 1908, only 10 per cent of homes in Britain had one by 1939. In other homes the cleaning, sweeping and polishing was all done by hand and done regularly for there was a fierce pride in many women to have a spotless home. To be a good homemaker and a good mother were the goals most women were taught to aspire to.

The fact that women had no economic power, no money and no right to a share of their husbands' money, was the main reason why labour-saving devices were not more advanced in Britain in the 1930s. A woman would have to persuade her husband of the need to buy an electric washer or vacuum cleaner and most men could see no need for such devices.

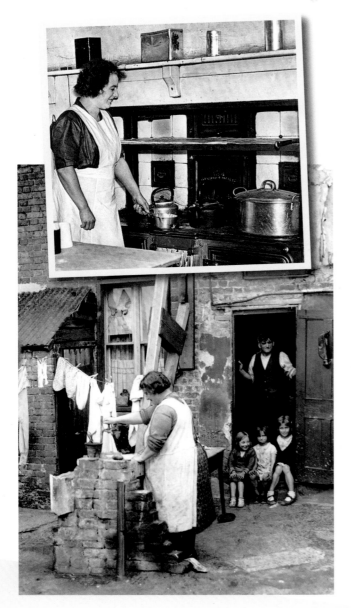

Above: A cookery demonstration. Before World War Two gas was used in many homes for cooking, water heating and also lighting. After the war electricity became a more popular source of power as the newly established National Grid carried the supply across the country and the newly built homes were equipped with electrical wiring.

Right: Actress Ellen Pollock tries out an electric washing machine at the Ideal Home Exhibition in 1935.

Left: For a large number of people who lived in poverty, wash day, usually a Monday, was a a grind.

Above left: In the 1930s many families used a range for cooking and heating.

The Abortion Laws Reinterpreted

A Ministry of Health Departmental Commission on Maternal Mortality which reported in 1932 admitted that around 45 per cent of the annual death toll was as a result of unskilled abortion. These figures did not reveal the numbers of women disabled or damaged as a result of self-administered or back-street abortions. Abortion was against the law and had been since 1861 when an Abortion Law determined that anyone, including a doctor or the woman herself, could be sentenced to imprisonment with hard labour for attempting or carrying out an abortion unless the mother's life was in danger.

Although the subject of abortion was not generally a topic for conversation or discussion, there was growing support during the 1930s for a change to the 1861 Act. Many people favoured legislation to permit abortion in cases of rape and incest, and a few supported the idea of abortion for married women living in poverty and overcrowded conditions, and there were a few, very few, people like the socialist Stella Browne who advocated abortion on demand. In 1938 came a court case which brought the subject into headline news.

A Harley Street surgeon, Dr Aleck Bourne, was charged with carrying out an illegal abortion on a 14-year-old girl who had become pregnant as a result of an 'assault' (men could not be charged with rape until the late 1950s) by a Guardsman in Whitehall. Dr Bourne had deliberately drawn legal attention to the case in order to test the existing law.

Aleck Bourne was found not guilty after the judge had directed that he thought the law's definition of endangering the life of the mother could be interpreted as meaning the health of the mother and that if the doctor genuinely believed the mother's mental or physical health would be severely damaged by the pregnancy then it could be terminated. The outcome of the trial was to establish a precedent for future abortion practice. Subsequently a doctor could perform an abortion if he and another doctor believed the mother's sanity or physical well-being was threatened.

A *Daily Mail* Leader following Dr Bourne's acquittal described the verdict as a 'decision that will be endorsed by the great majority of the British public'. Although the change was generally welcomed, the situation was still rather ill-defined and depended upon finding two doctors willing to accept this interpretation of the law. Parliament did not change the existing law for another 29 years.

WOMEN ARE LOGICAL

'Women – are they logical or illogical?' was a point debated in the Court of Appeal yesterday.

'Your lordships know the sex of my client,' said Mr Gilbert Beyfus KC, 'and that logic is not the strong point of that sex.'

And here are the replies that the statement drew:

Lord Justice Greer: I do not agree with that as a general rule.

Lord Justice Claison: That won't do at all. It is a heresy.

Lord Justice Slesser: If you look at the university exam results you will find that women take very high degrees in logic.

Mr Beyfus: I withdraw my remark.

Daily Mail, 2 April 1938

Left: Despite growing awareness of contraception, large families, especially among the poorer levels of society, were still common.

Right: Midwives from Queen Charlotte's Hospital defy the BMA ban on midwives administering analgesics. Here they set out on auto-cycles carrying pain-relieving equipment.

1930s Postscripts

July 1936: The Midwives Act was passed. This instructed local authorities to provide a service of trained midwives available to every expectant mother, whatever her circumstances.

September 1936: Beryl Markham landed in New York after flying solo across the Atlantic.

April 1937: An article in the *Daily Mail* claimed that because two women secretaries had been appointed to top government officials – one to the Director General of the Post Office, the other to the Minister of Labour – it had 'killed the reproach that women cannot keep secrets'.

June 1937: Mrs G. B. Miller was the first woman owner to win the Derby with her horse Midday Sun.

July 1937: Amelia Earhart went missing on her round-the-world flight.

July 1938: A Danish woman, Jenny Kammersgaad, became the first person to swim the Baltic Sea. She completed the 37 miles in 40 hours.

July 1938: Helen Moody won a record eighth Wimbledon Singles Final in 11 years.

December 1938: The American writer Pearl S. Buck became the fourth woman to be awarded the Nobel Prize for Literature, following Selma Lagerlof in 1909, Grazia Deledda of Italy in 1926 and Sigrid Undset of Norway in 1928.

February 1939: A Bastardy Bill was passed making blood tests compulsory in paternity suits.

May 1939: Oxford University appointed its first woman 'fellow' when Miss A. Bradbury became Bursar at Balliol.

Above right: The Princesses wearing matching coats in 1939.

Above: The royal family pictured at Windsor during the World War Two.

Below left: Women sign up for the Auxiliary Territorial Service in 1939.

Below right: The Blitz rendered many homeless.

Women on the Eve of War

The Second World War began officially at 11 a.m. on Sunday, 3 September 1939. But throughout the first eight months of 1939 people in Britain continued to hope, as they had done for the past few years, that war would not come. As they hoped and convinced themselves appeasement would work, the country and its people continued to prepare for war.

As early as April 1939 plans were in place to evacuate mothers with children under five, pregnant women, school children and other groups considered vulnerable, away from areas which would be targets for aerial bombardment. These evacuees were to be billeted in the relative safety of reception areas, sharing the homes of the local people.

Evacuation was one way of protecting the population from air attack but for the men and women left behind the Air Raid Precaution (ARP) system was essential. Many women volunteered as air-raid wardens. Indeed, many women signed up to do Civil Defence work which involved a whole variety of jobs from ambulance drivers to fire-guard duty; staffing emergency control centres and first-aid posts to helping rescue parties. Despite an initial resistance to recruiting them, as the war progressed women's help in Civil Defence jobs became essential so that by 1943 one in four of CD workers were women.

The other major voluntary force in which women were involved during the war was the Women's Voluntary Service (WVS). The WVS, or one of many other similar organisations such as the Townswomen's Guild, the Red Cross and the Salvation Army, was always there at the scene of a bombing to provide comfort, shelter, food and aid to the victims and the workers. The WVS also organised the collection of salvage, staffed rest centres and ran canteens in shelters, on the streets or anywhere they were needed.

Inside the home and within the family the effects of the preparations for war were clearly felt. The Military Training Bill which gave the government the power to conscript men into the Forces had been passed in May, so that women faced the next few months in the certain knowledge that should war come their husbands, sons, brothers and boyfriends all risked being called up.

Gas masks were distributed to everyone and drills held to make sure they could be donned quickly. Women with babies and young children faced the additional responsibility of getting their babies into gas-proof suits and helping youngsters put on their Mickey Mouse gas masks. Other protections against air raids involved the distribution of Anderson shelters or the preparation of some suitable cupboard or spot to shelter within the home if there was no access to, or wish to use, a public shelter. Windows had to be taped against the effects of blast and thin curtains lined or blinds made so that no chink of light could be seen during the Blackout.

Preparations for war within the home and within the various volunteer corps and organisations involved women in a great deal of extra work and the work increased as war became a reality.

Women of Britain 'Come into the Factories'

Modern warfare demands a huge workforce not only to keep fighting men supplied with weapons but to keep the home country running as smoothly as possible. By 1940 Britain had three and a half million men in the armed forces. Nearly all of them had left a job behind and women were the only pool of labour from which to recruit.

In January 1940 Winston Churchill, then First Lord of the Admiralty, called for a million women to become munitions workers. This was only one of many calls for female workers up until December 1941 when women described as 'mobile', that is they had no pressing responsibilities in the home, aged 19 to 30, were conscripted to do essential war work either in the Forces or in industry. Throughout the war the ages for conscription were extended so that by 1943 nine out of ten single women and eight out of ten married women with children over the age of 14 were either in the Forces or in 'essential work'. Many thousands more women classed as 'immobile' took on part-time jobs outside the home or became outworkers and made or assembled small machine parts at home.

'Essential work' covered a variety of jobs. Munitions production was obviously a priority. As many of their mothers had in the First World War, women took on jobs they had not previously been thought capable of doing. During the Second World War women were involved in a good deal of 'heavy' work, building ships, tanks, aircraft, barrage balloons and in fact generally extending the boundaries of what women could do, even beyond those set by women in World War One.

Munitions production also covered the manufacture of bombs, mines and bullets. Many women were employed in producing the casings to such items which were then sent to be filled in other factories, usually sited out of town because of the risk of explosion. Women working with explosives wore a cloak and beret of undyed silk, rubber galoshes and had to remove jewellery, corsets, hairpins or anything metal which might cause a spark and set off an explosion.

Food production was also an area of essential work and the Women's Land Army formed the core of women engaged in that, although many female factory workers along with school children, the Forces and men in reserved occupations could take a well-earned rest by having a free 'holiday' on a farm providing that they helped out!

However, women workers were not only required in war industries and in the manufacture of food and clothing, they were also needed to do many jobs essential to keeping society running as normally as possible, jobs such as glazing broken windows, road mending and bus and taxi driving.

Women who did 'go into the factories' or into any other work during the war found their lives arduous. Those with a home to keep found the time especially difficult. Compulsory overtime meant hours were long and it was usual to work at least a half-day on Saturday. Shops were closed by the time they got home from work, so, unless another family member could shop, the working housewife had to do it in her lunch hour. Queuing for everything took time and the lack of facilities for keeping food fresh meant shopping regularly. Sunday was often the only full day off in which to clean the house and do the washing, usually without the benefit of any mechanical aids.

Above: Women, or 'girls' as they were continually referred to in newspapers, working on drilling machines to make small parts for aircraft.

Above centre: Manufacturing 'Sten' guns at the Royal Ordnance factory in Theale, Berkshire.

Above right: Filling maritime distress flares.

Left: Tar spraying in Hampshire. The original newspaper caption suggests this is the first time women had done this job, ignoring completely the service of women in World War One.

Above: One of ninety training at the Beaufoy Institute in Lambeth, this young woman is learning how to use measuring callipers. The women had all paid £1 2s 2d (about £1.11) for a twelve-week course.

Joining the Services

The National Service Act passed in December 1941 made women, for the first time ever in Britain, liable to be conscripted to serve in the Military Services. Only unmarried women and childless widows could be called on to join the Armed Forces, but the Act also allowed for other categories of women to be 'directed' to do war work in industry or on the land.

After the end of the First World War the women's auxiliary corps to the Navy and the Air Force had been disbanded. They had to be re-formed in 1939, the Women's Royal Naval Service (WRNS or Wrens) in April, and the Women's Auxiliary Air Force (WAAF) in July. There was also the Auxiliary Territorial Services (ATS) which had existed between the wars as a reserve of trained women to aid the Army in the event of war. Apart from the three main Services there were a variety of smaller corps which undertook more specific duties –such as the Voluntary Aid Detachment (VAD) nurses; the Royal Observer Corps which staffed 24-hour watches in isolated lookout posts; and the Air Transport Auxiliary Service whose ferry pilots delivered planes and essential supplies wherever they were needed.

It was stressed continually that women in the Services would be unarmed, serve only in non-combatant roles and always be well behind the front-lines – but aerial bombardment meant that the front-line was Britain itself. Service women on duty in military command centres, barrack and air-base cookhouses, staffing anti-aircraft and searchlight batteries or driving bomb-disposal crews with their loads of unexploded bombs were all at risk of death or injury as a result of the bombing.

While on the whole not involved in policy decisions, women became crucial to the administration of the war. They were also important in maintaining the Services' transport and equipment including aircraft and torpedoes; feeding the men; staffing barrage-balloon sites and other defence posts. But women also undertook duties other than these, including some who parachuted into occupied Europe to help the Resistance movements and Wrens who served on warships as radio operators. By the end of the war of the 443,000 women in the three main Services 624 had been killed, 744 wounded, 98 were missing and 22 taken prisoners of war.

Above: Morning parade for the Women's Auxiliary Air Force (WAAF). Although women did not fly combat missions, their contribution in the auxiliary services was invaluable. The WAAF staffed radar stations while, among other duties, the women in the ATS manned anti-aircraft guns. Those of the Air Transport Auxiliary flew missions delivering new aircraft.

Above right: Wrens training to be torpedo mechanics, regarded as one of the most highly skilled jobs in maritime engineering.

Far right: A member of the WAAF plots a trans-Atlantic course at Prestwick air base.

Right: By the end of the war a quarter of a million women had served in the WAAF, more than 180,000 of them volunteers.

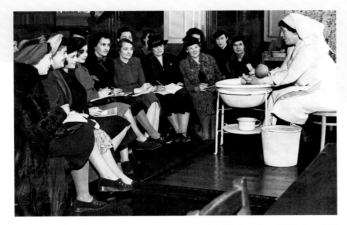

More than a million women will be required during the coming months, and 100,000 of them are needed at once.

It is hoped that women between 18 and 25 who have no occupation will form the majority of the 100,000 who are required in the main for the women's Services and to be trained in Government Centres for work in industry.

Plans are being made to round up the women of leisure who, living in the comparative safety of reception areas, might try to avoid registration. 'Women who deliberately fail to register will be prosecuted and the penalties will be heavy,' a Ministry of Labour official told me yesterday.

Daily Mail, 24 March 1941

Top: Women learn to be 'baby-minders' for state nurseries. Seen as a vital contribution to the war effort, nursery nursing was made a reserved occupation.

Above: 'Munitions grannies' work on parts for aircraft landing gear.

Above right: Recruits to the Women's Auxilliary Police Corps in Bedfordshire receiving instruction in morse and wireless telegraphy.

Right: Female labourers, employed by Islington Council to help clear air-raid debris, break for lunch.

1940s Postscripts

January 1940: In response to pressure from the public, who believed that it was necessary to ensure a fair distribution, the government introduced food rationing – butter, sugar, bacon and ham were the first items to be rationed.

February 1940: The government launched its 'Careless Talk Costs Lives' Campaign, often playing on the image of the gossip and Mata Hari stereotype women with lines like 'Be Like Dad – Keep Mum' and 'Keep Mum – She's Not So Dumb'.

October 1940: The government of Vichy France, which collaborated with Germany, banned married women from working in the public services.

January 1941: Amy Johnson, the famous aviator of the 1930s, was reported missing, feared drowned, when her plane developed engine trouble and she bailed out over the River Thames. She had been working as a delivery pilot for the RAF, transferring planes from aircraft factories to air bases.

March 1941: The government announced a scheme to train baby-minders so that women could go to work happy that their children were left in good hands in state-provided nurseries.

June 1941: Clothes rationing on a points system was introduced.

September 1941: Two women clerks became the first women on the floor of the Stock Exchange when they marked slips behind the Mining and Foreign Railway Counter.

Vision of a Welfare State

In December 1942 the economist Sir William Beveridge produced a report which laid the foundations for a Welfare State after the war. The Report had all-party support within the coalition government and each of the major parties committed itself to its implementation post war. The public, too, were enthusiastic and 635,000 copies of the report or its official summary were sold. It became something to look forward to after the war.

The concept and implementation of a Welfare State which was to provide care and financial assistance 'from the cradle to the grave' was especially important for women. The proposed National Health Service would bring free medical care to millions of married women not covered by existing insurance schemes.

The Beveridge Report also suggested a number of financial benefits including family allowances, a state retirement pension and unemployment pay. These latter two allowances would be of great help to a large number of women, who often worked in employment which had no insurance schemes to provide pensions or unemployment pay.

However, in many cases women would not receive equal allowances and pensions to men, much of the time because they would pay lower contributions. Again it was married women who had the worst deal. It was announced in September 1944 that married women would receive lower unemployment rates because they had their husband's earnings to fall back on.

1940s Postscripts

December 1941: Parliament passed a second National Service Act, widening the scope of conscription by making all unmarried women and all childless widows between the ages of 20 and 30 liable to call-up.

1942: The TUC elected Anne Loughlin as its first woman president and pledged itself to the principle of equal pay for women.

April 1942: It was announced that women of the ATS would staff the searchlights in anti-aircraft batteries – the most dangerous of all civil defence jobs.

August 1942: The rules banning American soldiers stationed in Britain from marrying local women were removed, eight months after the GIs first arrived.

February 1943: A Commons committee recommended equal war compensation payments for men and women after women (and the men who worked alongside them at the scenes of bombings) protested that men received 20 per cent more for injuries sustained as a result of enemy action. A Personal Injuries (Civilian) Scheme was

introduced but compensation was based on earnings and women earned less than men.

October 1943: A report in the *Daily Mail* said that Sunday was now 'washday'. For many British housewives it was their only full day at home and they could not take advantage of laundries as many had closed because of shortages of staff and washing materials.

March 1944: R. A. Butler, President of the Board of Education, said the ban on married women teachers working would be lifted as a reward for their 'great war effort'.

MORRISON HAS A CHARTER FOR MOTHERS
Happiest Homes Will Have Four Children

Mr Herbert Morrison, Home Secretary, yesterday outlined a charter of motherhood designed to clear away the obstacles to rearing families, and to the menace of the nation's falling birth rate...

He gave this warning: If the birth rate goes on at its present rate, Britain's population will be halved by 1999. 'None of our long-term reconstruction plans will be more than pleasant dreams if we don't alter this,' he said. The plan for the attack on the evils that have caused families to dwindle is made under these heads:

* Family Allowances.
* Complete health service for all.
* Pleasant homes for every family in pleasant surroundings.
* Work for mothers only if they want it. They must not be forced to take jobs to support their children.
* Nursery Schools for every child.

Daily Mail, 8 May 1943

Above: The Queen talks to women and children during a visit to a bomb site in the East End of London in 1940.

Below: Making stockings at the Howard Ford factory, Liverpool, in 1947.

Below: Anne Loughlin chairs her first meeting as President of the TUC.

Right: Mrs Flanningan repairs bomb damage to a railway arch.

Women and Money

For some women wartime gave them their first experience of handling money other than the housekeeping allowance given to them by their husbands. With husbands away in the Forces, sometimes earning less than they would in civilian life, women found themselves responsible for all of the family finances and often short of money; the soldier's pay would just not stretch to cover everything. Many of these women took on a job even if they had young children. State nursery provision for the children of working mothers was dramatically increased during the war, thus freeing women to go out to work.

When she took on her job the working Service wife found, like all other women during the war, that she was paid significantly less than a man working at the same job. A survey in 1943 found that women's average weekly pay, at £3 2s 11d, was only just over 50 per cent of men's pay, which averaged £6 1s 4d. The trade unions, as they had before the war, did little to try to win equal pay for women – although the TUC, with its female president Anne Loughlin, pledged itself to the principle in 1942.

The war did bring some financial freedom for some women. They were earning their own money even though there was pressure to donate at least a portion of it to the war effort and there was little to spend it on apart from basic necessities. However, a legal case in 1943 emphasised just how little financial freedom married women had, especially those who stayed at home. Mrs Dorothy Blackwell had deposited £103 in a co-operative society – money she had saved from her housekeeping allowance and had earned from taking lodgers into the family home. Her husband claimed that the money rightly belonged to him and the Court of Appeal agreed with all the lower court judgements that Mr Blackwell was indeed entitled to the money and that a wife had no right to any savings from the housekeeping.

Even those married women earning their own money could not save money without their husbands' knowledge. As the husband was responsible for completing a tax return for both of them he risked prosecution if he failed to declare the interest on his wife's savings. This was a situation which was to continue for many years.

Making Do and Mending

Britain's first manufacturing priority during the war was weapons. By the end of 1940 virtually all factories had turned to war production. A small amount of space in some factories was given over to making items for consumption on the home market. Cadbury's continued to manufacture some sweets and Yardley a limited line in cosmetics while the bulk of their factories produced shell casings and small parts for aircraft. It was considered necessary to maintain production of what were in effect luxuries in order to keep up morale in the country.

As the war progressed shops emptied of stock. Food rationing began in January 1940, in June 1941 clothes rationing was introduced and soap was added to the list in 1942. But there were many things, such as crockery, cutlery, household furnishings, furniture, toys and cleaning products, which were not rationed but were in short supply. Some of these items were simply not in production at some periods of the war and if it was possible to buy them in the shops, or on the black market, there was usually little or no choice of style, colour or quality.

Women spent many hours during the war mending or improvising items which could not be replaced. Radio broadcasts, special classes, newspaper and magazine articles, government propaganda, even product advertising all urged the housewife to 'make do and mend'. Tips and instructions were given on how to make children's clothes out of unwanted adult clothing; turn shirt collars; unravel old woollens and reknit the wool into blankets or use clothing to make rag rugs; repair shoes, patch towels; extend the life of bed linen by splitting worn sheets in two and stitching the less worn outer edges together; make a baby's cot from an old drawer; make polishes and cleansers for the home and face creams for the complexion.

The ingenuity of the advisers was endless but what they often overlooked was that in many cases it was difficult or impossible to find the ingredients or materials needed for repairs and renovations. Glue, sewing thread and needles, knitting needles, rubber for patching bicycle tyres or mending shoes were all in short supply. Salvage drives throughout the war netted many items of metal, rubber, paper and fabric that might have come in useful later on. Initially it was items that were unwanted and unused, although some no doubt donated a favourite pan or ornament in a spirit of patriotic fervour, but as the war progressed everything that could be recycled had to be cleaned and saved by the housewife ready for collection by WVS and other organisations. All salvaged material went into weapons' production and by 1944 British women and children had collected so much that 50,000 tanks could have been made from the metal alone.

Above: The arrival of the GIs meant that luxury items such as stockings became easier to obtain. Until then women often painted their legs to give the impression of having a seam.

Above right and far right: When clothing rationing was introduced in June 1941, 60 points were allocated to each person. Later this was reduced to 48 points.

Right: A ration card issued to members of the Newcastle Co-operative Society in November 1939, designed to deal with shortages before rationing was officially introduced.

Family Allowances

Eleanor Rathbone formed the Family Endowment Council in 1917 to fight for family allowances. The Council called for a weekly payment of 12 shillings 6d for wives, 5s for the first child and 3s 6d for all subsequent children to be paid directly to the mother. Rathbone felt it was important that the money went to the mother to ensure it was not squandered on beer by the husband. She saw, at a time when women had not yet been enfranchised, that the vote would not solve all of women's problems and that an improvement in the financial position of women was an important aim.

In 1945, after 28 years of campaigning, the newly elected postwar Labour government implemented the Beveridge Plan's suggestion for family allowances paid to the mother. But at 5s for all but the first child the payment was considerably less in real terms than Eleanor Rathbone had called for during the First World War.

The first payments to mothers were made in 1946, the year in which Eleanor Rathbone died.

Top: Thousands of people had to be rehoused after the war. This woman is pictured in her 'up-to-date' kitchen in a new experimental house on the outskirts of London.

Above: Women queue for fish in Streatham High Street in 1945.

Right: Charity Taylor, governor of Holloway Prison.

Far right: A modern cooker, with automatic ingnition, to be fitted in some of the prefabricated homes which were a quick solution to some of the post-war housing problems.

EQUALITY FOR WOMEN 'PERIL'
Warning by Churchmen

The way woman has used her newly won equality has created a danger to the state through the threatened decline in population, according to the report of a Church of Scotland Commission...

'There is little doubt that in the voluntary limitation of the family the woman's will largely prevails. It does so partly because she, in her days of economic self-sufficiency, has acquired standards of living which, naturally, she wishes as far as possible to preserve when she sets up home on her own.'

Daily Mail, 18 May 1944

1940s Postscripts

July 1944: Servicewomen arrived in France to feed the troops following the D-Day invasion in June.

1945: Charity Taylor became the first woman prison governor when she took over at Holloway.

March 1945: Women protested about plans to close day nurseries at the end of the war, arguing they should be used for the under-twos once the new nursery schools for all children aged two to five were set up.

May 1945: The war in Europe ended with the defeat of Germany.

August 1945: Japan surrendered after the dropping of atomic bombs on Hiroshima and Nagasaki and the Second World War finally ended.

March 1946: The government removed the ban on women becoming diplomats, but only if they remained unmarried. Monica Milne became the first woman to take up a diplomatic post.

May 1946: For the first time ever, bread was rationed – food shortages were even more severe than during the war as there were now 30 million people to feed in Germany, where the agricultural base had been destroyed.

April 1947: As shortages increased the government banned the use of gas and coal fires – most families' sole form of heating – until September.

'Not Worth Equal Pay'

During the war there had been a great deal of agitation by women for equal pay. The fact that in many cases women had been doing 'men's' jobs, and doing them well, often working alongside men doing exactly the same job but receiving far less pay than them, had forced women to rethink the argument that because men were generally the breadwinners they should earn more. Employers had many arguments against the women's claims: they required more training, created more waste and needed extra investment in terms of rest facilities. The unions paid lip service to women's claims for equal pay but were anxious to protect jobs for their male members when the war ended and many trade unionists feared equal pay would mean a reduction in men's earnings.

To accommodate the pressure for equal pay and examine all the issues the government set up a Royal Commission in 1944. The Commission of five men and four women reported in October 1946. Three of the women, including the trade unionist Dame Anne Loughlin, dissented with the report's conclusion that women were not worth equal pay.

There were three main reasons for this conclusion. First, that women's performance justified lower pay, although the dissenters argued that women were often excluded from trades where they could be more efficient. Second, the Commission agreed with the argument that equal pay would mean lower pay standards for both men and women. The third reason was that married men with families would become relatively the worst-off members of society.

The Report cited two linked factors of 'force of tradition' and 'economic factors' to explain how women were in the position which led the Commission to their conclusions. The Commission felt that women traditionally saw wage-earning as only a small part of their lives, working only until they married and had children. The fact that women's sick rates were higher was seen as an economic factor justifying lower pay, although the Commission also pointed out and seemed to accept as part of the 'force of tradition' that women were more poorly nourished than men. The report suggested that better feeding would improve women's health, reduce absenteeism and increase efficiency but offered no positive suggestions as to how to bring this about.

All in all the 1946 Commission on Equal Pay merely accepted and justified the status quo. Women in industry were paid less than 60 per cent of the average male wage. Women teachers, local government officials and civil servants, rewarded with rates of pay at 80 per cent of their male counterparts, were the best-paid woman workers apart from those very few women who earned equal pay with the men in their professions.

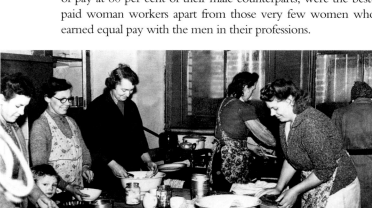

WIFE LOST ALL CHATTELS

Judge Kirkhouse Jenkins, KC, decided at Melksham, Wiltshire, County Court yesterday that all the furniture acquired by Mrs Maud Elizabeth Shrapnell, of Beanacre, Melksham, out of household expenses, now belonged to her husband, William George Shrapnell, of Oakfield, Battledown, Cheltenham, a valet-chauffeur.

Mr and Mrs Shrapnell had separated under a court order after being married for 21 years.

The judge also awarded to the husband a tea service acquired by the wife, who paid 1s a week into a club, and also a cutlery set secured by the wife as a free gift in exchange for gift tea coupons.

Daily Mail, 13 April 1946

Above left: A family in their quickly built temporary home.

Above: Preparing Sunday dinner in a communal kitchen. Until homes were built for them many families had to share facilities in hostels.

Left: Tenants in a newly built block of flats do their washing in the basement laundry fitted with coin-operated machines.

1940s

Below: After announcing her engagement to Philip Mountbatten in July 1947, Princess Elizabeth was married, wearing an embroidered satin dress by Norman Hartnell, at Westminster Abbey in November of the same year.

Right: Swedish model Hjördis Tersmeden looked glamorous when she and David Niven were married at South Kensington Register Office in 1948 six weeks after they first met.

A Tidal-wave of Divorce

In March 1947 the government announced that it would fund bodies like the Marriage Guidance Council to try to help stem what had been described in a House of Lords debate the previous year as a 'tidal wave' of divorce. The aim of this funding was to try, wherever possible, to effect a reconciliation between the couple. The divorce rate was indeed growing at an alarming pace. From a figure of 10,000 divorce petitions in 1938, to 25,000 in 1945, rising to 38,000 in 1946 and 50,000 in 1947.

By May 1946 there were 50,000 divorces involving Service personnel outstanding and the Attorney General, Hartley Shawcross, appointed 35 legal teams to deal with them. The following month the period of time between the granting of a decree nisi and a decree absolute was cut from six months to six weeks.

Real or faked adultery was still the main way of obtaining a divorce, despite the Herbert Act which had widened the grounds. In reality marital breakdown was the principal reason for the soaring divorce rate. Understandably, for there were so many points of possible friction. Six years of war had put a strain on everyone.

Soldiers at the front had obviously suffered the fear, mental and emotional stress, physical danger and actual injury connected with their role as fighters. Some men returned physically disfigured or mentally scarred by their war. Some were returned prisoners of war. The mere fact of having been away from home for so long in the company of other men made it difficult to resume a 'normal' life with their families.

The women and the men who had stayed behind on the home front had suffered too. They had experienced the bombing of British towns and cities, fear for the safety and welfare of their children and husbands, sons, brothers, loved ones serving in the Forces, as well as six years of hard work to keep the troops supplied and their homes and families together. But the war had also given women some new freedoms and the confidence to do many things they would never have dreamt of doing before. For many women it was not easy to go back to living with a husband who made all the decisions, controlled the family finances and saw himself as head of the household when for several years they themselves had fulfilled all those roles.

Health Services for Women

On 5 July 1948 the National Health Service came into being. It was perhaps the most momentous and revolutionary idea of the Beveridge Report and the 'crown jewel' of the 1945 postwar Labour government's welfare reforms. The National Health Service provided, for the first time anywhere in the world, access for every member of the population to a totally free system of health care.

For married women especially, the new Health Service was extremely important. Before 1948 most working men and women paid into sickness insurance schemes through their jobs, which meant that they had the right to free or subsidised medical care. Married women at home, and indeed a large number of working women who were in jobs such as domestic service which offered no insurance schemes, had no access to free medical care. The result was that they rarely sought medical help.

Women put up for years with a whole host of minor and less minor ailments – varicose veins, constipation and diarrhoea, gynaecological problems, problems with the menopause, thyroid conditions, toothache. Resorting to home remedies, over-the-counter preparations or simply ignoring the problem and carrying on were often the only way women dealt with their poor health. When the NHS started, doctors found a large number of women visiting a doctor for the first time ever, often with long-standing complaints.

Another benefit women derived from the NHS was the provision of a free national service for antenatal and maternity care. The Midwives Act of 1936 had allowed for local authorities to pay for a midwife, or a doctor if deemed necessary, but a national service was designed to remove any anomalies in the standard of provision throughout the country.

Above: A woman at work in the kitchen of a prefabricated home.

Above centre: A visit from the district nurse in 1948.

Above right: Helena Normanton arriving at the House of Lords to be sworn in as a King's Counsel in 1949. Normanton worked all her life to further women's rights. A suffragette in her youth, she was also the first woman to practice at the English Bar, the first married woman to obtain a passport in her maiden name and the first woman to prosecute a murder case.

Right: Thirty-year-old mother of two Fanny Blankers-Koen and Great Britain's Maureen Gardner (first and second right) compete in the 80 metres hurdles at the 1948 Olympics. Blankers-Koen claimed one of her four gold medals of the games, although both athletes are recorded as finishing in 11.2 secs.

1940s Postscripts

Spring 1947: Christian Dior launched his 'New Look'. Nipped-in waists with peplums, slash pockets, and jackets flaring over the hips to accentuate the bottom; busts pushed up and out; skirts longer than for several years; clothes which unashamedly used yards of material were all a reaction to the austerity of wartime clothing and postwar shortages. The government in Britain called for women to shun the New Look out of a sense of patriotism, to save cloth in the face of the economic crisis.

June 1947: Cambridge University finally agreed to award full degrees to women but they remained barred from the offices of Proctor and Esquire Bedell.

1948: A new Nationality Act allowed a woman marrying an 'alien' to keep her nationality unless she took steps to change it.

1948: Margaret Kidd of the Scottish Bar became the first King's Counsel (KC) in Britain.

February 1948: The Women's Service Bill provided for the ATS to become the Women's Royal Army Corps and the WAAF the Women's Royal Air Force and to be permanent corps, not to be disbanded as after WWI.

August 1948: Dutch athlete Fanny Blankers-Koen was the first woman to win four gold medals (100m, 200m, 80m hurdles and 4x100m relay) at a single Olympics at the London games.

5 July 1948: The introduction of the National Health Service gave everyone free access to healthcare.

1949: Simone de Beauvoir published her book *The Second Sex* in which she said that, 'One is not born a woman, one becomes one.'

1949: Rose Heilbron and Helena Normanton become the first KCs at the English Bar.

May 1949: Britain's first launderette opened in London for a six-month trial period.

Post-war Austerity

The ending of the war was not the end of rationing, going without and 'making do and mending'. Indeed for a period after the war food-rationing became more severe, with even bread coming on to the ration.

Britain's economy had been shattered. It had borrowed, principally from the USA, to finance the war and now the debts had to be paid. Industry had to be turned from wartime to peacetime production in order to earn money to fund repayment. There was the task of rebuilding, repairing and refurbishing the thousands of homes affected by the bombing. The government had also embarked on a bold plan of restructuring and nationalising many of the country's industries. It also had ambitious plans for establishing a Welfare State. All of these projects required the investment of money.

In 1949 Britain's balance of payments' deficit with much of the world was still drastic, the pound was devalued and the economic crisis severe. Although clothes rationing ended in 1949 this was the only hopeful sign for housewives who were exhorted by the government in speeches and pamphlets to save money, energy, food and materials, and to assume the responsibility for ensuring that the rest of the family did so too.

LONG SKIRTS TALK 'IS WASTE OF TIME'
Mrs Braddock Speaks her Mind

British women revolting against the longer skirt introduced by world fashion planners got support this weekend from Mrs Bessie Braddock, Labour MP for the Exchange Division of Liverpool. She described the trend as 'the ridiculous whim of idle people'...

'Most British women at present are glad to wear any clothes they can get hold of, and the people who worry about longer skirts might do something more useful with their time.'

Daily Mail, 22 September 1947

Top: Models wearing Norman Hartnell's first collection of utility clothing in 1942. From 1941 clothes were subject to restrictions which controlled the amount of fabric allowed per garment as well as the number of buttons and fastenings.

Above centre: Easter fashion at Kempton Park racecourse, 1948.

Above left: While not adopting the extravagantly full skirt of Dior's new look (*left*), the Princesses show a relaxation in austerity in spring 1948.

Above: An outfit in broad overstriped twill, features the square yolk which is becoming very popular, 1945.

The Baby Boom

Just as the 1920s and '30s had seen a dramatic decline in the birth rate, the '40s and '50s saw a 'baby boom'. So that while in 1927 only 85 babies were born for every 100 deaths, 20 years later in 1947 there were 121 births for every 100 deaths.

The low birth rate was blamed on the Depression but the economic situation during the war and for several years after was almost as bad. The rising birth rate from 1942 to 1945 seems to have been a direct result of the war itself as people sought not, as might seem logical, to prevent conception, but to reaffirm life in the face of death and destruction. Despite the austerity of the post-war years, the baby boom was fuelled by a powerful feeling of a brighter future ahead, and after 1952 the economy, as well as the birth rate, boomed.

There were of course a great many unwanted pregnancies, especially during the war as people's passions overcame conventional morals and good sense. Although it was still expected that a woman remain a virgin until marriage, there was a little more tolerance for those who did not. But for a woman to have an illegitimate child was a source of eternal shame. Many unmarried women who found themselves

pregnant in the '40s and '50s were frequently thrown out of the family home, asked to leave lodgings and their employment. Often there was nowhere for these women to go except charitable foundations where they could stay until they had the baby before giving it up for adoption. Women could even be committed to a mental home if they had an illegitimate pregnancy, and a survey in 1950 revealed that in 11 mental institutions there was a fair proportion of women whose only 'insanity' was that they had had an illegitimate child.

Birth control was becoming more widely known about and acceptable. It was, however, strictly for married couples. The Family Planning Association would only see, advise and equip married women with information and aids for birth control. To do anything other than exclude unmarried women from consultations would have risked the accusation that they were encouraging these women to act immorally.

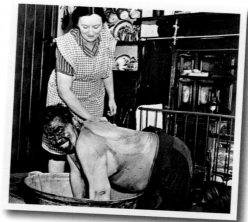

Left: Washing in a tin bath in front of the fire, like this miner being helped by his wife, was still common.

Below: Mothers and babies at a child welfare centre.

Above: Domestic help was only available to a few in the 1950s. The 1891 UK Census showed there were 1.38 million indoor domestic servants. This number fell dramatically during the early part of the 20th century. – the effects of both wars was particularly felt as many women who had taken on traditional male working roles in factories

and elsewhere while men fought did not wish to return to domestic service.

Opposite: A promotional picture of the new Hoover washing machine presents a smiling housewife in her labour-saving kitchen. However, many women had no choice but to tackle the jobs without such help.

1950s Postscripts

May 1950: Following the Communist takeover in China the new government began to bring in new laws, many of which improved the lives of women – laws banning polygamy; infanticide, of which girls were the principal victims; and child marriage, especially difficult for girls in a society where the wife left her parental home to live in the home of her husband's parents.

June 1950: In Croydon grocer J. Sainsbury opened the first self-service store in Britain.

1951: There were 178,000 domestic servants working in Britain.

January 1951: The BBC announced that all eight regular newsreaders would be men because, 'People do not like momentous events such as war and disaster to be read by the female voice.'

March 1951: MP Eirene White introduced a Private Member's Bill to make it possible for a couple to divorce after a separation of seven years, in effect for a divorce to be granted

because the marriage had broken down. It had a large majority on its second reading, but White withdrew her Bill when the government promised a Royal Commission to review the subject.

May 1951: The government agreed to pay old age pensions from the age of 65 for men and 60 for women. This was because women, on average, were five years younger than their husbands and the age differential meant that married couples would be eligible to draw their pensions at the same time.

The Average Housewife

A study by Mass Observation published in 1951 showed that the average housewife in Britain worked a 15-hour day, spending 25 per cent of her time in the kitchen. The study concluded that children and the preparation of meals were the two things which most restricted her freedom to organise her day.

It is not surprising that Mass Observation revealed a working day of fifteen hours for most women. Even vacuum cleaners by far the most common labour-saving device, were only found in one in two homes and other surveys in 1951 showed that six per cent of British homes had no internal water supply, five per cent had no cooking stove, while 23 per cent shared a stove with another one or more families; 15 per cent had no indoor toilet and 38 per cent no plumbed-in bath. Vera Brittain writing at just this period said in her book *Lady into Woman*: 'Foremost among the married woman's handicaps has been the primitive home still imposed upon her owing to the convention which still regards her as a domestic slave, and her own inexplicable failure to organise and protest.'

With hindsight it is easier to see why women failed to 'organise and protest'. It was still expected and accepted by most women that this was their lot in life. Schools still trained girls in 'domestic science' and boys in woodwork. Girls were not supposed to express, let alone assert, their needs and desires. The images and ideals of what it was to be a woman were nearly all to do with working to make a home for a family. There were still only a handful of, usually single, women in positions of authority and power to act as role models for other women.

With few women in any position to make their voices heard, houses, plumbing systems, labour-saving devices were all designed by men and did not always function to the best advantage of the women who used them. The individual housewife's lack of financial power meant that she still depended on her husband to purchase any of the equipment necessary to aid her in her working life. If she could not persuade him of the need for a washing machine, refrigerator or vacuum cleaner she would not get them. However, as the 1950s progressed and the British people as a whole became more affluent, there was a huge growth in the purchase of labour-saving equipment for the home so that by 1959 the average housewife's work was probably less physically demanding – but probably not less time-consuming – than in 1951.

The 1950s Perfect Figure

Ten years after the 'New Look' was created by Dior in 1947 it continued to dominate the female silhouette, even if the dresses narrowed to the sheath dress, which was popular alongside the classic 1950s' waisted, full-skirted and full-busted styles. Hollywood had reinforced and emphasised the hourglass figure by promoting women like Marilyn Monroe and Jane Russell.

Exercise and women's sport in general were not as popular as they had been in the 1930s. In fact vigorous exercise was rather frowned upon as unladylike. So for most ordinary women to obtain the perfect figure it required control over their diet either the hard way or the 'easy way' through the use of 'diet' or 'slimming' pills, the most effective of which later proved to be addictive. Corsets and padded bras helped trim the figure or supplement the bustline if it was lacking.

Make-up was used to draw attention to the eyes, particularly the eyebrows, and strong lip colours to emphasise the mouth, although towards the end of the 1950s pale pink lips as worn by Brigitte Bardot became fashionable. Bardot's backcombed and dishevelled hairstyle was also copied and marked a change from the neat cuts and waves for short hair and long hair smoothly held in a bun or roll.

Stiletto-heeled and pointed-toed shoes which flattered the legs of the wearer first made their appearance in the mid-1950s and became popular as skirts shortened.

1957 marked a watershed in the style of women's clothing when the 'sack dress' was the new shape to be shown that year. Its unfitted line and shorter length was a distinct reaction to the postwar 'New Look' and presaged some of the ideas for women's dress in the 1960s.

Right and above: The girdle was heavily advertised in the 1950s. Constructed out of new materials such as nylon and latex, it helped to smooth the stomach and flatten the bottom. The breasts were the erogenous zone most favoured by fashion at that time, and circular stitched bras gave a distinctive pointed look to breasts.

Above right: Open necklines were often filled in with multiple strands of beads or soft scarves in the early 1950s.

Left: The perfect hourglass figure in a tight-fitting pencil skirt.

Opposite top: Film stars Jane Russell and Brigitte Bardot (right) in dresses which emphasise the bustline.

Opposite middle: Models preparing for a catwalk show illustrate contrasting styles: the pencil skirt and a fuller skirt – both teamed up with hat and gloves.

Opposite bottom: Make-up in the 1950s was dramatic. Heavy foundation creams emulated the pan-cake look Max Factor had created for the movies. Eyebrows were strong and eyeliner and block mascara were heavily used. The Italian cut, featuring all over waves, introduced by Italian stars such as Gina Lollabrigida, became popular in the early part of the decade. The French Pleat, and later the beehive, were also worn by many women.

THE SECRET

... of sane slimming

BY JANE ALISON

WORKING women—and that's most of them—often start a slimming regime, then give it up after a week or so because they feel that work and diets do not mix.

The secret of sane slimming, that will make you feel fitter than ever, is not to stop eating flesh-forming foods but to cut them down to safe proportions.

Here are two meals, one light and one heavy in calories :

6oz. steamed cod with ½lb. of sliced mushrooms simmered in a very little milk. That is approximately 155 calories Add a slice of wholemeal bread with a scraping of butter for 120 calories, and for a filler, a salad of lettuce and tomato, approximately 25, and there is a sensible well-balanced meal for 300 calories.

Suppose, instead, you take 2 pork sausages, chips, and a roll and butter. That meal will cost you about 870 calories almost the whole of the daily allowance.

However, if you really long for those sausages and chips you may have them, *but* you must have only a couple of starch-free rolls and a small portion of sugarless marmalade for breakfast, with black coffee, and a salad and coffee for the other main meal. Sprinkle the salad with at least 2 tablespoonfuls of lemon juice. This will bring out the flavour of the salad, make it crisp and appetising, and add not a calorie. You may even spend another 100 calories, but you must knock them off tomorrow's allowance.

That is the point of our 'Slim and Enjoy It" idea.

Eat balanced meals, eat, to a large extent, what you like, but compensate on the other meals of the day.

Women in Government

Florence Horsbrugh became the first woman appointed to a Conservative Cabinet when her post as Minister for Education was promoted to Cabinet level in 1953. She was only the third woman to be given a Cabinet post. Margaret Bondfield was in Ramsay MacDonald's Labour government from 1929 to 1931 as Minister for Labour and Ellen Wilkinson was in the Cabinet as Minister for Education from the 1945 election of the Labour government until she died in 1947.

In 1953, of the 625 parliamentary seats available, only 17 were taken by women. They had been elected in the 1951 General Election and they represented, more than 30 years after women had first become eligible, only three per cent of the membership of the House of Commons. In fact, the number of women elected in 1951 was a reduction from the 21 returned in 1950 and seven less than the record number of 24 women elected in 1945. Before the war there were never more than 15 women MPs.

Dorothy Evans, who campaigned vigorously to end discrimination against women, organised a pressure group, Women for Westminster, during the Second World War to try to encourage more women to stand for Parliament. She died in 1944 and the group did not last much longer but it undoubtedly had some impact as in the 1945 election there were 87 women candidates. These women had all had to overcome the selection procedure of their particular political party, a procedure dominated by men who were fearful that even in a safe seat many of the party's traditional supporters would refuse to vote for a woman.

Women's profile in local government, especially outside London, was only slightly better than in Parliament. On the London County Council about a third of the members were women in 1952 and this was the best ratio of women to men on local government councils anywhere in the country. In the same year only seven per cent of mayoral posts were held by women and in Scotland only three out of 106 Provosts were female.

In the 1950s women were seriously under-represented at all levels of government, but most notably in Britain's second chamber, the House of Lords, which still had considerable power to amend legislation. The Lords was an all-male body to which women could not be appointed until the passage of the Life Peerages Act in 1958.

Women and the Church

Despite the fact that throughout the world women comprised the majority in the congregations they had no voice in the hierarchy of many of the Christian Churches of the world, especially the older and established Churches which forbade any ecclesiastical positions to women.

There were some exceptions: the Quakers and the Salvation Army had allowed women as preachers since their inception and some of the more recently established Churches in the USA and Canada had allowed women to become deacons and elders. A few of these Churches, such as the American Methodist Church, had even ordained female ministers. In Denmark legislation was passed in the 1940s to allow for the ordination of women as ministers in the State Lutheran Church.

However, none of the mainstream Churches in Britain had women in any similar capacities. One exception was the Presbyterian United Free Church which ordained its first female minister in 1935, and there were a number of women who had studied theology as lay members of the other Churches. The issue of women priests had been to the fore in Britain for some years, promoted by groups like the Society for the Equal Ministry of Men and Women in which the actress Sybil Thorndike was a prominent member.

Opposite top: Jennie Lee with her husband Aneurin Bevin in 1957. When Lee was elected to Parliament as Labour MP for North Lanark in 1929 she was the youngest member of the House, at the age of 24.

Opposite middle and bottom: After the death of her father in February 1952, Princess Elizabeth was crowned Queen at Westminster Abbey in June 1953.

Above: Dorothy Macmillan, the wife of Conservative politician Harold Macmillan, canvasses for votes in 1955.

Below: Men and women take part in a protest march demanding equal pay for female employees of the British civil service in 1952.

Right: Margaret Bondfield, Britain's first female Cabinet Minister, who died in June 1943.

Far right: Princess Margaret in velvet, 1953.

1950s Postscripts

February 1952: Princess Elizabeth is proclaimed Queen following the death of her father, King George VI.

May 1952: Maria Montessori, Italy's first woman physician and a pioneer in the education of young children through discovery and less rigid organisation, died at the age of 81.

1952: The House of Commons voted in favour of the principle of equal pay for women and John Boyd-Carpenter, a Treasury Secretary, said new pay structures would be introduced but it would have to be done in stages.

June 1953: The Coronation of Queen Elizabeth II took place at Westminster Abbey.

August 1953: Dilys Cadwaladr became the first woman to win a Bardic Crown at the Welsh National Eisteddfod.

December 1953: Harold Macmillan, the Housing Minister, announced that 301,000 new homes had been built in 1953 – all part of the drive to replenish the housing stock following the losses during the war and to reduce overcrowding.

The End of Rationing

Food rationing had started in Britain in January 1940 as a result of wartime shortages. Prices had begun to rise steeply and there was a public clamour for rationing and price controls to ensure that what food there was would be distributed fairly. The following year clothes rationing was introduced on a points system that allowed people to choose from the limited styles and items available how they wanted to 'spend' their allocation – although of course they had to pay money for the goods as well as points. The success of the points system, which was in fact copied from a German scheme, was extended to 'luxury' foods such as dried fruit, biscuits and tinned food later in 1941.

After the war, for a period, rationing became even more severe but gradually throughout the late 1940s and early '50s more and more items came 'off the ration'. Sometimes, as with sweets, restrictions ended more than once.

Although rationing affected the whole of the population it affected women, in their role as homemakers, most. It was women who had to plan and prepare meals with a limited amount and variety of ingredients. It was women who were urged to save cooking and heating fuel in the home. It was generally women who queued for everything from basic rations to rare luxuries. It was women who patched, darned, sewed, repaired, cut down and remade clothing, tablecloths, towels, curtains and bedding. It was women who had to keep themselves, their children and their homes and clothing clean on rationed soap and cleaning equipment and materials in short supply.

Clothes rationing ended in 1949 and restrictions on soap the following year, leaving only a few items of food 'on the ration'. Problems with the balance of payments with sugar-producing countries meant sweet and sugar rationing did not finally end until 1953.

By 1954 only butter, margarine, cooking fat, cheese and meat were rationed on the domestic market. Gradually throughout the year the restrictions on their supply to the public were removed and on 3 July 1954 meat was the last item to come off the ration, almost exactly fourteen and a half years since rationing had first begun.

Top: A cut in the meat ration in 1952 prompted this butcher to put a display of mourning in his window.

Middle: A family, including a baby in a high chair, eat together at their kitchen table in the early 1950s.

Bottom: A member of the Housewives' Association ceremonially tears up her ration book in Trafalgar Square to mark the end of rationing.

1950s Postscripts

1954: Television was becoming an increasingly popular rival to radio. The ratio of applications for TV licences to radio licences fell from 5:1 in 1953 to 3:1 in 1954.

October 1954: The Swedish Parliament approved the introduction of a National Health Service.

December 1954: Divorce was legalised by Juan Perón's government in Argentina.

July 1955: Ruth Ellis was hanged in Holloway prison for the murder of her lover. She was the last woman to suffer the death penalty and her case again stirred debate on the issue.

October 1955: Princess Margaret announced that she would not marry the divorced Group-Captain Peter Townsend. Although the public looked favourably on the couple's marriage, the Establishment made it clear that it was not willing to accept the marriage of a member of the Royal Family to a divorced man.

1956: Women civil servants, teachers and local government workers were were awared equal rates of pay with their male colleagues.

October 1956: In an address the Pope urged women to subordinate all other activities open to them in order to fulfil their prime function. He said, 'Her sublime mission is maternity.'

April 1957: A survey by the National Council for Women showed that 3,570,000 married women worked outside the home. The great majority of them for economic reasons rather than because they were 'bored or lonely'. The survey also 'found that most husbands are accepting the fact that their wives should work, and were co-operating by helping with housework'.

SEX IS HERE TO STAY

Dr Kinsey solemnly reports that 50 per cent of married women sleep in the nude. He says, 'There is every indication that the percentage is still increasing, much to the consternation of the manufacturers of nightclothes.'

Figures and alleged statistics dot the pages of the book, but the net effect is confusing. How did Dr Kinsey and his associates reach their conclusions? They say that they interviewed 5,940 females aged from two to 90 of various religions and occupations . . .

You don't often get 250,000 first printings of a book which sells at eight dollars a copy. Sex is undoubtedly here to stay.

Daily Mail, 20 August 1953

Above Left: Women in pinnies entertain a child dressed in rompers in East London.

Above: Six-year-old Prince Charles and his sister Princess Anne watch with interest as their mother organises her stall at a sale of work at Abergeldy Castle, during a family holiday at Balmoral in 1955. During the years immediately following the coronation the Queen Mother took an active role in looking after her grandchildren while their mother embarked on a tour of the Commonwealth.

Above: People queue to view a new house in Maidstone in 1957. Building regulations were relaxed in 1954 and between 300,000 and 400,000 homes were built every year during the decade. Most boasted modern amenities, such as running water and plumbed-in baths.

Below: For many, living conditions did not improve until the 1960s.

How U
OR NON-U
is your home?

THE way you talk, the way you hold a knife can both fix your U or non-U rating. But the biggest giveaway of all, says a famous interior decorator, is the way in which you furnish your home. He is Mr. John Gillett, of Beauchamp-place, Knightsbridge, who for 20 years has been advising the top people how to decorate their stately homes. In a trade which today attracts more than its share of chi-chi, brides from Debrett still go to quiet Mr. Gillett for guidance ("Mummy always did").

Years spent studying the best homes in Britain have given Mr. Gillett a fairly clear picture of what constitutes current U and non-U taste in furnishings.

"The best homes," he tells us, "are slightly shabby, a little untidy, in fact, an elegant hotchpotch of period-furniture. You come out thinking what a lovely home . . . without remembering details. If you go away with vivid memories of a handsome sideboard, it was most probably non-U and ostentatious."

Edited by AMY LANDRETH

Mr. G's guide

Here is Mr. Gillett's guide to good taste:

It's non-U to have . . .

Three-piece suites, bedroom suites, carpets with a too-deep pile, linoleum (except for kitchens and bathrooms).

To have too much shine . . . shine in textiles, shellac shine on furniture is bad, so is new looking gilt.

Elaborate flower arrangements, like a florist's window. Potted plants in living rooms.

Plastic or paper lampshades, ding-dong door chimes, ashtrays on stands, harlequin glass or coffee sets.

Tinted glass walls, wallpapers with borders and panels. Folk weave fabrics. Blue rooms, red bedrooms.

Leaded windows, "baronial" chimney pieces and grates.

Ruchings and fringe pipings round cushions and chairs.
It's U to have . . .

Rooms without definite colour schemes with back-to-nature colours and flower - printed fabrics.

Odd chairs and sofas with non-matching covers. Covers with self piping and a simple fringe round the bottom. No ruchings.

Waxed floors and furniture.

Rare old carpets, or new ones in soft plain colours. Fitted plain carpets with Persian rugs on top.

Surprise !

Luscious furry rugs in your bedroom (but not living-rooms).

Regency stripes (surprise !) but they must be in traditional colours.

Lace table mats. Plenty of silver on the table.

On the subject of Contemporary, Mr. Gillett is undecided: "*Of course, some of it is very nice, but none of my clients ever want it.*"

Marriage and Motherhood

Marriage and motherhood were what every girl or woman in the 1950s aspired to, or at least was supposed to aspire to. There was a very real feeling after the war that family life needed to be rebuilt and re-established. Enforced separation of young children from parents by evacuation, and fathers, older sons and daughters being called up to the Forces or to do war work had all severely disrupted families.

The expectation on everyone's, including the government's, part was that women would reassume their role as homemaker, pull the family together and hold it together. Government policy was conceived with this in mind. The nurseries that had been opened for working mothers during the war closed, some even in the week the war ended. The financial structuring of the Welfare State assumed that wives and mothers would stay at home.

Women in the 1950s had fewer children than their mothers so that the period of their life spent pregnant or caring for young children was reduced from perhaps 15 or 20 years to around five. Motherhood became much more of a career, a job to be done well. Research by the psychologist John Bowlby suggested that children separated from their mothers in the early years had problems later in life. A mother had to be there when her children came home from school

and even taking a part-time job suggested that a mother was not giving her full attention to her family. Growing juvenile delinquency was blamed on mothers not giving their children enough attention.

The image of marriage and motherhood was promoted everywhere, from Hollywood films to the popular radio programmes like *The Archers*. Advertisers, too, used the image of the wife and mother caring for her family, desperately worried in case she was failing them by not buying the right brand of soap powder, polish or baked beans. The marriage of film star Grace Kelly, who announced that she was giving up her career to be a full-time wife to Prince Rainier of Monaco, was the social event of 1956.

The reality for many women was far from the fairytale marriage of the film star and the prince. Post-war housing programmes relocated and isolated many new mothers from family and friends. Clearly many women enjoyed the time they had with their children but as the children grew more independent many felt trapped and bored at home. Most women had had the benefit of a secondary education, had worked before they married and, increasingly, had remained at work until their first child was born. They knew they could do more than look after a home, husband and growing children.

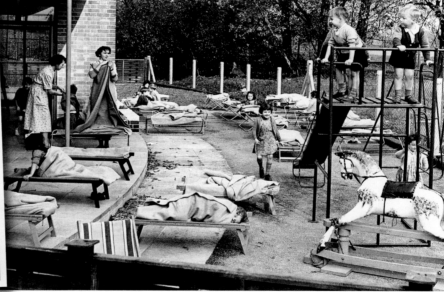

Left: After meeting Prince Rainier of Monaco in Cannes in 1955, 26-year-old Grace Kelly married the prince in a lavish wedding ceremony reportedly watched by more than 30 million TV viewers across the world. After her marriage Princess Grace retired from acting to concentrate on her official duties as Rainier's wife, and later looking after their three children. Despite offers of work from Hollywood, she never appeared on film again.

Above: Children at rest and play in a nursery attached to the National Health's first purpose-built comprehensive health centre.

Right: Family at dinner – father carving.

Those Infuriating Men

THEY are impervious to acute discomfort when absorbed in games, racing, sailing, and on holiday. But if they find anyone in their favourite armchair they sulk.

THEY will wear magnificent clothes, elegant clothes, drab clothes, and clothes no woman would be seen dead in, all with an unself-conscious air of being absolutely right. But let a woman make one mistake, such as nylons with country tweeds or high heels in a boat, and their disapproval will shrivel her.

THEY will eat revolting food at their clubs without a murmur of reproach; but look pained if the joint is overdone at home.

THEY will sit up all night with a sick dog; but sigh ostentatiously if the baby wakens them from a doze.

THEY accept compliments as a right; and offer them as if they were conferring a once-in-a-lifetime knighthood.

THEY want their homes beautifully run, but don't want to hear about it. They wash up once and feel virtuous for a week. They can never understand why their wives can't be with them, cool and unflurried, for a leisurely hour *before* a meal is served.

SALUTE to the women who understand them:

WHO look entranced while hearing, for the 50th time, how they carried their bat for 73, did the hat-trick, holed in one, and made their contract.

WHO know exactly the kind of clothes they like, even to the seed pearls (because they're real), even to the spray of roses (because they're fresh), and who succeed in dressing well in spite of it all.

WHO manage, heaven knows how, to get home first, cook an admirable meal, change, and look as though they'd had all day to do it in.

WHAT I HEAR

THE best diet gimmick yet. Mrs. Heidi Simpson, wife of Dr. Leonard Simpson, high-fashion store owner as well as doctor, says: Just order the SAME MENU for lunch and dinner.

It's best if it can be based on plain proteins like steak. But if you can't resist rich dishes and you order the same thing twice a day it kills your appetite. You just can't face it. A brilliant idea and so simple.

Above: A family-planning poster offering help and advice but only for married couples. The Family Planning Association advertised for the first time on London Underground trains in 1960 but were forced to withdraw the ads following complaints.

Women as Professionals

Throughout the 1950s newspapers were full of stories of women storming the last bastions of masculine preserves. Women gaining entry to the House of Lords in 1958 was one such story. But there were women who entered a wide range of, especially professional, jobs that had previously only been done by men.

Margaret Kidd in Scotland and Helena Normanton and Rose Heilbron in England had become King's, later Queen's, Counsels at the end of the 1940s. Hilda Harding had become the first woman bank manager in Britain in 1958 and John Lewis had appointed a woman managing director, Miss M.J. Ahern, in 1951.

Women were beginning to make careers for themselves outside the home. It was made easier for them by the fact that the marriage bar had disappeared from all spheres of work but there were still many obstacles in their way. In the 1950s there remained a number of areas where women were only permitted to a portion of the whole sphere of operations. Sometimes this was the result of rules barring them as with the Stock Exchange where they were not permitted 'on the floor'. But more often it was a lack of courage to appoint women to posts for which they were eminently suited. For example there were a number of women with the qualifications to be Ambassadors as early as 1952, but it was not until 1962 that Britain appointed its first woman Ambassador.

The chief obstacle in the way of any woman, especially a married woman, who wished to have a career was social pressure; it was still maintained that a woman's place was in the home. It is interesting to note that many of the women who were successful at this period were either unmarried or did not have children.

Should 'Forty' Marry Miss 'Twenty-One'?

ANN TEMPLE'S
Human Casebook

My only son is in his early forties and proposes to become engaged to a girl of 21.

His mother and I are very concerned owing to the disparity in their ages. I have pointed out to him that when he retires at 60 she will still be in her thirties.

We have never known or heard of a man of his age marrying one so young. There is nothing brilliant or striking about the girl. I feel he is making a great mistake, but our only concern is for his happiness. What are your views on this?—FATHER.

THEY have been considerably jostled by my experience in this column. Like you, I used to think so wide a disparity must work out badly. But facts do not bear that out.

I really have been surprised by the numbers of letters I receive from couples of widely differing ages (in some cases the wife being the older partner) who assure me that their marriages have been most successful and proof against the risk of differing interests in the later years.

I still think twenty years' difference when the girl is only twenty-one rather risky. In such cases the young wife often suffers from loneliness, feeling herself cut off from friends of her own age. And I should certainly think it disastrous for a man of twenty-one to marry a woman much older than himself.

A very young man is given to liking the companionship of older women but also to making a violent *volte-face* in the thirties. I should not worry too much about this marriage if I were you.

After all it is your son's choice, and, goodness knows, he must be old and wise enough by now to know whether he and the girl have sufficient interests in common to give them an enduring companionship.

COMMERCIAL ART

My daughter is very good at art, and has had a painting accepted at an art gallery.

I feel that on leaving school she should try something in the commercial art line. Could you please tell me what training is required and what are the openings?—P. O.

IN fairness to you I feel I must point out that many experts hold that the art schools of the country have been turning out more students with an art training behind them than there are salaried jobs or even free-lance openings.

Your daughter may find it very difficult to take up art after her training. A commercial artist needs to have a tremendous perseverance and "push" quite apart from her capabilities in her work.

The usual training is to take a three-year course at an art school which has a department for commercial art. After general training a pupil studies design and then applies it to the branch of work she is most interested in — advertisement lay-out, book and magazine illustration, fashion drawing, lettering, package design, posters, brochures, exhibition design, etc., industrial design : textiles, glassware, wallpaper, etc.

Above: Launderettes were becoming popular for those who could not afford the initial outlay for a washing machine for their own home.

Left: Members of the National Union of Women Teachers and the National Association of Women Civil Servants protest in support of equal pay for women in public service in 1955.

Opposite: The perfect outfit for summer.

Equal Pay for Some Women

Despite the conclusion of the Royal Commission on equal pay in 1946 there were a number of areas in which successive governments had said that they approved the principle of wage equality. Women teachers had been promised pay parity with men during the war at the same time as the marriage bar was lifted, yet when salaries were reviewed in 1950 male teachers received £630 per annum and women £504, exactly 80 per cent of the male rate. Women in the Civil Service had long been promised equal pay. Even the 1946 Royal Commission had singled out the Civil Service as the one area where there should be parity.

The new post-war argument why women should not have equal pay was that the country could not afford it. Women teachers, civil servants and local government officers finally grew tired of the government backing off from its commitments and in 1951 organised a campaign to bring about equal pay. The campaign took four years to bear fruit: in 1955 women in the Civil Service, teaching profession and local government were were awared equal rates of pay with their male colleagues.

It was a victory of sorts for it showed what women could do if they organised and protested but it still left millions of women without equal pay. Even within the Civil Service and local government the awards were only granted to professional grades not manual grades, and many other women, such as nurses, in the public sector were also excluded, as were women in industry, financial institutions, agriculture and business.

Above: (L-R) Members of Parliament Edith Summerskill, Patricia Ford, Barbara Castle and Irene Ward with a petition demanding equal pay in 1955.

Left: Britain's first female bank manager Hilda Harding at her desk in London.

Below left: Doris Day epitomised the 'nice girl' image of the 1950s. Movies still had a strong influence on popular culture and promoted a series of female stereotypes from the girl-next-door to the blonde bombshell image of Marilyn Monroe, almost all of them helpless without a man.

Below far left: Workers at the Templeton carpet factory in Glasgow in 1953.

Opposite: Glamour 1950s style.

A RIGHT TO BE IN THE UPPER HOUSE

The government wants women to be admitted to the House of Lords, the Earl of Home, leader of the House said yesterday.

The peers, crowding their benches for a two-day debate on House of Lords reform, took the news manfully. There were even a few cheers…

'The admission of women,' he went on, 'is a recognition of the place which they have created for themselves as a right in modern society.'

Daily Mail, 31 October 1957

1950s Postscripts

May 1957: The Church of England allowed remarried divorcees to take the sacrament if a bishop permitted it. They had been barred from communion before because they would be, strictly speaking, 'living in sin' with their new partner.

July 1957: Prime Minister Harold Macmillan told the people of Britain that they had 'never had it so good' as the country enjoyed prosperity and a booming economy.

1958: Britain abstained from voting when UNESCO passed a resolution calling for full political rights and equal pay for women.

April 1958: The Church of England gave its unequivocal blessing to the use of artificial methods of birth control, accepting the idea of planning the number of children and frequency of their birth as a moral one.

July 1958: Britain's first list of life peers included 14 women. Four baronesses were created including Baroness Wootton. Women who inherited a peerage were still not allowed to sit in the House of Lords.

October 1958: Marie Stopes, pioneer of birth control in Britain, died.

Drawings by FRANCIS MARSHALL

Marriage? It's Like Being Run Over by a Bus'

—SAYS ONE, BUT TWO DISAGREE

by CAROLE FINDLATER

MARRIAGE, they say, is an institution heavily publicised by women but regarded with wary suspicion by the average male. Therefore, most women's magazine propaganda is directed at how to get—and keep—your man.

Are men really so reluctant to be caught? As an earnest seeker after this great truth, I have asked a bachelor, a "twice - married - and - never - again" cynic, and a heavily and happily married man.

Peter Bryant, familiar to all addicts of TV's Grove family, is one of the most eligible bachelors in his profession. Slim, fair-haired, he lives with his parents in a London suburb, readily admits that he would like to marry.

"The snag is if you leave it too long it becomes more difficult to choose a wife. You become too selective, too critical."

I asked for specifications for an eligible candidate.

"She must be intelligent. I loathe stupid women—heaven protect me from the dumb blonde. I don't agree with men who say that women talk too much—I'll listen for hours as long as they are saying something worth listening to."

Essential quality

WHAT, I asked, did he think was the most essential single quality his wife would have to possess. There was no hesitation. "A sense of humour, of course."

He looked idly across the bar, then added quickly: "She must also have good legs. That's the first thing I notice."

I wondered whether there was any one aspect of marriage which had kept him a bachelor for so long. There was.

"I have a dread of possessiveness, and, so often, wives do become possessive and demanding. I think a man must retain a measure of independence, don't you?"

Politely I agreed.

I asked twice-divorced big and burly American film star **Steve Cochran**. In a red T-shirt, blue jeans, knitted socks, and no shoes, he slouched comfortably on a tousled he slouched comfortably on a settee in his elegant London (temporary) home and gave me his strong and decided views on marriage.

Clever to be dumb

"**M**ARRY again? Look, honey, a man can be run over by a bus once, even run over by a bus twice, but he'd be one heck of a fool to be run over by a bus three times.

"The trouble with marriage," he elaborated, "is that it's so dull. You know a girl—it's fun. You marry her—it stops being fun. You get dragged down by duty.

"Polygamy?" His toes curled reflectively. "Yes, I'm all for it."

Tentatively I asked how many wives he would suggest. He grinned. "I can't give you the exact number, but this I do know: one wife at a time is one too many —anything over, things improve."

"Do women talk too much? Of course, much too much." He became expansive. "You know, what you women think of as clever women aren't clever at all. The clever girl is the one who keeps her mouth shut — and that's just the girl that you all call dumb. Do you see what I mean?"

Mutely I nodded.

I asked **Rossano Brazzi**, fast and deservedly winning the title of the screen's most romantic male star.

I lunched with him at Shepperton studios, where, between shooting his new film "Loser Takes All," he let his meal get cold while he told me his views.

"Sometimes I feel that I was born married," he reflected. "I met my wife when I was a 17-year-old student; we've been married for 16 years. At first I was too busy trying to make a career to think seriously about my marriage. I made pictures, worked hard—and I am still married.

"I think the main reason a man marries is because he fears loneliness." He looked sad. "Loneliness—now, there's a terrible thing. Also, he has in him always a trace of the little boy, and every woman has in her a maternal instinct."

On respect

HE warmed to his subject. "Where people are wrong is to think of marriage as love. It begins as love but marriage is really a very special relationship between two people which is created over the years.

"The foundation of marriage is based on respect. The day I ceased to respect my wife, the day she ceased to respect me, our marriage would end."

He prodded a poached egg reflectively. "Do women talk too much? No. I would rather talk to women than to men."

Taking a deep breath, I asked him what was the first thing he noticed about a woman.

He raised his eyebrows, implying that it was surely unnecessary even to ask. "But of course —the eyes. The eyes tell you everything."

Hastily I stared hard at my leg of lamb.

The most telling comment I have heard on the whole thing was made as I left Shepperton— "It's a pity you didn't have a chance to meet Mrs. Brazzi," somebody said. "Now, there's a clever woman."

Left: British actress Anna Neagle puts the finishing touches to Elizabeth Taylor's hair before her wedding to Michael Wilding – her second marriage – at the Caxton Hall in London, February 1952.

Above left and right: Lady Angela North and PJH Whitely at St Margaret's, Westminster, in 1955 (left) and model Jane McNeil with the Earl of Dalkeith outside St Giles Cathedral in Edinburgh. During the 1950s many brides chose to use lace, which had not been manufactured during the war and immediate post-war period, in their dresses. Designed by Helen Rose of MGM's costume department, Grace Kelly's dress with it's lace-covered bodice was an inspiration to many.

Marriage and Money

In the 1950s one of women's major disabilities, as it had been before and still remains, was a lack of money. Dr Edith Summerskill, who had been a Minister in the previous Labour government, recognised this fact and in April 1952 introduced a Private Member's Bill to try to ease the burden of worry about finances for some women.

Dr Summerskill's Women's Disabilities Bill ran out of parliamentary time before it could become law or make a real test of the House of Commons' opinion on the matter. The Bill proposed to give a woman whose husband had failed to pay a maintenance order the right to be paid the arrears directly by the husband's employer under a court order. The Bill also made provision for a wife still living with her husband to be able to take him to court for an order to be made for the payment of a reasonable housekeeping allowance. Failure to comply with such a court order would mean that property could be transferred into the wife's name. A further suggestion in the Bill was that a husband's savings could be divided equally on divorce.

**DEBATORS OF OXFORD VOTE
TO LET WOMEN JOIN**

The Oxford Union Society last night decided by 383-294 votes that women undergraduates should be admitted to debating membership.

But the vote was not conclusive because the anti-feminists demanded a poll. If 150 members of the society support this demand in the next two days, all the 2,000 resident members of the society will be able to vote on the issue.

Since its foundation in 1823 the society has been exclusively for men.

Daily Mail, 27 November 1959

In the same year, indeed in the same month, a row broke out within the Married Women's Association on the subject of women and money. Its President, Helena Normanton QC, resigned after being accused of insulting women by suggesting to the Royal Commission on Marriage and Divorce that wives should be given an allowance by their husbands provided they spent it sensibly. The Association said that this was contrary to their policy which was that the only way to give economic security to wives and children was to ensure that the housekeeping money was adequate and jointly owned by both husband and wife.

In Britain wives still had no right to any money they did not earn themselves, unlike wives in some of the Scandinavian countries. Sweden had passed a Marriage Act in 1921 which made it a legal requirement for all income and property to be pooled and divided equally on marriage. In Norway, too, housewives had a right to share their husbands' income and property as a recognition that although they were not earning money they were making a contribution to the maintenance of the family. British wives had no such recognition. Apart from the State family allowance and their own earnings, they were dependent upon whatever their husbands saw fit to give them and had no recourse to law should he choose to give inadequately or not at all. However, at least in Britain in 1952 wives had had for seventy years the right to own their own property and income; in France a husband could dispose of a wife's property without consulting her unless she had made a special legal arrangement with him prior to marriage.

Above left: Clocking in for a shift at a factory in 1952 and *(above right)* the end of a shift.

Above centre: Workers put the finishing touches to cutlery at George Ibbenson & Co., Sheffield, in 1957.

1950s Postscripts

November 1958: Hilda Harding became the first woman bank manager in Britain when she took over the Hanover Street, London, branch of Barclay's Bank which had been specially planned to attract women's accounts with 'a ladies' waiting room and a powder room, both in pastel shades and with deep carpets.

December 1958: Some early suggestions were made linking the anti-sickness drug for pregnant women, thalidomide, to a number of babies born with malformations.

February 1959: A poll of the male electorate in Switzerland rejected the proposal to give women the vote.

1959: In India Prime Minister Nehru's daughter Indira Ghandi was elected as President of the ruling Congress Party.

October 1959: The Conservative Party was elected for the third time in succession and Margaret Thatcher won her first parliamentary seat.

An Education for Girls

Post-war education policy in England and Wales had been to offer a secondary education in grammar, secondary modern and technical schools for all, but in strictly segregated schools.

There was also overt and hidden segregation in the curriculum – boys' subjects and girls' subjects. Girls' schools were equipped for domestic science and needlework while boys' schools had woodwork and metalwork rooms. Even in girls' grammar schools it was rare to be offered a wide range of science subjects; most had just biology or general science on offer. Nearly all science teachers were male, reinforcing the idea that science was a boy's subject.

A number of government-commissioned reports in the 1960s, such as *Half Our Future*, sought to address the question of what should be included on the curriculum for boys and girls. In 1960 the Crowther Report was published. It said that it was a fact that in the last years at school, boys' first thoughts were most often about their careers and only secondly about marriage and the family, but the opposite was true for girls. The Report's solution to this situation was not to try to widen girls' horizons but, much to the protestation of the National Union of Women Teachers, to suggest that girls be 'specially directed to preparation for marriage and motherhood'.

Outside education circles the attitude that it was a waste of time to bother with much in the way of advanced education for girls was still prevalent. Girls who did well at school could still find their chances of sixth form or higher education sacrificed for the sake of a brother having the opportunity to continue his education.

Nevertheless most girls in the 1960s had an education which, while it might not have equalled the boys of their generation in terms of opportunity, was certainly superior to that of their mothers and probably their fathers.

Above right and above: Women receive instruction during a typing class in 1963. The manual typewriter *(on display above)* was the key office machine in the 1960s, a heavy, noisy, and relatively slow device but in the right hands much faster than writing, though not shorthand, that other important office technology. By the end of the decade the electric typewriter was making life much easier and the IBM Selectrics were the state of the art.

Right: A young girl demonstrates the phonetic alphabet in 1961. By the time this girl was ready to take formal exams, participation by girls had increased. In 1956 in England and Wales boys made up 65 per cent of the candidates for O-Level maths and 55 per cent of entrants for O-Level English. In the case of maths, this gap decreased gradually in the 1970s and, since 1986, the gender split has been evenly balanced. In English the balance had reversed by the early 1970s and since 1986 the gender split has been even. In science, only 16 per cent of those taking the Physics O-Level in 1966 were girls.

MP SEEKS 'SEX BOARD'

Labour MP Mrs Joyce Butler yesterday moved the setting up of a 'Sex Discrimination Board' with powers similar to the Race Relations Board.

Mrs Butler (Wood Green) said in the Commons, 'There has been a failure by society to appreciate the full value of women.

'Fifty years ago they were granted the vote and ever since they have been struggling for something more tangible.

'Nine out of ten don't get equal pay,' she complained, and when pressure was put on the government, demands were met with 'constant procrastination'.

Her Bill, backed by other women MPs of all parties, was given an unopposed first reading.

Daily Mail, 8 May 1968

Above right: The 1962 Ideal Home Exhibition shows all the latest in kitchen design, including a built-in oven and counter hotplate. Greater attention was paid to design as the kitchen became a centre for entertaining and relaxing rather than simply a place to prepare food.

Above left: Minimalism and futuristic designs were in vogue.

Left: Home fashion on display at the 1968 Ideal Home Exhibition shows the influence of modernism in domestic furnishing and the latest technology on offer, including a portable television.

Below: Hatchetts coffee bar in Dover Street, London, epitomises continental modernist style, which made it a cool place to hang out and drink Italian coffee.

The 1960s Housewives' Top Ten

The years of prosperity in the 1950s had seen a huge increase in the labour-saving devices in the average British home. Manufacturers and advertisers had pushed their wares telling housewives how much easier they would make their lives and insisting that 'every home should have one'. Indeed, many homes did have and the rest aspired to having any one or all of a whole range of household items. In May 1962 the *Daily Mail* published the Housewives' Top Ten, presumably in acquisition order – vacuum cleaner; refrigerator; spin dryer; electric iron; sewing machine; washing machine; gramophone; electric toaster; television; electric floor polisher.

Also in 1962 Betty Friedan published her book *The Feminine Mystique*. In it she claimed, from her experience in the USA, where a larger percentage of women than in Britain went on to higher education, that the American manufacturers had manipulated women into spending a disproportionate amount of time, effort and money caring and buying for their home and family. Educated, and often highly educated, women at home were set goals to make the job of homemaker seem a more valuable one. Save up, buy the washing machine, then sort out all the various types of fabrics for the different washing cycles, and then experiment to find the best soap powder.

A similar thing was happening in Britain. Women at home were being called on to do more. While labour-saving devices freed them from much of the grind of housework they also created more work. Clothes were washed more frequently, houses cleaned more thoroughly, homes redecorated more often. Then in the free time left there was also the gardening, sewing, knitting or handicrafts to be attended to. Women with young children at home were also expected to provide a happy learning environment for them to grow up in. For some women this filled their time and fulfilled them but for many who had the benefits of education and had experienced the freedom and independence of paid work, it was not enough and they found themselves bored and unfulfilled.

The Pill

In January 1961 the oral contraceptive Conovoid was allowed to go on sale in Britain. By the end of the year it was possible to get the Pill, with a capital 'P', as it became known, on prescription through the National Health Service. Despite the fact that almost immediately doubts were raised over its safety, that it was virtually 100 per cent effective meant it became a vital ingredient in a revolution in women's sexuality.

It is doubtful whether the 'Swinging Sixties' would have been quite so swinging without the Pill. Women could control their own fertility without having to mess about with caps or rely on the man to use a sheath. They could go to their GP or more likely a Family Planning Clinic where, if they were single, they would often pretend to be married, or at least not enlighten the clinic to the contrary. Once on the Pill, all it required was that the woman remembered to take her pills at the right time.

The immense publicity for the Pill and the freedom from fear of unwanted pregnancy it gave women also meant increased knowledge about, and the freedom to

enjoy, sex. But it also put pressure on some women to have sex with a man when they weren't ready or did not want to. Unwanted pregnancy was no longer an excuse and as the 'permissive society' grew it became distinctly old-fashioned not to have sex before marriage and increasingly it was regarded as a good thing for women to have many sexual partners. Pleasure and love were the aims and pursuits of the culture of the 1960s and sex was a route to both.

Controversy over the safety of the Pill has been constant since its introduction. It has been linked to thrombosis and other circulatory diseases and some forms of cancer. Subsequently some of these links have been proved, others remain speculation. There are also numerous reported more minor ailments or side effects, such as weight gain, headaches, dizziness and breast pains. Over the years, on the grounds of safety, more and more women have been excluded from using it, so that it has not fulfilled all its early promise, or perhaps expectation is a better word.

Although there were negative aspects of the Pill and the sexual revolution associated with it, it certainly gave women power over their fertility and the beginnings of power over their own sexuality, so that women began to think about their own bodies and responses to and enjoyment of sex. It also brought these issues into the open so that they were talked about in newspapers, magazines and the media generally, and sex education began to find its way on to the curriculum in schools.

Doctors Warn About
THAT PILL

Britain's leading doctors came out today with their gravest warning about that pill and say it may be 20 years before they can give it safety clearance.

Only six years of evidence has so far been gathered by research doctors. The Lancet says: 'We must accept for the present that this form of contraception could be dangerous, and we must try to balance this against its advantages.

'The balance struck will plainly be influenced by the circumstances of the individual or community for whom the contraception is proposed.'

Daily Mail, 1 June 1962

1960s Postscripts

1960: Maureen Nicol, who suggested the idea, helped set up the National Housewives' Register with the aim of putting women at home in touch with each other to offer support facilities to one another but also to talk, read, paint and discuss together.

July 1960: Sirimavo Bandaranaike, widow of the assassinated Prime Minister, became the world's first elected female head of state when she took office as Prime Minister of Ceylon.

November 1960: D. H. Lawrence's novel *Lady Chatterley's Lover* was found not to be obscene following a colourful trial at the Old Bailey,

during which the prosecution asked the jury, 'Is this a book you would wish your wife or your servant to read?'

April 1961: A government report revealed that 8,272,000 women were now working and earning money outside the home.

September 1961: The first Mothercare shop was opened in Kingston-upon-Thames.

1961: The BBC announced that only men compères would appear in women's television programmes. Doris Stevens, head of BBC TV's Women's Programmes said, 'Men make better

compères and women viewers accept a man much more uncritically than their own sex'.

March 1962: Mrs Thelma Casalet-Kier, one of two women among the nine governors of the BBC until she left in 1961, was quoted as saying that the BBC was unfair to women as only four of the top 150 jobs were held by women and there were only three female television department heads – in Planning, Women's Programmes and Wardrobe.

HAVE WOMEN LOST THE ART OF COOKING?

IS your marriage a marriage of convenience? Don't get me wrong. What I mean to ask is whether your family is a "convenience food" family.

The Ministry of Agriculture, Fisheries and Food —which we will henceforth call "Ag and Fish" — calls "convenience" foods all "labour-saving, prepared or semi-prepared products."

Ag and Fish has just published a 142-page red-covered report, costing 8s. 6d., which contains some fascinating facts about "convenience foods," and other food trends.

Quicker

IT shows quite plainly that housewives are grabbing the tin-opener, the packet, and the frozen pre-cooked package with increasing enthusiasm.

So much so that if things go on the way they have been going in the last few years the idea of preparing and cooking a meal from scratch will seem as ridiculous and unnecessary as, say, washing clothes by hand.

The facts are that four shillings out of every pound that was spent on grub in 1959 went towards "convenience foods." That is an increase of about a quarter on the 1955 figure.

There is, of course, one slight inconvenience attached to "convenience" foods. They cost more than, how shall we put it . . . the real thing.

Easier

THIS means that although we have all been spending more on food we have not necessarily been getting an equivalent extra amount back in what Ag and Fish calls "nutritional value." So that although we may never have had it so easy or palatable, we may certainly have had it as good.

As the report puts it : " When there is increased expenditure on the more desired foods such as meat, bacon, fruit, green vegetables and convenience foods '—and this is accompanied by decreased expenditure on bread, flour and potatoes, the intakes of many nutrients, especially of protein, calcium and riboflavin, will not necessarily be improved."

Families with four or more children seem to have got the worst bargain out of this trend towards spending more and getting less back than any other group.

WHAT THE AFFLUENT SOCIETY EATS compared with pre-war	
Dairy Products excluding Butter	UP 41%
Meat	UP 2%
Fish	DOWN 15%
Poultry, Game, Rabbits	UP 31%
Butter	DOWN 25%
Margarine	UP 67%
Tea	UP 3%
Coffee	UP 157%

Dearer

IT has been discovered that, first, their total spending on food has increased in recent years less than any other group's.

Not only that, but they have diverted more of their spending to foods like fish, poultry, eggs, canned vegetables, fresh fruit, chocolate biscuits, and breakfast cereals. These are all "more expensive sources of nutrients" than the humdrum old stuff they have bought less of, such as dried milk, potatoes.

As a parallel to this state of affairs the report points out that recent studies have shown that children in smaller families are, on average, taller and heavier than those in correspondingly larger families.

But we needn't get too gloomy about this. Ag and Fish. says that our general diet in 1959 was "adequate." We are getting 5 p.c. more calories than we were in the years between 1934-39. But how our national eating habits have changed since then.

For one thing we are drinking 157 p.c. more coffee than we did. Our butter consumption has gone *down* by 25 p.c., but we are spending 67 p.c. more on margarine.

We are drinking more milk, but we still haven't reached a national pinta per head, per day. (We drink just over five pints per head, per week.)

The roast beef of old England has dropped in favour, although, thanks to the broiler industry, we are eating double the amount of poultry. We are eating fewer oranges and lemons, but a lot more nuts.

We are drinking 3 p.c. more tea, but eating 15 p.c. less fish.

We should all feel healthier. In particular—thanks to the calcium from the extra milk—we should all be producing some splendid teeth.

The only thing which seems problematical to me is whether coming generations of housewives will be bothered to prepare anything worth biting.

Above: Fanny Cradock, best known as the TV cook who partnered with hen-pecked husband Johnnie. As this picture shows, Fanny had authentic English eccentricity! Although not a trained cook, she had broad experience as a restaurant critic and was a tonic to a nation just emerging from the grip of post-war austerity, with her no-nonsense approach and her practical recipes that could be dressed up as something special.

Above middle: Britain lagged behind the USA in the introduction of self-service grocery shops. In 1950 there were around 50 supermarkets in Britain, increasing to some 500 by the beginning of the 1960s. However, that number had swelled to nearly 3,500 by the end of the decade.

Above: Margaret Thatcher was elected MP for Finchley in 1959, one of 25 women in Parliament who made up just 4 per cent of MPs.

Her first ministerial appointment came in 1961 when she became a parliamentary secretary in the Ministry of Pensions and National Insurance. Here she is pictured with her eight-year-old twins Carol and Mark.

Opposite left: The Pill.

Opposite right: Women with their prams outside a supermarket on a rainy day in March 1964.

Rising Hemlines

Mary Quant had opened her boutique 'bazaar' in London's King's Road in the mid-1950s and by the early 1960s she had been joined by a number of other shops selling fashionable clothing to young people. Quant and other young designers like her had a tremendous influence on the style of clothing that was to become emblematic of the 1960s.

The beach fashion of 1963 was for mid-thigh-length beach dresses and shirts worn over swimsuits and bikinis, reflecting a trend set by designers such as Quant, who had already been selling clothes with hemlines above the knee. At the beginning of 1964 she condemned Paris fashion as out of date; by the end of that year Paris too had raised its hemlines and the mini skirt was well on its way to becoming established. Throughout 1965 and 1966 skirts got shorter so that a skirt length of 18 inches (46 cm) was not remarkable even for some of the more staid clothing manufacturers. Dress styles were much simpler and freer, relying on pattern, detail and colour for interest rather than cut.

Hairstyles early in the 1960s were backcombed and piled up, a style which reached its peak in the beehive. By the mid-1960s Vidal Sassoon had begun to change hairdressing and simple stylish cutting became more important than shampooing, setting and backcombing. Mary Quant adopted a Vidal Sassoon cut and helped popularise the look.

Fashionable clothing was by now mass market, not just for the rich, although the styles were very much for the young, reflecting the increasing power of youth culture. The mature, full-busted woman was no longer promoted as the ideal. Boyish adolescent figures like that epitomised by the model Twiggy became the accepted and sought-after shape. In many ways the shape of women in the 1960s mirrored that of women in the 1920s with a flat-chested, waistless and bottomless silhouette, although the 1960s one was altogether much thinner.

In all decades one style does not reflect the whole period of time and the 1960s was represented by more than just the mini. There were unisex clothes such as trouser suits and the kaftans of the flower power period. There were also attempts, which had some limited success, to introduce mid-calf- and ankle-length dresses (the midi and the maxi), but the mini dress on a woman with a slim boyish figure has become the stereotypical image of the decade.

Sporty

Those skinny sweaters and kilts, and the lean jersey dresses that are fast emerging as this winter's uniform, need low-heeled, sporty shoes, very country style down to the buckles and chains. But in non-country colours, like the yellow and red ones on the left.

Gloves are equally sporty, like the riding gloves on the left; but again, get them in some unlikely colour, like purple.

Best with the kilts are textured stockings or knee-socks with a cable stitch down the side. But the last thing you want with them are hearty earrings. Better some that glow in the dark like the papier - mâché golf-balls on the left, that come in a variety of colours. Or those orangy-pink globes with a stylised flower painted on them.

The bag to carry with the daytime uniform is no longer that quilted Chanel mini-bag which has been safe (like black shoes) for years. The tiny, square satchels in unbelievable blue and pink patents and PVCs are more interesting.

There's still more shine for the evening. To go with the silver stockings and shoes, there are a silver and gold leather watchstrap and some earrings painted with luminous paint to light up the discotheque twilight.

Above: Up until the 1960s the fashion houses of Paris, with their clientele of wealthy, mature women had dictated what was in vogue. Mary Quant was one of a new breed of designers whose clothes were aimed at the young and who took inspiration from the street.

Above right: A polo-neck skinny rib sweater, slim fit trousers and lace-up shoes complete an androgynous look.

Opposite: Simple shapes and strong geometric patterns were hallmarks of the 60s style.

What s-h-a-p-e is a woman?

THEY can't sell corsets in the Caribbean, or girdles in Mexico, and women won't flatten hips and backs or build up busts in Buenos Aires. This shocking piece of news has been announced by **Mr. Fred Gann**, who is trying to sell American foundations to Latin-American women.

"It is all a matter of status," says Mr. Gann.

"Men treat their women much as European men did 50 years ago. Economically, the majority of women are completely dependent on their husbands or fathers.

"Consequently they must dress to please their men, whereas American and European women often dress to please themselves or one another.

"Latin-American men," he goes on to say, "like their women to show their curves and favour the hour-glass figure, with tiny waist, accentuated bustline, plump hips, and natural back."

New move

MR. GANN'S firm is so worried about the sales that they are attacking the problem with advertising.

"We are creating a psychological erosion," he states. "Through advertising women are being influenced to think in terms of chic rather than of comfort and of simply pleasing the men."

I do not envy salesman Gann his epic task.

But I am jealous of the uncivilised Latins who actually want to dress to please a man. Who are prepared to think in terms of a man being the boss and paying the bills. Who will even tolerate having hips and a waist and a natural back.

But I suspect I'm writing in the wrong country.

Above: Style icon of the 1960s and 70s Jackie Kennedy, pictured here with her children greeting the Queen. A fan of Paris designers such as Chanel and Dior as well as American Oleg Cassini, Jackie Kennedy's cool, understated style is still admired more than 50 years after she became First Lady.

Right: A United Airlines hostess models a new uniform reflecting the fashion of the decade but still including a hat and gloves. Stewardesses were starting to fight contract terms which prevented them from marrying or having children while working for an airline.

DRESS AS YOU LIKE

ANY girl off to a party knows the feeling of excitement at the thought of meeting lots of interesting new people.

She also knows the apprehension that she is underdressed or overdressed, the other guests will be too highbrow—or lowbrow—and worst of all, she won't know a soul and will be left to wilt in a corner all night.

She wants to be able to contribute something herself, either in appearance, ravishing, or conversation, witty, but preferably both.

She wants men to be whispering : " Who is that beautiful and clever girl ? "

Basic party philosophy is fairly obvious : if you feel good, then you look good— and if you look good, the net result is usually a wonderful evening.

And this season party wear couldn't be easier. The Whips are off, the Party Line is relaxed.

You can wear what you please, how you please and this freedom extends right from the cocoa party through to the hard liquor party.

It means you can dress the way you feel happiest and most relaxed and *not* feel a social outcast who will never be asked again.

Opposite: If Mary Quant was the designer most associated with the rise of London as the fashion capital of the world – Twiggy was the face of Swinging London. Five foot six inches tall and weighing 8 stone, Twiggy was on every major magazine cover.

Below right: Joanna Lumley models a space age outfit – topped with a hairstyle that looks like a precursor to her famous Purdy cut of the 1970s. Low maintenance geometric haircuts were associated with celebrity hairdresser Vidal Sassoon.

Below left: 'Big hair' was also fashionable in the early 1960s – as worn here by Barbara Windsor.

Right: Hippy style – beads, kaftans and long hair became the look of the late 1960s and continued to influence fashion well into the next decade.

Above left and below far right: The 60s space race and the manufacture of new materials, such as vinyl and polyester, strongly influenced some designers – particularly André Courrèges, who had originally trained as an engineer.

MEAN MEN

MEAN MEN give you the housekeeping money two days late, borrow part of it back almost immediately and don't return it.

MEAN MEN say they hate Christmas because they like to give presents on the spur of the moment—only they never give presents at all.

MEAN MEN say they *like* margarine.

MEAN MEN don't pay housekeeping when you're on holiday.

MEAN MEN say 'Let's have scrambled eggs at your place' (not only mean men, of course).

MEAN MEN never order a taxi : they say 'We'll pick one up at the bus stop.'

MEAN MEN demand the family allowance money back and say that they pay for it in tax at the end of the year anyway.

MEAN MEN always buy the first round, because someone might come along later to swell the group.

Above: Dorothy Crowfoot Hodgkin won the Nobel Prize for Chemistry in 1964, the third woman to do so after Marie Curie and Irene Joliot-Curie.

Right: Elizabeth Lane, Britain's first High Court Judge.

Far right: Twenty-year-old Sonia Ross is crowned Miss Britain 1966. Pictured with her are runners-up Nanette Slack (left) and Maureen Lidgard-Brown.

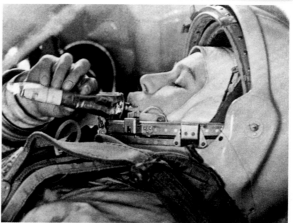

Women With Careers

On 30 September 1965 Elizabeth Lane was sworn in as Britain's first woman High Court Judge. It was still rare to see a woman in such a position and many areas of life, such as financial institutions, in which power and authority were wielded, still barred or restricted entry to women.

Few women pursued a career; it was expected that they would give up work as soon as they had their children, if not when they married. Even women who had spent several years qualifying for a professional job would give it up with no intention of ever returning. The idea of taking a break to have a family and then returning to work was only just surfacing.

In 1963, there were 1,960 women practising as barristers. This was an almost fourfold increase on the numbers in 1953, but there were in both years many more women qualified as barristers who were not working but who felt their duty was to stay at home.

There were also 670,000 women in the Civil Service. As the Service did not offer part-time work at this time the female employee profile would have been much the same as in the legal or any other profession. A large proportion would be young women working until they married. A few would be returners and a few would be women pursuing a

career. Of these career women most would be single, some perhaps widowed or divorced, and if they were married it would be extremely rare for them to have children. Apart from the fact that it was not expected for a woman to have a career and children, absolutely no allowances were made for having children.

While most professional women such as doctors, lawyers, teachers, accountants and architects were paid equal salaries to men, a break in employment to have children would not be taken into account as a benefit when promotions were considered. Even in teaching, where having your own children might be thought to be beneficial, a woman returner resumed the position on the pay scale she had left on, with no credit allowed for her years of motherhood.

Outside the professions there were often more effective bars to the career structures for women as when they were actively excluded from doing many jobs, especially in industry, which would lead them up the promotion ladder to satisfying and well-paid positions. A report entitled *Justice and Prejudice* published in 1965 by the National Federation of Business and Professional Women's Clubs found that women were still being treated as inferiors in most jobs and were seen as 'cheap labour in trade and commerce'.

Married Women's Property

At the beginning of the 1960s, whether or not a married woman worked outside the home property and possessions usually belonged to the husband. It was rare for a couple buying their own home to put the property in their joint names. Any cars or household items would be regarded as owned by the husband unless a woman could prove they were bought with her earnings. Hire-purchase applications had to be signed by the husband so that even if the wife's money paid the premiums the item would legally belong to him. Nothing had changed since the Blackwell case in 1943, in that the husband still had a legal right to any savings from the housekeeping money. A wife could not secretly save money because her husband was required to declare the interest on his wife's savings in his tax return.

The Married Woman's Property Act of 1964 put into law the recommendation of the Royal Commission on Divorce that a wife should have a right to half of anything she might have saved from a housekeeping allowance. However, the Act did nothing to change the position of women with regard to their right to live in the family home and in theory if a husband had sole ownership of the house he could have his wife evicted. A further law in 1967, the Matrimonial Homes Act, gave both men and women the right to occupy their home. These two Acts removed some of the inequalities in marriage but the State's underlying assumption, in terms of tax affairs, pensions and unemployment benefit, was still that women were their husbands' dependants and as such did not need to be treated as individuals in their own right.

Left: Seventy-one-year-old Florence Nagle outside the High Court in 1966 after she had won the right for women to be awarded a licence to train horses. Having eventually triumphed in her battle against the Jockey Club, Nagle also took the Kennel Club to court over their insistence on male-only membership.

Opposite below left: Every large company employed women on the switchboard.

Opposite below right: Russian cosmonaut Valentina Tereshkova in training for her space mission.

Left: Five of the 20,000 female shop stewards in Britain take part in a course to improve their skills for the role. Training had previously only been open to men.

Above: Nan Winton interviews Labour MP Barbara Castle. Winton was the first woman to read the national news on BBC TV, beginning in June 1960. However, her tenure was short-lived as audience reaction was unfavourable. It was not until 1975, and the appointment of Angela Rippon, that the main BBC news was presented regularly by a woman.

1960s Postscripts

June 1962: Sophia Loren and her husband Carlo Ponti were charged with bigamy in Italy as Italian law did permit divorce and therefore did not recognise Ponti's divorce from his first wife.

November 1962: Lady Edith Summerskill, MP and a former Health Minister, urged a ban on the prescription of oral contraceptives until the results of a committee appointed to assess the reports that the Pill might 'predispose to thrombosis' were published. Lord Brain of the Family Planning Association dismissed the connection between the Pill and thrombosis.
January 1963: The BBC ended its ban on mentioning politics, royalty, religion and sex

in its comedy shows. This paved the way for programmes like *That Was The Week That Was*.

June 1963: Lieutenant Valentina Tereshkova, a Russian cosmonaut, became the first woman in space when she orbited the earth in a spaceship. In the USA, 13 women had passed astronaut tests but none of them had been selected for a mission.

1963: A Leader in the *Daily Mail* suggested that the time was long past for the eight million working women in Britain to have equal pay with men and not just the ten per cent who had achieved it by 1963. It also pointed out that husbands still legally

owned any savings from the housekeeping money. In 1964 women were awarded half.

April 1964: West German Geraldine Mock became the first woman to fly solo round the world.

July 1964: The first Brook Advisory Clinic opened giving birth-control advice to unmarried couples.

December 1964: Briton Dorothy Crowfoot Hodgkin was awarded the Nobel Prize for Chemistry for her work in using X-rays to determine the structures of biochemical substances.

Divorce Reform

By 1969 anyone wishing to divorce still had to rely on the 1937 Matrimonial Causes Act which required one partner to prove the other guilty of desertion, insanity, adultery or cruelty. Even if both partners wanted a divorce, because blame had to be attributed, the process was messy and unpleasant.

During the 1960s legislation had been passed allowing a wife, and a husband in the rare cases where the woman owned the house, security of tenure in the family home. Further legislation had allowed her to keep any savings she had made from any money her husband might have given her. Laws like these, which gave women a little more financial security, and a general feeling that they were not prepared to put up with unhappy marriages and situations their mothers might have accepted, were part of what brought a growing pressure for a change in the divorce laws.

A Divorce Reform Bill was introduced into Parliament and passed in 1969, although it did not come into effect until January 1971. This new Act allowed for either partner to sue for divorce on the grounds that the marriage had 'irretrievably broken down'. After a couple had been apart for two years, if both agreed, a divorce could be granted; if one partner objected to the divorce a separation of five years was required.

The new Act did not always make divorce any less unpleasant but it did remove the necessity to apportion blame. However, it did not remove the need for partners to challenge one another over the major issues which follow from divorce. Couples still battled in the courts over custody of, and access to, any children of the marriage; maintenance payments and their upkeep; the division of the family home and property. The Divorce Reform Act made divorce easier to obtain and the dramatic 25 per cent increase in divorce petitions showed just how many unhappy marriages there were.

Above: John Lennon and Yoko Ono were married in Gibraltar in 1969 and honeymooned in Amsterdam, where they staged their famous 'bed-in' at the Hilton Hotel.

Left: Film director Roman Polanski and actress Sharon Tate at their wedding reception in the Playboy Club, London, in 1968.

Women in the Universities

As Britain sought to keep up in a rapidly changing and developing world there was an expansion in the numbers of university places available and increasing numbers of women took up those places. Several new universities were established and polytechnics created to offer a wider range of degree courses. Women formed just under 30 per cent of the total university population. However, at Oxford and Cambridge less than 10 per cent of students were female in 1962, which was hardly any improvement on the percentage in 1922, and all of those women were in women-only colleges.

In 1964 New College, Oxford voted to be the first men's college to admit women but the decision was reversed the following year after lobbying by the women's colleges who feared it would severely damage the standard of applications to their institutions. The women's colleges admitted 300 applicants each year, while the men's colleges took in almost 2,500. It was not until 1972 that women were granted admission to any men's colleges.

Those women who did gain a university place often worked far harder than their male counterparts, perhaps feeling they had to justify their presence in such establishments. A study by the University Grants Committee found that in 1965–6 almost 82 per cent of women passed their finals as against just over 76 per cent of men.

Above: Sophia Loren and her husband Carlo Ponti were charged in Italy with bigamy as Italian law did not recognise Ponti's divorce from his first wife, indeed did not legally accept any divorce.

Above: Pop singer Lulu married Bee Gee Maurice Gibb in February 1969, keeping out the winter chill with a white, mink-trimmed cossack-style coat and a white silk mini-dress.

Top: Sirimawo Bandaranaike became the first female elected head of state in 1960 when she succeeded her husband as Prime Minister of Ceylon (now Sri Lanka).

Above: Indira Ghandi, daughter of India's first Prime Minister Jawaharlal Nehru, became the country's third Prime Minister, serving from 1966 until she was assassinated by two of her bodyguards in 1984.

Right: Golda Meir was appointed Prime Minister of Israel in 1969.

Wanted: Angry young women

IT should anger every woman in the land.

Pussyfooting and meanness **by** the Government and the mandarins **of** medicine are delaying the eradication of cancer of the cervix.

Each year cancer of the neck **of** the womb kills 2,500 women in Britain. The great majority of these deaths are preventable.

They go on happening for two reasons. The Ministry of Health will not spend enough on screening facilities for early detection of the disease.

And a row among medical men **on** the efficacy of screening looks likely to swamp the issue in years of sterile committee wrangling.

To take the second point first. A working group of medical experts, appointed by the Nuffield Provincial Hospitals Trust, has come down against cervical cancer tests because, they say, not enough is known about the disease, screening procedure and treatment.

Ignorance

And Lord Cohen of Birkenhead, president of the General Medical Council, seems to agree. He speaks of 'public ignorance' or imperfect understanding putting pressure on the Government to set up a service whose worth is not fully known.

Happily, his view is not shared by the Queen's gynæcologist, Sir John Peel, who is president-elect of the Women's National Cancer Control Campaign.

Sir John says: 'The cure rate for *pre*-cancer diagnosed by the smear test is nearly 100 p.c. Cancer of the cervix is therefore **in** theory a preventable disease.'

Even in clinically diagnosed and established cancer of the cervix the cure rate in Britain **is** 50 p.c.

He has a powerful ally in Professor H. G. McLaren, of Birmingham University, who found 300 cases of *pre*-cancer with the smear test. Not one developed cervical cancer.

Professor McLaren's message is that it is *fit* women who should take the test. The trouble is that 'a young mother of several children is always busy and thinks of herself and her health very rarely. She is, however, the key figure in any family or community.'

The test can be had in any National Health Service hospital. But not many fit young mothers have cause to go to hospital.

Closing

And Ministry of Health screening clinics throughout the country are closing, says Lady Donaldson, chairman of the Women's National Cancer Control Campaign.

The campaign has launched an appeal for £100,000 for mobile clinics which would tackle cervical cancer in factory yards and at country crossroads in much the same way that tuberculosis was tackled.

But what is more urgently needed is an evaluation of the impressive statistics given by Peel and McLaren, a massive publicity campaign, and *action*.

And no woman should let her anger abate until these things happen.

BRING ON THE BLUE STOCKINGS

Sir Denis Brogan, retiring Professor of Political Science, calls for more university education for women.

'Our greatest untapped source of ability', he said, 'is education for girls. If I had money to give away I would spend it on getting more women into the universities. That's where we are missing the bright ones. I don't think we are missing very many bright boys.

'The argument that it is a waste because they get married is bogus. We should make it easier for them to go back to their jobs ten years after they have their children…And anyway if a clever woman remains a wife and mother what is wrong with having clever wives and mothers?

Daily Mail, 4 March 1966

1960s Postscripts

January 1965: Yvonne Pope was the first British woman to pilot a scheduled aircraft. A shortage of male pilots as air travel increased had given her the opportunity for the job.

November 1965: The Customs and Excise Department changed the criteria for assessing what would be classed as children's clothing, and thus not taxable, from dress length to bust size so that mini-length women's clothing would not escape tax.

January 1966: Following the death of Prime Minister Shastri, Indira Gandhi was elected

and sworn in as Prime Minister of India by the members of the ruling Congress Party.

June 1966: Barclay's Bank issued their Barclaycard credit card. In cases of joint accounts only the husbands were issued with cards, but most husbands returned them and asked that their wives also be issued with one.

July 1966: Florence Nagle won a long fight with the Jockey Club, eventually taking them to the High Court, over being allowed a trainer's licence. Mrs Nagle described herself as a 'ghost trainer' as she had trained racehorses for almost

30 years under a licence given to her head lad.

October 1966: The Law Commission was charged to examine the practice by which the marriage prospects of a widow or single woman had to be taken into account when a court was assessing an award of damages.

1967: MP David Steel sponsored an Abortion Law Reform Bill, which became the Abortion Act. Technically the law did not legalise abortions but provided a legal defence for those carrying them out under certain conditions.

A New Abortion Law

With the growth of the 'permissive society' and much more open discussion about sex and contraception there was a growing public feeling that something had to be done about the existing abortion laws. The law dated back to 1861, despite a ruling in 1938 in the Bourne case which reinterpreted the expression 'unless the mother's life is in danger' to mean her physical or mental wellbeing. However, many doctors (and the agreement of two doctors was required to allow the abortion to go ahead) were not willing to risk judgement on whether a women's health would be so disabled by continuing the pregnancy as to leave her a 'wreck', and in the majority of cases it was patently not the case. The only alternative was an illegal or 'backstreet' abortion.

Many plays and novels of the time, such as *Up the Junction*, dealt with or included the situation of a woman becoming pregnant and seeking an illegal abortion. They described graphically the often insanitary conditions and the risks to the mothers' health. It seems surprising that women would endanger their lives in a backstreet abortion but during the 1960s, for all the talk of permissiveness and although there had been some softening of attitudes, the unmarried mother still faced rejection by society and often by her family.

In October 1967 the Medical Termination of Pregnancy Bill became law despite a campaign by anti-abortion groups such as the Society for the Protection of the Unborn Child formed in January of the same year. The new law effectively ended the practice of backstreet abortion by permitting abortion up to 28 weeks on the grounds that to continue with the pregnancy would cause injury to the mother's mental or physical health. Abortion was also permitted if the baby was at risk of being physically or mentally malformed.

The National Health Service was charged to make provision for abortion operations. However, it was not always simple to obtain an abortion on the NHS as not all hospitals provided facilities, and some doctors, morally opposed to abortion, were unwilling either to refer women for, or to perform, the operation. Once in hospital a woman waiting for an abortion operation could find herself in an ante-natal ward alongside women anxiously trying to prevent the unborn child within them from spontaneous abortion.

The shortcomings of the NHS in relation to abortion lead to the establishment of bodies such as the British Pregnancy Advisory Service which offered contact with doctors willing to sanction and perform abortions and a more sympathetic treatment in private clinics.

The new law brought tremendous benefits to women: they no longer had to suffer for life the results of an unwanted pregnancy, or physical pain or terrible damage from an illegal abortion, although the law could not remove the mental and emotional suffering such an operation brings.

Top: After taking the fertility treatment gonadotrophin, in 1968 Sheila Thorns underwent a caesarean section at Birmingham Maternity Hospital with 28 medical staff at the delivery. She gave birth to Britains first recorded sextuplets.

Here she is pictured with her three surviving children – Susan, Roger and Julie.

Above: A mother having her baby weighed at a child health clinic in 1960.

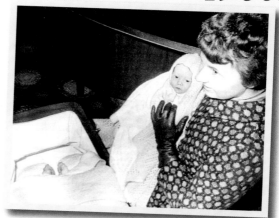

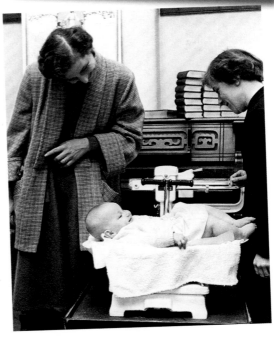

MOTHERS with babies who want at all costs to be seen to be trendy, colourful and above all *different* when it comes to nursery accessories are going to have the time of their lives in 1970.

The only difficulty will be making a choice from among all the new-look ideas.

PRAMS, for example, are going into PRINT. On show at this week's Pram Fair in London is the Sandown baby carriage by Royale. With bodywork, hood and apron in Stylon (a new fabric of washable Bri-nylon and PVC), it's printed all over with a swirling William Morris design in red, blue or gold, and it costs about £30.

A strong colour contender in this year's pram stakes is a delicious new honey tan, a follow-up to last year's successful orange. 'Heavy-knit' vinyl for pram bodies looks like being another popular newcomer, while the traditional white pram interior is now very much an also-ran.

by ANGELA BROADBRIDGE

silks—and in 12 designs, from about 38s.

CARRY-COTS are getting BOLD—the latest, imported from Italy, are in shiny scarlet, brilliant yellow, green or white, £7 10s. at the new Bilba Boutique, Kensington.

Most hilarious idea around at the moment is the musical potty. In the shape of a pink or blue duck, it has a string trailing from the duck's mouth which the child can pull—and be rewarded by a cheerful little song.

Enough to give any child a musical hang-up for life, we'd think.

More practical is the Kiddi-rail, a telescopic handrail for fixing to a staircase at child-height. In silvery or ivory metal, it adjusts to any staircase up to 12ft. in length. By Bells of Southport, 59s. 6d.

Final colour note: a big plump rabbit in bright pink, to use as a table mat, with matching bib in towelling and a cotton wallet to store the bib 30s. the set, by Bassetti.

Practical

Today it's navy—smart, dark and much more practical—which looks like taking the prize here.

CANOPIES are going PSYCHEDELIC, in huge, printed abstracts or florals in mixtures of deep green, pale green and sugar pink. By Morlands of Glastonbury, they come in cotton or a new, shiny satin—as stunning as a jockey's

Birth Control Under Attack

Pope Paul published his Encyclical Letter entitled *Humane Vitae* (Of Human Life) in 1968. The Vatican's deliberations on the subject of birth control had been awaited by Roman Catholics throughout the world with great expectation of a dramatic new approach. In the end most were severely disappointed, for the Papal Encyclical stated that any form of artificial birth control was against divine will, although it did approve the 'rhythm method' of birth control where a couple had to avoid having sex at the woman's most fertile period. It was some small acknowledgement by the Church that sex was not solely for the procreation of children.

For many Catholic women this ruling put them in a very difficult moral position. Their Church ruled against artificial forms of birth control which were by far the most effective, and yet they felt that in terms of their own family's wellbeing and the world's population, to say nothing of the immense benefits to their own life and fulfilment, a strong moral case could be made for contraception.

If they chose to defy the Church's teachings, and many did, there was a growing range of possible alternative methods of contraception. There was of course the cap, the sheath and the Pill (although scares about the safety of the Pill had caused many women to stop taking it, sometimes only for a period until they could be reassured but often abandoning it altogether as a suitable method of contraception).

The Intra Uterine Device (IUD) became available a few years after the Pill and despite it not being as widely publicised, it quickly became popular, especially among older women who had had their family and were at greater risk on the Pill. Wives, however, needed their husbands' consent before having the IUD fitted as once in place it made the woman temporarily sterile and only a doctor could reverse that sterility. By mid-1966 there was a year-long waiting list for the IUD, partly because of its popularity and partly because there were not enough doctors trained to fit it.

Sterilisation was another, if drastic, method but a number of women chose that route although it was usually only offered to those with large families. Male sterilisation, or vasectomy, was an alternative but usually only in cases where the wife was not considered fit enough to undergo a sterilisation operation.

Left: Mother and baby are on trend in 1968 – the mother in a mini length fun-fur coat and the baby sports the Union Jack, used in many designs as Britain became synonymous with fashion and style.

Right: Entrepreneurial spirit on show at the 1967 Woburn Abbey Flower Child Festival. By the late 1960s ethnic clothing and jewellery were the height of fashion. The hippies of San Fransisco had led the way but love beads and long hair, batik and bell bottoms were worn by the young everywhere.

1960s Postscripts

February 1967: A Bill was passed allowing local authorities to give contraceptive advice to married and unmarried men and women.

July 1967: The Sexual Offences Act became law, decriminalising homosexual acts in private between consenting men over the age of 21. Lesbianism had never been illegal as it was not acknowledged to exist by the law makers of earlier centuries.

1968: Epidural pain relief was first introduced for women during childbirth.

June 1968: Women machinists at Ford called off a strike for better grading of their jobs after Barbara Castle, the Minister for Employment and Productivity, stepped in. She did not gain them better grades but the company ended the practice of setting separate rates of pay and the women were paid the same rate as men on the equivalent grade.

October 1968: Sheila Ann Thorns gave birth to sextuplets after having been treated with a fertility drug.

February 1969: Lloyd's of London announced that it would admit women from the beginning of 1970.

1969: Scientists at Cambridge revealed that they had fertilised a human egg in a test tube but they said that there was a long way to go before this advance would have any practical use.

March 1969: The Israeli Labour Party elected Golda Meir to be Prime Minister following the death in office of Prime Minister Cevi Eshkol.

The Women's Liberation Movement

After the Second World War Simone de Beauvoir, Vera Brittain and Betty Friedan had all published books drawing attention to the overt and subtle forms of oppression exercised over women. In 1970 Germaine Greer published a new work on the subject challenging the way in which men had stereotyped women and set out ways in which it was acceptable for them to behave, and the way in which society trained girls to be unassertive, undemanding and compliant to men. *The Female Eunuch* had a dramatic effect when it was first published, and a great deal of media attention, through which its message reached women who would never have dreamt of reading the book.

In 1970, responding to what they felt was a need, a number of women, including the feminist historian Sheila Rowbottom, organised the first national Women's Liberation Movement Conference. The conference, like Germaine Greer's book, was only part of a growing women's movement which questioned the role women were being forced to play in society. Very like the suffragettes before the First World War, the Women's Liberation Movement held marches and demonstrations and lobbied Parliament and politicians on issues which affected women. Indeed, they had success in terms of legislation. Several new laws were passed removing many of the inequalities women suffered in the legal system. The Movement was also international and brought changes in the legal position of women in countries such as France, which was the first country to appoint a Minister for Women. It also brought changes in the social position and women's awareness of themselves and their value to society in countries with such vastly different cultural heritages as the USA and Japan.

The Women's Liberation Movement also drew attention to the way society and men in general perceived and treated women. Attacks on the exploitation of women and their bodies, with demonstrations at events like the Miss World Contest, had some impact. While at first the media dismissed such protests and did not treat them seriously, the message was strong enough to change public consciousness. There is now no longer the same media attention given to beauty contests and the winner of Miss World would be lucky to make it to the front page of even the tabloids.

There were critics at the time who said the Women's Liberation Movement and the 'bra-burning, scrubbed-faced, dungaree-wearing women's libbers' went too far and denied their femininity in order to gain their freedom. However, there would be no argument now that these women had an important effect on future generations of both men and women, and felt they had found a freedom for themselves while making freedom for other women a possibility.

Below: Feminist writer and campaigner Germaine Greer.

Below left: Margaret Thatcher, soon to become leader of the Conservative Party, arrives at the polling station in Finchley to cast her vote.

Bottom: A slim pair of legs seems to be one of the main selling points of the Triumph Stag.

Opposite middle: Despite the efforts of the Women's Movement it was becoming more common to see naked women used in advertisements. This one of model Vivien Neves caused a sensation when it appeared in *The Times*.

What's a nice girl like you doing in a firm like this?

FISONS

Above: The Women's Liberation Movement demonstrate in London's Hyde Park in March 1971.

Below: Marsha Rowe (left) and Susie Boycott founded the feminist magazine *Spare Rib* in 1972. In contrast to the many magazines for women which focused on topics such as beauty and romance, *Spare Rib* explored the issues surrounding women's rights,

covering matters such as equal pay, domestic violence and abortion.

Below right: Many women may have been eschewing traditional feminine charms but glamour was alive and well in the Miss World competition. Seen here is Mary Stavin, Swedish winner of the 1977 contest, who went on to become a Bond girl.

BETTY FRIEDAN, the high priestess of Women's Liberation, started it all with her book 'The Feminine Mystique.'

She is founder of the National Organisation of Women, professional women working to end job discrimination, repeal the abortion laws and establish creches.

'Discrimination was crystallised in my mind when I went to Boston researching for my book. I had an hour to kill before my appointment, so I went into a large hotel for a drink. But the barman would not serve me because I was a woman alone. He said he would take me to where I could have a drink.

'He led me to the ladies' cloakroom.

'All I really did in my book was to put into words what millions of women have probably been thinking for years. That everything is against them.'

1970s Postscripts

February 1970: The House of Commons gave an unopposed second reading to the Equal Pay Bill, introduced by Barbara Castle, the Minister for Employment and Productivity, which said that women and men doing the same job would have to be given the same rates of pay by January 1976.

May 1970: Ann Hays and Elizabeth Hoisington became the US Army's first women Generals.

June 1970: The Methodist Church announced that women would soon be permitted to be

ordained as ministers and be granted the same pay and status as men.

January 1971: The first decree was granted under the new Divorce Act which allowed 'irretrievable breakdown' as grounds for divorce.

May 1971: It was announced that 'ladies in hot pants' would only be allowed into the Royal Enclosure at Ascot if the general effect was satisfactory.

March 1972: The US Senate passed an Equal Rights Amendment to the Constitution making it against the law to discriminate against a person on the grounds of sex.

March 1972: The British government warned employers to make moves towards bringing women's pay into line with men's ready for equal pay in 1976 or they would bring in interim legislation to give women 90 per cent of men's pay by January 1974.

Fair Shares

During the 1960s and early 1970s legislation had given a wife more rights in terms of a share in the family's assets when a marriage broke up, so that although divorce frequently brought financial hardship for both partners, especially where children were involved, the burden fell less on the wife with children than it had done in the past. However, the same rules did not apply to common-law wives. A woman living with a man where he had ownership or tenancy of the property could be evicted by him and maintenance need only be given for any children of the relationship once paternity was proved.

By 1972 it was not an unusual occurrence for a couple to set up home together without getting married. In fact it had almost become a regular thing for couples to live together before making the commitment to marry. Sometimes couples decided to live together with no intention of ever getting married, others decided to live together until they had or decided to have children.

A case in 1972 reported in the *Daily Mail* illustrated clearly the position of a woman living with a man without the legal benefits of marriage. The woman, whom the judge described as 'a mistress' (her partner was described simply as a man), was granted a right to a share in the home they had built together. An initial court case decided that she was entitled to a twelfth share of the property and on appeal the percentage was increased to a third but not the half she had claimed and to which she would have had a right had they been married.

Above: Princess Anne married Captain Mark Phillips in November 1973.

Right: Mick Jagger and Bianca Pérez-Mora Macias, who married in 1971, were one of the golden couples of the early 1970s.

Top: Erin Pizzey in the Chiswick women's refuge.

1970s

Domestic Violence

In 1970 Erin Pizzey opened her first refuge for women seeking shelter and protection from violent partners. Throughout the 1970s the issue of violence within marriage was brought into the open and the term 'battered wife' was coined. Of course the violence was not always against wives. Often the women in question were not married to the men who assaulted them but felt just as helpless and fearful, trapped by children and financial dependence, just like wives who would have to go through the courts to gain a legal separation. A woman living with a man could, if she had the emotional strength and a willing police force, have a violent partner charged for an attack. Wives had no such recourse to law. In 1976 pressure from women's groups brought about the Domestic Violence Act which gave wives more protection from violent husbands and the police powers to arrest husbands who breached injunctions.

Before the issue of domestic violence was brought out of the confines of the family home many people simply ignored or were ignorant of its existence. There was also an underlying inheritance, especially among the victims and the perpetrators, that it was somehow acceptable for a husband to beat his wife and indeed, in the days when a wife quite literally belonged to her husband, society accepted that she was his to do with as he liked. In marrying she gave away her rights.

This last issue of what a woman was giving up when she married was the crux of a ruling which said a husband could not rape his wife. In the eighteenth century a judge had ruled that when a woman makes her marriage vows she gives away all rights to refuse to have sex with her husband for the rest of the marriage. A case in December 1975 had reaffirmed this to be the legal position in Britain with regard to rape within marriage. However, some states in the USA had changed their laws to allow for a man to be prosecuted for raping his wife. And in 1978, in what was believed to be the first case of its kind, a man in Oregon was prosecuted for raping his wife while they were still living together. He was found not guilty after claiming that his wife consented voluntarily to sex, because the jury felt there was insufficient proof of guilt. It was not until 1991 that rape within marriage became a crime in the UK, after the House of Lords, on appeal, removed the marital rights exemption.

GIVEN the chance, two-in-five of Britain's housewives would take a job. And another 19 p.c. are thinking about doing so.

Their reasons, discovered by the National Opinion Polls survey, are that extra bit of money to do with as they please; the boredom of home life; and the companionship of people at work.

But of the 40 p.c. happy with their lot at home, a half said they wouldn't take a job—or go back to their old job—because they would have to do the housework at night.

As one young housewife with two children commented: 'Well, you don't have time for sex, which is the most important thing, because you're too tired. I think working wives *must* be irritable.'

Others said they would hate having to rush everything, and that the children would suffer. An accountant's wife in Devon commented: 'The house wouldn't be in the same condition that it's in, and my son would be annoyed if I was not there at 4 p.m.'

Among full-time mothers, 46 p.c. spend 41 hours or more a week on housework, including cooking, shopping and washing. At the other end of the scale, 11 p.c. of working housewives spend less than 15 hours on the same tasks.

Sixty p.c. of non-working women disagreed with the suggestion that married women can't find enough to occupy their minds just running a home.

But 79 p.c. agreed that it was important for a married woman to have some money of her own, illustrating the frustration of those who would like to work but can't — usually because of the children.

More than half (53 p.c.) think working wives are less bored than themselves, and 45 p.c. think that women who work make more interesting companions for their husbands. (Only 34 p.c. disagreed with this.)

An inhibiting factor for those women who would like to work is the lack of nurseries and nursery schools —63 p.c. said their area needed more.

As to what effect all this has on a marriage, it is curious to find that, where the largest proportion of working wives think there are fewer rows in their home because they go out to work, exactly the same number of non-working women disagree.

WOMEN, according to many medical researchers, are beginning to pay the price of their liberation — increasing ill-health, stress and loss of sex drive and fertility.

They are smoking more, drinking more, attempting suicide more, taking more pills; and the incidence of heart disease, cancer and VD is rising.

Professor Ivor H. Mills, whose team of researchers at Addenbrooke New Hospital, Cambridge, has been studying the problem for eight years, says: 'My view is that women are gradually cracking up under social, sexual and business pressures. At present they seem biologically less able to withstand these pressures than men.'

'If women push themselves too hard, their personalities — and even their hormone balance — changes. The result is a drop in sex drive and fertility.'

'Fertility rates are dropping dramatically, and I am convinced this isn't due only to the pill.'

The birth rate dropped from 18·6 per thousand women in 1964, to 15·8 in 1971. But it went down to 14·4 in 1972, and was 12·7 last year.

'It is dropping so fast that our population is no longer replacing itself,' said Professor Mills. 'Yet our infertility clinics are swamped with desperate women.'

Professor Mills also points out that with the age of puberty having dropped to around 12, pressure is now put on girls at a much earlier age.

Right: This model combines two trends of the decade. Chunky knitwear, with a hand-knitted look, and an ethnic feel. Peruvian jumpers, prints from India, padded jackets inspired by Chinese and Tibetan styles, embroidered peasant-style blouses and crocheted tops all had their moment in the 70s.

OLD LAW ENDS LIFE OF SHAME

Ann McLean kept a secret for 28 years from her son and her neighbours.

The shame of the ex-nurse was that she was not married to the man she lived with. But yesterday, 20 months after her 'husband' died, a judge in Edinburgh decided that under an old Scottish law she had been married by 'habit and repute'.

Miss McLean, of Kirkintilloch, near Glasgow – now officially Mrs Frederick Roberts, 66, was granted a marriage decree.

She told the court that when in 1953 she returned to the village of Lattermorar in Kintyre, she and her husband had a son. She did not dare admit that she was not married.

Daily Mail, 8 June 1978

WOMEN'S BOREDOM LEADS TO BABIES

Father-of-four Lord Beaumont of Whitely was in trouble last night for saying that women often have babies because they can't think of anything better to do.

Lord Beaumont, former President of the Liberal Party, told peers debating the world's population problems:

'Towards the end of a period when women have two or three children, if there is not a chance of finding a worthwhile job, they find themselves lonely.

'And there is a great subconscious wish just to go on being a mother with more children.'

Daily Mail, 11 February 1971

HOW DOES A WOMAN SPEND HER SPARE TIME?

Watching TV	Crafts & Hobbies	Reading	Social Activities	Gardening	Going for walks	Doing nothing
80%	71%	57%	46%	44%	37%	2%

1970s Postscripts

September 1972: At the Munich Olympics Olga Korbut won three gold medals and one silver, capturing the affection of the crowds in a gymnastics competition where the USSR and East Germany and their 'perfectly formed' and trained gymnasts won every medal except one.

September 1973: A report entitled *Equal Opportunities for Men and Women* proposed the setting up of an Equal Opportunities Commission which would have legal backing to ensure that neither sex could be discriminated against in employment, training or education.

September 1973: It was recommended in a government report that mothers bringing up children on their own should be given a weekly cash allowance which could also be given to fathers in the same position.

May 1974: In the USA the Dalkon Shield contraceptive was taken off the market amid fears that it had caused infections, sterility and even death amongst its users. It remained in use in Britain although it was not a very popular form of contraception.

November 1974: Helen Morgan, newly crowned Miss World, resigned when she feared that she would be named in a divorce case. The rules stated that only unmarried women were eligible as contestants and the implication was that they were virgins.

Entering the Establishment

Part of the work of the Women's Liberation Movement was challenging what the press continually referred to as 'the last bastions of male supremacy'. There were many, some of them trivial, some of them in areas which wielded power and authority over society. 'Gentlemen's clubs', which were meeting places for directors of businesses, financial institutions, high-ranking civil servants and politicians, denied membership to women, only allowing them to enter the club premises when accompanied by a male member. In these clubs men met and talked, and influenced direction and policy in many areas of British life.

One major financial institution which removed its final barriers to women in 1973 was the Stock Exchange. Since its foundation women had been excluded from trading on the 'floor' of the Stock Exchange building. Although there were a number of women working as stock brokers the governors of the Stock Exchange always maintained that the hectic pace and stress of work on the 'floor' would be too much for a woman, that they needed to be protected from such harsh and rough conditions. However, in February 1973 several women, amid much media attention, took to the floor of the Stock Exchange as traders.

While the Stock Exchange and men's clubs were very obvious places which excluded women from the Establishment which ran Britain, there were other factors which made it, and still make it, difficult for women to be part of it. Parliamentary hours, set to allow those in the legal profession to work by day and legislate in the evenings and nights, do not suit most women with a family. The selection process for candidates frequently favours men as they appear

to be a safer bet – no one in the electorate is likely to object to them simply because they are a man. The whole system of parliamentary 'debate', the shouting, abuse and insults MPs hurl at one another, is not something which appeals to many women. All these factors accounted for the abysmally low percentage of women MPs in the 1970s, and on into the 1980s and early 1990s.

In business, too, women, especially those with children, were still expected to leave work to bring up children, and although most women who did so planned to return to work when their children were older there were no allowances given for taking time out to have a family. In 1973 no company or institution even paid lip service to the idea of a career break. Even in the Civil Service part-time workers could only work on the lowest grade.

GOOD GOD, SIR!
A Woman at the Carlton?

The Carlton Club, male bastion of the Tory Party, was last night faced with the greatest dilemma in its 140-year-old history. For members of the exclusive club in St James's Street, London, must now decide whether to break with tradition and allow Mrs Thatcher to join.

In the past every Conservative leader has been invited to join if he was not already a member. But to offer membership to a woman – the very prospect set some members shifting uncomfortably in their leather-studded armchairs, while other traditionalists sought comfort in large gulps from even larger brandies.

Women considered it a breakthrough when, in 1963, they were first allowed into the Carlton as guests of members.

Daily Mail, 12 February 1975

Above: Anna Ford prepares herself for her newsreading debut as ITN's first woman newscaster on the major evening news slot in 1978.

Above middle: One of the three women allowed on to the Stock Exchange Floor in the early 70s.

Right: The Sex Discrimination Act became law on 29 December 1975 and these women journalists tried to be served a drink at the bar of El Vino in Fleet Street which clung to its men-only tradition and refused them.

Above right: Flexible working hours in offices was introduced in the early 1970s. Staff of a City insurance company are pictured here clocking in.

Opposite top: The 'pregnant man' poster which caused great controversy when it was first introduced.

Opposite right: Nannies from the Princess Christian Training College wheeling their charges. The college which took in 'unwanted' babies was closing as better contraception, easier abortion and a more tolerant climate for unmarried mothers had combined to reduce the numbers of children who needed care.

Opposite left: The Women's Liberation Movement claimed the right to enjoy the same social and sexual freedoms as men. Abortion was legalised in Britain in 1967 but a heated debate continued across Europe and in the US through the 70s as pro-life and pro-abortion supporters tried to persuade governments to alter laws in their favour.

Free Family Planning for All

From April 1974 family planning advice and contraceptives were free on the National Health Service. For several years the government had been campaigning actively to encourage the use of contraception, especially among young people of both sexes not ready to carry the responsibility of parenthood. Sex education in schools also included information and discussion about contraception. But until 1974 anyone requiring contraceptive advice had to go to a special family planning clinic, which could be funded by the local authority. After that date an ordinary GP could dispense contraceptive advice and any prescriptions were free of the standard prescription charges.

The move towards more freely available birth control was not without controversy. There was debate about whether it put pressure on young people, especially young girls, to start on sexual relationships before they were emotionally mature enough. There was also a great deal of argument as to whether doctors should be able to prescribe the Pill to girls under the legal age of consent.

However, the biggest controversy over birth control in 1974 was caused by a speech by Sir Keith Joseph, the Shadow Home Secretary. His call for better birth control amongst the poor recalled the eugenicists of the pre-Second World War period. He said, 'The balance of our population, our human stock is threatened by the rising proportion of children born to mothers least fit to bring them up...' He was referring to a growth in the figures for births to young unmarried girls from the poorer sectors of society.

Would you be more careful if it was you that got pregnant?

Contraception is one of the facts of life. Anyone married or single can get advice on contraception from the Family Planning Association. Margaret Pyke House, 25-35 Mortimer Street, London W1 N 8BQ. Tel. 01-636 9135.

TOP PILL RISKS

A table of women who should not use the Pill is given in a report published today for family doctors.

The young wife who has yet to start her family and the woman over 40 head the list as the type for whom the oral contraceptive is least advisable.

The report, the first of its kind to guide GPs on the groups of patients who could suffer unnecessary risk from the drug despite government reassurances on its relative safety, is prepared by Social Technology Associates of Manchester, and appears in the Journal of the Royal College of General Practitioners.

The report assesses the present death rate from blood clotting and unwanted pregnancy among women on the existing pill – a combination of the hormones oestrogen and progestogen – as 13 a year.

Daily Mail, 6 March 1972

1970s Postscripts

1975: The year was designated International Women's Year by the United Nations with a view to promoting women's rights and position and campaigning on issues concerning women throughout the world.

1975: The Sex Discrimination Act makes it illegal to discriminate against women in work, education and training.

1975: The Employment Protection Act was passed giving women the right to maternity leave with some pay and for their job to be held open for 29 weeks after the birth.

February 1975: Margaret Thatcher, described as the wife of a wealthy businessman and mother of twins, was elected leader of the Conservative Party.

1975: The Sex Discrimination Act makes it illegal to discriminate against women in work, education and training.

1976: Angela Rippon became the first woman to regularly read the main evening news on BBC television.

August 1976: Betty Williams and Mairead Corrigan began the Women's Peace Movement

in Northern Ireland in an attempt to end the bloodshed. They were later awarded the Nobel Peace Prize for 1976 but did not receive the award until October 1977.

September 1976: Dartmouth Naval College admitted its first women cadets.

1977: New adoption laws gave adopted children the right to seek out their natural parents. But the law did not give natural parents the right either to refuse disclosure of their name and address to the child or the right to trace a child they had given up for adoption.

Far left: The mid-1970s 'page boy' hairstyle was a rediscovery of the 1950s style made popular by glamour model Betty Page.

Left: Hot pants were an alternative to the maxi skirt in the early part of the decade.

Below left: The halter neckline was employed in a huge range of clothing, including swimwear, evening gowns, catsuits and maxi dresses with cutaway armholes.

Below centre: At the British Footwear Show in 1973 platform heels were all the rage, coming in all colours, shapes, and sizes. Heel heights ranged from two to five inches, and platform heights from half an inch to four inches.

Below: The maxi skirt was as fashionable as the mini skirt in the early 1970s. The model is wearing a black velvet skirt, with tartan taffeta cummerbund and white crepe pintucked blouse.

Flares, Hotpants and Punk

Flares, hotpants, platform soles, midi skirts, trouser suits, Laura Ashley designs, jogging suits, military styles and of course denim jeans were just part of the multiplicity of styles in the 1970s. The '70s seemed to mark the beginnings of more rapidly changing clothes styles, as well as a wider range of styles being worn by any one individual. Advertisers created a market for fashion by promoting changes and crazes. This was part of a whole movement towards increasing the sales of consumer goods of every description but the method was always the same: change or update the product and then persuade the consumer that they needed the latest version.

Unisex fashions, emphasised by men growing their hair longer, were a strong feature of the early 1970s. In fact men became increasingly concerned over how they dressed and how they looked and smelled, promoting a huge growth in the range of skin and body-care products for men. While men grew more aware of how they looked many women, bolstered by the feminist movement, refused to spend hours shopping, dressing and making up.

Towards the end of the decade Punk fashions which, for both men and women, challenged the conventional ideas of how people should look, was a style which was developed on the streets and by the promoters and performers of punk music. The fashion industry took up, copied and refined punk fashion.

During the 1970s the first Page Three Girls began to appear in national newspapers. This exploitation of women was a strange paradox to the growing women's movement. Nudity, promoted by shows such as *Hair* and *Oh, Calcutta!* was classed as a 'good thing'. But the majority of nude bodies anyone ever saw were those of young women – either in the tabloid press or being used to sell a product.

Nevertheless there were important spin-offs from a growing concern with body image in the late 1970s. While dieting came to rule some women's lives, people became more aware of what was a healthy diet. Better, more wholesome nutrition and the fact that more and more women were taking up exercise would in the future have a beneficial effect on the general health of women. Women more than men embraced more wholeheartedly the advice and education about a healthy lifestyle.

Top: Soft, romantic hairstyles accompanied Laura Ashley's Edwardian- and Prairie-style dresses.

Above: Marsha Hunt wears the 'afro'.

Top right: A dramatic and luxurious fireplace and boldly printed wallpaper were two hallmarks of 1970s home design.

Middle right: Innovations in the kitchen during the 1970s included food processors such as the Magimix, and later the microwave oven. But for many it was the freezer that revolutionised domestic eating habits, with one in ten British households owning one by 1974, and specialist frozen food outlets opening on the high street.

Far right: Punk brought brightly coloured hair and extreme styles such as the Mohican, which was held up using everyday products such as eggs and sugar as well as gels and hairsprays.

Right: Fashions with a 1920s twist were echoed in films such as *The Boyfriend* (1971) and *The Great Gatsby* (1974).

1970s Postscripts

December 1977: Rosalyn Yalow was awarded the Nobel Prize for Medicine for her discoveries relating to hormones.

1977: Florence Nagle, the first woman ever to hold a racehorse trainer's licence, was one of three women admitted to membership of the previously all-male Jockey Club.

February 1978: A Life Assurance Company reported it would cost £6,000, one and a half times the average male salary of the period, to replace the services of a woman looking after a home and children.

June 1978: Naomi James arrived in Britain after sailing her yacht around the world in two days less than Francis Chichester's record time.

June 1978: The Inland Revenue announced that future correspondence about wives' tax affairs and any rebates owed to them would be sent to them and not their husbands.

September 1978: France appointed Monique Pelletier as Minister for Women. With government commitment and funding the Ministry made some strides on women's issues, particularly that of abortion, but after the first few years the funding and commitment faded.

March 1979: Lee Marvin's long-time girlfriend, who took his surname, sued him for 'palimony' after their relationship broke down. She claimed that she had given up her own career to be with him and so deserved half of the £3.6m he made during the six years they were together.

May 1979: Margaret Thatcher, MP for Finchley, became the first woman Prime Minister of

Equal Opportunities

From the beginning of 1976 women were given equality with men. At least that was how the media interpreted the implementation of the Equal Pay and Sex Discrimination Acts. Indeed the year marked a change in the way women could be treated in a whole range of areas. In education girls had to be given the opportunity to do technical subjects such as woodwork, and boys the chance to take domestic science subjects. All training places offered in colleges and by employers had to be open to both men and women. Women could not be discriminated against by a system of quotas, such as operated in medical schools, which in effect controlled the number of female doctors.

In the supply of goods and services women were not to be discriminated against. In theory women would no longer suffer the indignity of being refused a mortgage simply because they were female and they could not be asked for a male guarantor to the deal. Job adverts could no longer request 'dolly birds' or 'pretty secretaries', or even say whether they wanted a man or a woman for the job. Employers interviewing women for a job could not ask her questions they would not have asked a man, such as whether she would be leaving to have a family.

There were, however, exceptions. Men and women were still not treated equally in retirement and pensions (women having to retire five years earlier than men), tax affairs and social security benefits. Some jobs in areas such as mining were still barred to women. Some organisations and institutions such as private clubs, the Army and religious organisations were exempt from the law.

Apart from these exemptions there were employers and organisations who actively sought to get round, or use loopholes in the law, to maintain the status quo. As with all legislation of this nature the change in the law was really only a first step to changing society's attitudes and perceptions; no overnight successes could realistically be expected. By December 1978 a survey of 575 companies revealed that only 25 per cent had made any plans aimed at giving equal opportunities to women and only two per cent had actually taken steps to implement such plans.

Top: NUPE workers picket outside Queen Mary's Hospital, Roehampton.

Above: Mairead Corrigan (left) and Betty Williams surrounded by some of the 10,000 people who took part in the first demonstration for peace in Northern Ireland. The pair won the Nobel Prize for Peace in 1976 for their work.

Above right: Pickets outside Grunwick photo-processing Laboratory in Willesden, London, in 1977.

WOMEN GET THEIR CHARTER
Equal jobs for girls – and boys who want to work as midwives.

Women will be guaranteed equal treatment in almost every walk of life under plans announced by the Home Secretary, Mr Roy Jenkins, yesterday.

Anyone who refuses a woman a job or a mortgage or a pint of beer just because she is a woman will face legal action.

And so will anyone who refuses to employ a man as a secretary just because he is a man.

The rules would break some old barriers. Men would be able to work as midwives and women prison officers could be recruited for men's jails.

But there would be some exceptions. The Army won't have to employ dolly girls in the front line and the Church won't have to ordain women priests.

Daily Mail, 7 September 1974

Getting round the law!

IT IS not so much what you say—it's the way that you say it.

Advertisers, in search of their elusive ideal requirement, are finding that a tongue-in-cheek approach can land the staff they want when they are not supposed to discriminate between the sexes.

Managing director Colin Hooton, for instance, got almost exactly what he wanted — an attractive mini-skirted receptionist. He advertised for one without actually breaking the Sex Discrimination Act.

His advertisement in an evening newspaper simply said what he could *not* do . . . : 'What we really wanted was a mini-skirted blue-eyed blonde but under the Sex Discrimination Act we cannot advertise for her. So we'll just say that we require a receptionist.'

The advertisement, quite within the bounds of the law, brought 60 replies. None of them were from men.

Mr Hooton, of Repete Publicity, Wellingborough, Northamptonshire, interviewed about 20 applicants and appointed 17-year-old Deborah Farden.

Eton College were less fortunate. They popped an advert in the Slough and Windsor Express under 'Person Wanted' seeking a dining room assistant to 'share a room with another lady.' Most of the inquiries came from men.

The BBC's *That's Life* programme have had quite a collection sent in. This is among the better ones from the Romsey Advertiser :

'Experienced storekeeper, either sex, provided that they have at least five years' experience, are fluent in German and look like Marlene Dietrich in her early Twenties'

The Sidmouth Herald was a little more blunt. They published this one : 'Mechanic required, essentially fully qualified person. Responsible well-paid job, permanent. Sex immaterial provided they are prepared to share gent's toilet.'

Frivolous

And the Warminster Journal : 'Dental nurse-person required, either sex. Experience an advantage or suit recent school leaver with interest in people and sense of humour. Uniform comprising white coat, blouse and skirt.'

The sartorial theme is quite popular in the amusing adverts. The Weston Mercury carried this appeal : 'Bar Staff required mornings and evenings— ability to look good in women's clothing.'

The Northern Echo ran one for 'promotional team vacancies with the proviso: 'female costume will be worn.' .

And an advertisement in the Evening Gazette, Blackpool, offers as a perk for a sales consultant job: 'Grooming and hosiery allowance.'

How many men are going to have the nerve to apply for that one?

The Equal Opportunities Commission however, don't find them all that funny. An official said the 'more frivolous advertisements nearly all showed a blatant disregard for the spirit of the law '

Most of the complaints they receive, they say, are serious, and these are receiving attention. But, sooner or later, they could well get around to the funny ones—'and then they may not be quite so funny after all.'

Above: Jaclyn Smith, Farrah Fawcett-Majors and Kate Jackson, stars of the US TV series *Charlie's Angels*. The show was unusual in having three female leads – although they sometimes fought crime wearing bikinis!

Above left: Blonde and beautiful, Lindsay Wagner as the bionic woman – who like Charlie's Angels fought her battles without the help of a man.

Above right: Charlotte Cornwell, Julie Covington and Rula Lenska, starred in the innovative musical comedy drama *Rock Follies*, which traced the fortunes of the fictional girl band The Little Ladies.

Above: Teenage girls still had their idols. By the early 1970s singers such as Donny Osmond, David Cassidy and David Essex had taken over from The Beatles, The Rolling Stones and The Monkees as the teenagers' pinups. Here hysterical fans of Scottish pop group the Bay City Rollers, which by 1975 was one of Britain's biggest-selling acts, show their devotion.

1970s Postscripts

May 1979 (continued): Britain when the Conservatives won the General Election.

July 1979: Portugal's first woman Prime Minister, Maria Pintassilgo, took office.

October 1979: Athlete Greta Weitz won the New York Women's Marathon in 2 hours, 27 minutes and 32.6 seconds and beat the 2 hours 30 minutes barrier for women runners over the distance.

November 1979: The Swedish Parliament voted 165 to 21 with 147 abstentions to grant the right of succession to the Swedish throne to the monarch's first-born child. This meant that two-year-old Princess Victoria would take precedence over her six-month-old brother, Carl.

November 1979: An Employment Tribunal ruled that an employer who sacked a woman from her job because she was pregnant was not guilty of sex discrimination. The tribunal said that because there was no male equivalent to pregnancy the woman should sue for redress through the Employment Protection Act, not the Sex Discrimination Act.

December 1979: Mother Theresa, the Albanian nun who had worked for years with the poor, the sick and the dying in Calcutta, was awarded the Nobel Peace Prize.

Babies from a Test Tube

Nine years after scientists in Cambridge first announced that they had succeeded in fertilising a human embryo outside the womb, the world's first test-tube baby, Louise Brown, was born on 26 July 1978 amid huge publicity. Her birth brought hope to thousands of infertile couples, although the treatment was originally only available privately at specialist clinics like the one run by Dr Patrick Steptoe who treated Louise's parents.

In the 1960s several infertility treatments were developed, including artificial insemination and the use of fertility drugs. Many of these treatments were a result of research into contraception which demanded a better understanding of both male and female fertility. Infertility became another of the issues which were far more openly talked about in the 1970s. The fact that there was more help available meant couples no longer had to suffer in silence over what were now often curable conditions.

Test-tube fertilisation might have captured the public imagination but science could not provide the cure to every form of infertility. In America, there was a growing practice of surrogacy, where one woman, usually paid for the service, was impregnated with the sperm from a man whose partner was infertile. The woman carried the child and when it was born handed it over to the father and his partner. Agencies were set up to introduce infertile couples and surrogate mothers and arrange the payment of fees.

The huge advances medical research and practice had yielded in the 1960s and 1970s in the field of human, and especially female, fertility gave women much greater freedom and choice. They could choose when and how many children they wished to have and if they found getting pregnant was more difficult than they expected there were medical treatments available to help. But there were disadvantages. Multiple pregnancies, with all the attendant dangers to both mother and babies, often resulted from the use of fertility drugs, especially in the early days, and this problem was transferred to pregnancies resulting from in-vitro fertilisation. As fertility, contraception and birth itself became more scientific and hi-tech, doctors, and especially male doctors, took much more control over all these processes. It was a balance which women themselves began to address in the 1980s with calls for less medical intervention in pregnancy and childbirth.

Above right: The world fell in love with Soviet gymnast Olga Korbut at the 1972 Munich Olympics. The diminutive 17-year-old inspired thousands to take up the sport.

Above left: Tracy Austin was another young sports star who hit the headlines.

Below: In 1973, the same year that she graduated from High School in Fort Lauderdale, Florida, Chris Evert reached the finals of both the French Open and Wimbledon, coming second to Australian Margaret Court and fellow American Billie Jean King respectively.

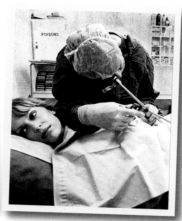

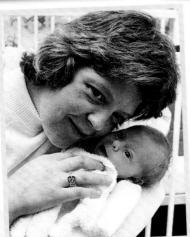

Above left: 1977 Nobel-prize winning scientist Rosalyn Yalow.

Above right: The Marie Stopes Well Woman clinics began to offer female sterilisation on an outpatient basis in 1977.

Left: The world's first 'test tube' baby, Louise Brown, was born by a Caesarean section at Oldham District General Hospital on 25 July 1978. Patrick Steptoe, a pioneer of in-vitro fertilisation, had spent more than 12 years perfecting the technique along with fellow scientist Robert Edwards.

Work and Marriage

In 1951 only 20 per cent of married women in Britain worked outside the home but by 1980 official statistics showed that the figure had risen to 50 per cent. In most other European countries the percentages were lower – 35 per cent in Germany, 22 per cent in the Netherlands and 25 per cent in Italy. A study suggested that the main reason for this high percentage of married women in paid work was the relatively low wages paid to men in Britain. The study's conclusion was that economic necessity had driven women to find work and not equal pay opportunities. By the end of the decade the number of married women doing some kind of paid work had steadily increased so that at least two out of every three had a job outside the home.

Changes to employment laws to allow women to take maternity leave meant many more mothers were able to pursue a career and remain in full-time work. However, large numbers of women felt that working full time, bringing up a young family and assuming most of the responsibilities for household chores was simply too demanding. They wanted to have a career but they also wanted to spend time with their family.

Part-time work had, since the war, been popular with married women, especially those with children, as it has advantages in terms of hours worked outside the home. For despite a growing willingness of men to help with child rearing and domestic duties, the main burden of responsibilities still fell on women. Part-time working allowed more time for household duties and more energy to deal with the emotional demands of a growing family.

However, part-time work had many disadvantages. Pay rates and employment protection levels were generally lower than in full-time work. Crucially part-time workers were rarely considered for promotion, which meant that a large number of women found themselves stuck in boring and often menial jobs far below their capabilities simply because they had chosen to spend more time with their families. Small changes such as job-share schemes and more flexible hours made it a little easier for mothers to work part-time while also taking on more stimulating and interesting roles.

NOT A PENNY FOR THE LOVER OF 20 YEARS

A woman who kept home for her lover for 20 years and bore him two sons was not entitled to a share in their home when they split up, three Appeal Court judges ruled yesterday.

'I think she can justifiably say that fate has not been kind to her,' said Lord Justice May of 40-year-old Valerie Burns. But together with Lord Justices Waller and Fox he could offer her only sympathy because the law did not give her the same rights as a wife.

She 'has no rights against him,' said Lord Justice Fox. 'But the unfairness of that is not a matter which the courts can control. It is a matter for Parliament.'

Daily Mail, 27 July 1983

The Changing Family

Society at the beginning of the 1980s was based on the assumption that most people lived in a family with a mother married to a father living together and bringing up their own children. In this family, father went out to work and mother stayed at home. A startling report in 1981 showed that this was the case in only 15 per cent of families. The report also found that one child in every eight was living in a single-parent family, that in only a third of families were both parents living with their own children and that one in four marriages ended in divorce.

There were also growing numbers of children being born outside marriage – by 1986 the figure was 20 per cent. Many of these children were born into stable relationships but there were still a large number of women left with a baby and no partner to help financially, physically or emotionally. Unmarried mothers were no longer shunned to the extent they had been in the 1960s and earlier. The State did provide money and housing, but for a young mother bringing up a child or children alone and relying on State provision it was not a particularly easy life. Statistics show that they were, and still are, often among the poorest in society.

Children born to unmarried parents in a stable relationship were usually better off emotionally and financially. But if that relationship broke up the mother still was not entitled to the same rights as a wife. Her partner could evict her from the family home if he was the sole owner or tenant and she would have to sue for maintenance for herself and any children of the relationship and be required to prove paternity if the case was contested.

Some women with children found that a lesbian relationship provided a more fulfilling life for themselves and a stable home for their children. There were also a number of lesbian couples willing to have a baby by artificial insemination or to foster children. The fact that local authorities accepted lesbians as foster parents demonstrated just how much perceptions of the family unit were being challenged, although it was not without a great deal of controversy.

Do Britain's babies lose out?

STATISTICS released today will be viewed by many as nothing less than an indictment of the National Health Service : at least 5,000 babies dying—unnecessarily—at or near birth every year and a further 5,000 handicapped for life.

The call, from the Parliamentary Social Services Committee following a two-year investigation, is for **MORE** midwives, **MORE** paediatricians and **ROUND-THE-CLOCK** cover for maternity hospitals by experts in resuscitation—the absence of which is one of the main causes of these deaths. On figures alone, comparisons in this area are disquieting to say the least : more than double the number of babies die in Britain than in Scandinavia, and far more than in the Netherlands or Japan. Is the ante-natal care in these countries significantly better . . . how does having a baby in Britain compare . . . what, if any, are the lessons to be learned ? FEMAIL reports . . .

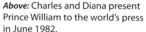

NORWAY'S campaign to encourage women to have babies in hospital has been so successful that only 0·3 per cent. of babies are now born at home.

Most hospitals have specially-trained resuscitation teams and there are only a handful of maternity homes still operating which deliver fewer than 5 per cent. of the country's babies.

The infant mortality rate is 9·2 per thousand births.

FRANCE is so determined that every mother has proper ante- and post-natal care that they 'fine' those who do not attend clinics.

Women are entitled to grants of about £250 before each birth, £300 after the birth of the first two and £750 for subsequent offspring—but only if they register their pregnancy with the local health service by the third month and attend three compulsory clinics before and after the birth.

THE NETHERLANDS have more babies born at home (more than 60 per cent. !) than in hospital, yet the infant mortality rate has dropped dramatically from 23·1 per thousand in 1965 to 12·5 per thousand two years ago.

Expectant mothers have a team of three to help them through a home confinement : their local doctor, community nurse and midwife. Obstetricians can also be called from the nearest hospital.

DENMARK is one of the few countries where checks for abnormalities like mongolism are made on *all* women during pregnancy instead of being restricted only to those most at risk (usually over the age of 35).

In addition a health visitor calls on the mother and her baby nine times during its first year.

Above: Charles and Diana present Prince William to the world's press in June 1982.

Left: As more women worked outside the home childcare became an important issue in the 1980s. Nannies were for the well-off – most working women relied on nurseries, child minders or relations to looks after their children.

Left below: Victoria Gillick feeding three of her ten children. Gillick began a campaign in 1980 in response to a Department of Health circular giving doctors guidance on prescribing contraceptives to under 16s without parental consent. The question of the competence of an under 16 to control his or her own medical treatment was considered by the House of Lords, which ruled that in some situations a minor was able to give consent without their parents being allowed to veto.

Far right: From 1983 a tax had been imposed on employees using workplace nurseries as they were deemed a 'benefit in kind'. Following pressure from campaign groups involving both employers and employees, the tax was abolished in 1990.

Left: Graham and Janet Walton pictured with their six daughters born in November 1983 after Janet Walton had been treated with a fertility drug.

1980s Postscripts

1980: A working Paper on sexual offences published by the Criminal Law Revision Committee recommended that husbands who forced their wives to have intercourse should be liable to prosecution for rape.

January 1980: The government announced that Child Benefit (Family Allowance) would be paid monthly and not weekly as had traditionally been the case. Existing recipients could elect to continue to collect the benefit weekly.

January 1980: The US Surgeon General warned that lung cancer was the leading killer cancer.

June 1980: Vigdis Finnbogadottir became Iceland's first woman President. The Icelanders claimed her as the first freely elected female Head of State as she was voted into office by the people and not because she was leader of a political party.

1981: The House of Lords had its first woman leader when Baroness Young was appointed.

February 1981: Gro Harlem Bruntland took office as Norway's first woman Prime Minister.

April 1981: Oxford were steered to victory in the Boat Race by Susan Brown, the first woman cox in the history of the event.

July 1981: Following a campaign promise by Ronald Reagan, Judge Sandra O'Conner was appointed to the US Supreme Court. Her pro-abortion and women's rights stance ran counter to the moral majority campaigners who had a great deal of influence over the administration.

Left: Ike and Tina Turner divorced in 1978, Tina citing her husband's physically abusive behaviour as one of the reasons for the split. It took eight years for her to find international success again – her album *Private Dancer*, released in 1984 and including the hit single 'What's Love Got to Do With It', sold 20 million copies worldwide.

Far left: Whitney Houston's self-titled debut album became America's best-selling album of 1986. Critically acclaimed, it included hits 'Greatest Love of All' and 'Saving All My Love for You'.

'Contributory Negligence'

Until 1958 a man who forced a woman to have sexual intercourse against her will would be charged with 'indecent assault' and not rape. The penalties if found guilty of a serious indecent assault were severe, but frequently women did not report such an assault. Even after the law was changed, and in the supposedly more permissive and open 1960s, rape victims frequently remained silent. Exposure of the crime often led to more censure and victimisation of the woman than of the guilty man by both the police handling the case and society at large. Many women and their families, especially if the victim was unmarried, did not want to admit that anything had happened. The woman might be regarded as 'damaged goods', perhaps severely affecting her marriage prospects. There was no anonymity for rape victims until the mid-1970s so that newspapers were allowed to publish their names.

The judge at any trial involving a sexual offence had to warn the jury then not to convict on the basis of the victim's evidence alone. This was not required in any other type of trial and places the victim of such an offence in a weaker position than any other witness, as their testimony could not be believed without corroboration, which is usually supplied by forensic evidence.

In 1982 there was a great deal of discussion about a rape case which reflected the long-held attitude that somehow the victim of rape had to bear some of the guilt for the crime. In January of that year Lord Hailsham rebuked a judge who said that a woman who was raped was guilty of 'contributory negligence' by hitch-hiking. The man in the case admitted his guilt and was fined £2,000 and not jailed. There was a public outcry against the judge's comments and the leniency of the sentence. But it was not the last such case to be reported in the 1980s where judges deemed that in some instances women 'led a man on' or where men were rewarded by ludicrously lenient sentences because they pleaded guilty and gallantly saved the woman from testifying.

Despite these much-publicised cases, or perhaps because of the very fact that they brought the issue into the public eye, reports of rapes increased dramatically. Rape victims were more sympathetically treated by both society and the police. Following the broadcast of a documentary about the Thames Valley Police in 1984 which included an interview with an alleged victim of rape where the woman was treated most insensitively, the police began to change the way they deal with such cases.

Peace Women

In the early 1980s, before the advent of President Gorbachev and *perestroika* and *glasnost*, the Soviet Union was continuing to put much of its energy into its armed forces and military hardware. With President Reagan in the White House, the US response was to increase its military spending and to plan to deploy nuclear weapons in Britain and Continental Europe. Despite talks and treaties aimed at reducing arms on both sides, the military and particularly the nuclear capability on each side had escalated to such a degree that many people considered it madness.

In such a climate movements such as the Campaign for Nuclear Disarmament, which had been popular in the 1960s, re-emerged to express great public disquiet and to press for peace. A change from the 1960s CND movement was that in the early 1980s the movement for peace became very much associated with women. In the peace movement many women, such as Joan Ruddock, found their political voice. Great stress was placed on women's history as givers, nurturers and sustainers of life against men's history of death, destruction and the creation of killing machines.

The focus of attention and a symbol for the whole peace movement in Britain became the American Military Base at Greenham Common. In 1982 it was announced that Britain would allow the USA to deploy Cruise, its newest nuclear missiles, at Greenham from where the weapons could strike at the heart of the Soviet Union. From September 1981 a group of women established a protest camp outside the base's perimeter fence. The makeshift camp became the scene of a permanent vigil for several years and Greenham Common saw many demonstrations and protests throughout 1982 and 1983. In December 1982 over 20,000 women joined hands to encircle the airbase in protest and in April 1983 a fourteen-mile human chain linked Greenham to two other defence establishments at Aldermaston and Burghfield.

All the protests failed to stop the deployment of Cruise missiles but the point had been made to politicians, not just in Britain but throughout Europe and the rest of the world, that people were seriously worried by the escalation in the nuclear arms race. Subsequent moves to call a halt to this and the removal of many missiles were claimed as a success for both the policies of the doves of the peace movement and the hawks like Margaret Thatcher and Ronald Reagan who insisted on outfacing the Soviet Union.

Above left: Margaret Thatcher interrupts reporters' questions to hurry President Reagan on his way. The two leaders became renowned for their close relationship based on similar conservative views on government and economics.

Above right: Protesters outside the US base at Greenham Common. A 'peace camp' was maintained at the base from 1981 until 2000.

Below: In April 1983 CND supporters formed a human chain that linked Burghfield (location of a nuclear weapons factory), Aldermaston (home of Britain's Atomic Weapons Research Establishment) and Greenham Common.

Feeling Fit and Looking Good

Jane Fonda's *Workout Book* sold 160,000 copies almost overnight when it went on sale in Britain in 1982. Capitalising on the fashion for jogging and a healthy lifestyle that emerged in the late 1970s, Jane Fonda became something of a high priestess of fitness. Her message was to 'go for the burn', and that if it wasn't hurting it wasn't doing any good. Aerobics became the fitness craze of the early 1980s and following Jane Fonda's there were many similar books, and women on television exercising the nation in the early mornings. As in the 1970s it was mainly women who took the fitness message to heart and aerobics became almost exclusively a female pastime.

The fashion for fitness and health continued and developed to include dance and less vigorous forms of exercise, such as walking, appealing to and enabling a wider range of women to participate. There was also a massive increase in the whole fitness and leisure business with more sport and leisure centres opening, more courses on offer, more books and magazines dispensing advice about what to eat and how to keep the body in perfect shape.

The search for the perfect shape and the desire to remain youthful looking led to a boom in cosmetic surgery, particularly in the USA, although it was being promoted more and more in Britain. Even girls as young as 16 were considering changing the shape of their noses or their breasts to make them more attractive.

In many ways women in the 1980s became freer to dress as they pleased. There was a wider range of styles, from the power dressing of the woman at work to floaty, flowery Laura Ashley designs or comfortable leisure and jogging suits. Older women were no longer required to wear either young fashions or be left with frumpy styles. On the other hand, there was continued pressure in the media promoting images of how a woman should look, from the Princess of Wales who became an icon – the glamorous working wife and mother – to the continued use of women to advertise products, to Page Three Girls, to Joan Collins and other television and film stars who remained young looking at 50.

Eating disorders became more talked about, with cases of bulimia being reported as well as anorexia nervosa which surfaced in the 1970s. The tip of an iceberg had been revealed and some dieticians reported that the iceberg was growing with younger and younger people, mainly girls, being afflicted by eating disorders. Many attributed this growing problem to the images of women portrayed in the media. This argument could be seen as simplistic but the issue is in part to do with body and self-image and the way girls have been conditioned to feel about themselves.

Opposite left: Ice skating duo Torvill and Dean won gold for Britain in ice dancing at the Winter Olympics in Sarajevo in 1984. They wowed the judges with a flawless performance set to Ravel's 'Boléro' and were the only pair to score top marks from every judge.

Opposite above centre: British swimmer Sharron Davies models fitness equipment in a fashionable leotard.

Opposite above right: Olympic gold-medal-winning javelin thrower and heptathlete Tessa Sanderson takes part in the shot putt.

Opposite below: Fitness was one of the great fads of the 80s. Here Angie Best, estranged wife of soccer star George, joined in as 774 women in leotards, and men in T-shirts and shorts, sweated their way through a rigorous routine in the bright sunshine.

Above: No one was more photographed during the 1980s than Princess Diana, who's struggle with bulimia was revealed in Andrew Morton's book: *Diana: Her True Story.*

Above right: Singer Karen Carpenter, pictured with her brother, who died of heart failure caused by complications related to anorexia nervosa.

Above: Jerry Hall puts the finishing touches to Angelica Huston's make-up. Hall was one of a group of 'supermodels' which included Cindy Crawford, Christy Turlington and Linda Evangelista.

Below: Naomi Campbell became the new face of the decade after she was spotted while shopping.

What you can do if your child stops eating

BOYS as well as girls are at risk of becoming anorexic. Dr Bryan Lask, head of a group of specialists at Great Ormond Street Hospital for Children, says that at least 25 per cent. of new cases are male.

Dr Lask says: 'Parents tie themselves in knots trying to find the reason why their child gets it. The truth is, there are many complex factors. One common strain is the issue of staying in control. Children who do not like what is going on in the family, find very quickly that by stopping eating they become the centre of attention and occupy a strong controlling position in the family.

'It is very addictive. It is often the bright conscientious child who does this. And once started it is very hard to stop. Any parent should keep a close watch on their child's weight. If they lose half a stone they are in trouble and need professional help. And families will need therapy to try to find out the underlying difficulties.'

At Atkinson Morley Hospital, Professor Arthur Crisp runs a regime where anorexics are put on a calorie controlled diet of 3,000 calories a day. A spokesman said: They are kept in bed and they have to agree to give over their willpower to us. If they do not make that agreement then we don't take them on. Those who stay have a good prognosis.

'We treat the whole family in pyschotherapy sessions. Often the parents will have to change their ways with dealing with problems or look very hard at their marriage.'

1980s Postscripts

November 1981: The Church of England Synod voted overwhelmingly in favour of admitting women to Holy Orders as deacons, enabling them to conduct weddings, funerals and baptisms but not to give Holy Communion.

1982: The Greenham Common camp opened.

June 1982: NALGO, the National Association of Local Government Officers, decided to amend its rule book to acknowledge the existence of 50 per cent of its membership. Reference would now be made to 'he/she' and

'him/her' instead of just he and him. NALGO also reported that two thirds of women were in clerical grades while half of their men members were in professional grades and that half of the men earned over £8,000 while only four per cent of women did.

April 1983: Jenny Pitman became the first woman trainer to win the Grand National when her horse Corbière was first past the post.

May 1983: Mary Donaldson was the first woman Lord Mayor of London since the office was created in 1192.

July 1983: A judge ruled in a case brought by Victoria Gillick that doctors who prescribed the Pill to girls under 16 were not guilty of aiding and abetting a crime by encouraging an underage girl to have sex but were medically encouraging contraception to limit the results of such a crime. The judge also ruled that it was not a crime for a doctor not to inform the parents that a girl under 16 was on the Pill as there was no law requiring this.

Left: Powers suits, with extreme shoulders and short skirts, were a major trend in the 1980s. Here Ungaro puts a twist on the idea by swapping the jacket for a frock coat.

Top: Mousses and gels allowed for experimentation with hairstyles.

Above: Lyrca, which had existed since 1959, began to be incorporated into clothing. French designer Azzedine Alaïa's tight-fitting dresses, often incorporating Lycra blends, became a must-have item among the fashion conscious and soon high street chains followed his lead.

1980s Postscripts

December 1983: Barbara McLintock of the USA was awarded the Nobel Prize for Medicine.

March 1984: The 250,000 members of SOGAT '82 elected Brenda Dean to head the union, the first woman to lead a major trade union.

March 1984: British Airways announced that all cabin staff would in future be placed on five-year contracts and the maximum starting age would be 26 so that no one would be over 31. Before the Sex Discrimination Act came into effect in 1976, the maximum age for women was 35 and 55 for men, following

the Act the maximum age for both sexes became 55.

July 1984: In the USA Democrat Walter Mondale named Geraldine Ferraro as his running mate. Women had become powerful within the Democratic Party and the selection of the first woman to such an important position reflected this.

August 1984: The first Women's Olympic Marathon was run at the Los Angeles Games.

1985: The Equal Pay (Amendment) Act was introduced with the aim of ensuring that

women would be paid the same as men for work of equal value.

January 1985: Surrogate mother Kim Cotton gave birth to a child whom she gave up to the father. Her case brought the issue of surrogacy, which had been practised for some years in the USA, to the attention of the British public and a law was passed banning commercial surrogacy.

February 1985: In the face of a threatened Aids epidemic the Dail in Dublin passed a Bill legalising the shop sale of condoms to people over 18.

Of Equal Value

The Equal Pay Act which was passed in 1970 and finally implemented in 1976 said that where a man and a woman were doing the same job they should be paid the same wage. However, there were many areas of work, which despite the Sex Discrimination Act, had remained through tradition and practice all male or all female. Where jobs had no male pay structure because there were no male employees before 1976 the pay structures remained the same. If a man was not doing the job it was likely to be low-paid. So many women doing what had by tradition become women's jobs were unaffected by the Act.

It became evident in the years following the implementation of the Act that in many cases women were doing work of 'equal value' to a man in a different job within the same company or institution. Following a ruling in the European Courts the British Government were forced to amend the Equal Pay Act in 1984 to allow women to be given equal pay for work of equal value. This of course was a less clear-cut law to implement and required a court ruling in some instances to define 'equal value'. In 1988 a cook won equal pay with joiners, painters and insulation engineers in the same company when an industrial tribunal ruled in her favour. And in 1989 Lloyds Bank had to increase the pay of 5,500 secretaries and typists to match that of senior messengers. A tribunal said that the difference had originated because of the traditional assumptions that 'the messenger was a family man and needed to be paid a family wage'.

In some areas of work, such as factory production lines which are exclusively female and where there is no man's job to compare the value of their work, the tradition of women workers, with their past willingness to work for lower wages and their lack of trade-union organisation, has established rates of pay which male workers and unions would not have accepted.

Right: Barbara Dean, General Secretary of the print union SOGAT between 1985 and 1991, was one of the best-known faces of the trade union movement, especially during the bitter dispute between the print workers and Rupert Murdoch.

Left: Czech-born US tennis ace Martina Navratilova won her fifth consecutive Wimbledon Women's Singles title in 1986. It was not until 2007 that the winner of the women's title would receive the same prize money as her male counterpart.

Rght: Women campaign for equal rights to employment opportunities outside the Labour Party Conference in Brighton. The banners demand one woman be short-listed for every job opportunity.

Equal Pay?

Figures in 1988 showed that women's average pay was still only 74 per cent of the average man's pay. Thirteen years on from the Equal Pay and the Sex Discrimination Acts women still were not anywhere near the equal pay the law had seemed to promise.

In 1989 there were almost 10 million women out at work, four and a half million working part time, the rest full time. A study by the Equal Opportunities Commission showed that in Britain women workers in non-manual jobs earned only 61 per cent of the pay of men working in equivalent jobs. Part-time workers fared even worse earning below 50 per cent pro rata of their full-time male equivalents.

Domestic ties have been the major and abiding reason why women's pay has remained so far behind men's. In the 1980s most women, especially if they are wives and mothers, still bore the responsibility for the bulk of the housework whether or not they worked outside the home. A government report called Social Trends, published in 1989, bore out this fact and confirmed the EOC report that women were being paid less than men. With responsibilities for children and housework, most women looked for jobs which gave them flexibility of hours and an employer who would not make too much fuss if they had time off to look after a sick child. Very often they were willing to forgo higher pay and some of the job perks they might find elsewhere to have the conditions which most suit them. The trouble was that many employers implied that women working hours to fit round a family were of detriment to the company or institution while ignoring all the beneficial advantages of having a mature, well trained, experienced and committed worker.

In 1989, before the economy went once again into recession, there was much talk about the future need for many more women in the workplace and of how employers would have to change their attitudes and work practices to allow women to return to work in large numbers. There would need to be provision of crèches or payment of childcare vouchers, more flexible working hours and job-share schemes. Once these were accepted as normal working conditions and women were really needed, the theory was that equal pay would come. In 1989 the future looked fairly bright for women at work.

Above: Shirley Williams with Roy Jenkins. Williams' desire for concensus politics was a major reason for her popularity.

Above right: George and Bush wave as they board *Air Force One*. Barbara Bush's image was very different from that of her predecessor as First Lady, projecting a more homely image.

Right: Raisa Gorbachev attracted as much attention as her husband when they visited London in 1984.

Left: First Lady Nancy Reagan brought some style and glamour back to the White House following her husband's inauguration in January 1981. She also used her influence to pioneer the 'Just Say No' campaign to stamp out recreational drug use across America.

1980s Postscripts

October 1985: The Law Lords reversed a ruling made by a lower court in February which banned doctors from prescribing the Pill to girls under 16. The ban had been won following campaigning by Victoria Gillick.

June 1986: Sixty-three per cent of voters in a referendum in Eire rejected a government proposal to amend the constitution to allow divorce.

November 1986: Following 278 deaths and 548 cases of Aids in Britain so far the government launched the largest ever health campaign to try to combat the spread of the disease.

1987: Legal and General took Rosalind Hines as a typical example of a woman at home looking after children and estimated that she worked on average 92 hours per week and that the cost of replacing her labour would be £19,253 per year.

1987: A survey showed that a quarter of all small businesses were run by women.

June 1987: In the general election in which Mrs Thatcher was the first prime minister this century to win a third successive term in office a record 41 women were also elected to Parliament – still only six per cent of the total membership of the House of Commons.

March 1988: A survey revealed that nine out of ten women were dissatisfied with the facilities for screening for cervical cancer – a completely curable cancer if treatment is administered early enough, and the incidence of which is growing.

April 1988: A Bill introduced by MP Clare Short to ban the publication of sexually provocative pictures of women in newspapers was given support by a large majority of MPs who had been told by women that they found such pictures degrading. The Bill, however, did not become law as it ran out of time.

A Growing Divorce Rate

In the period between the Divorce Act coming into force in 1971 and the mid 1980s, there had been almost a threefold increase in divorces. In 1985, one in every four marriages ended in divorce, affecting large numbers of women, men and children. Wives and children were in theory reasonably well provided for when a marriage broke up but of course finding enough money to keep two households going generally made everyone less well off. Problems occurred if the husband remarried and had a second family to support. Statistically a husband was two and a half times more likely to remarry than his ex-wife who usually had custody of any children. Keeping maintenance payments regular and at a reasonable level was, and remains, a perennial problem for divorced people.

In 1984 a law was brought into effect which allowed for divorce after only one year of marriage. The Matrimonial and Family Proceedings Act concentrated on providing maintenance for any children of the marriage. Where no children were involved and both partners were self-sufficient they could make a 'clean break', divide up their property and sever financial ties with one another. Where there were children maintenance was allocated to them and then the wife, where it was deemed necessary for her to look after them. When the children left home or the woman remarried, her maintenance from her ex-husband would cease and she would have to provide for herself.

There are obvious benefits to more easily obtained divorce. Couples no longer have to remain tied to a relationship that is unhappy, violent or simply emotionally dead. But there are disadvantages. Many people now no longer regard marriage as a lifelong commitment which means it is no longer the secure and stable institution it once was; although of course in Queen Victoria's reign as many marriages were ended within sixteen years by the early death of one or other of the partners as are ended by divorce today.

It is the mother who more often has to cope alone, for even if the father is granted access it is common for fathers to no longer have contact with their children only a few years on from the divorce. Bringing up a child or children alone and coping with all the demands they make emotionally, physically and intellectually is not easy. Without a partner for support single-parent status leaves women at a severe disadvantage in terms of career prospects as it is difficult to take a demanding well-paid job and childcare costs make lower-paid jobs uneconomic.

Opposite below left: Coronation Street celebrated its 21st anniversary in 1981. Millions of viewers tuned in to watch the wedding of Ken and Deirdre Barlow, timed to coincide with the royal wedding of Prince Charles and Lady Diana Spencer in the summer of that year.

Opposite below right: The first episode of the award-winning *EastEnders* was broadcast in February 1985. Here the cast is photographed on set at the BBC's Elstree studio.

The facts and figures that go to prove why the British woman is anything but average

LOVE

THE average woman makes love once every 3·8 days—96 times a year—and will burn up about 200 calories doing so.

First choice of location for lovemaking for 96 per cent. of women is the bedroom. As an alternative, 78 per cent. chose the living room, 46 per cent. elsewhere in the house and 41 per cent. in the car.

Most women receive a formal proposal, over dinner, and generally are engaged for 19 months. Today, 52 per cent. of all weddings are in a register office. The average single woman marries when she is 22·3 years old, single men 24·5. Second-time around women are 33·4 years of age, men 35·8.

Once married, she'll stay that way for 44·5 years—longer than at any time in history.

HOME

The average home is a house—beating flats into second place by four to one. One-third are terraced, one-third semi-detached and the remainder are split equally between detached, bungalows and 'others'. The average fuel bill in the average home is between £450 and £500 a year.

Most women do NOT have a tumble dryer (in only 27 per cent. of households); video recorder (33 per cent.); home computer (25 per cent.); microwave oven (8 per cent.); blender/ liquidiser (47 per cent.); pressure cooker (44 per cent.); deep-fat fryer (25 per cent.); toasted sandwich maker (44 per cent.); slow cooker (14 per cent.).

Every day we put 50,000 tons of rubbish into our waste bins. In a year the average dustbin contains enough paper to save six trees, enough waste to keep a garden in compost and half a ton of glass, metal and plastic.

When it comes to accidents in the home, it's women and children first. Children under five are involved in 27 per cent. of all household mishaps. Every day 300 women fall out of bed and more than 200 crash into doors—many of which are made of glass.

WORK

Today, 60 per cent. of women work—against only 20 per cent. in 1954—and women make up 40 per cent. of the total UK work force.

Fifteen years after the Equal Pay Act and nine years after the Sex Discrimination Act, women earn only two-thirds as much as men.

Most people work 40 hours a week which breaks down into 37.2 hours a week for women and 41·4 hours for men.

The average working man and working woman puts the earnings into a joint account from which both partners can draw. One in five men puts his money into a personal account ; one in three working wives do too. One in three men give their wives all or most of their earnings. Four in ten give wives a housekeeping allowance.

The average time a woman with a job must spend working to pay for household goods is :

1 pint milk, 4 mins ; 125gm tea, 7 mins ; Large white sliced loaf, 8 mins ; 1 pint beer, 12 mins ; 1 dozen medium eggs, 13 mins ; 500gm butter, 19 mins ; 20 cigarettes, 20 mins ; 100gm instant coffee, 22 mins ; Cinema admission, 34 mins ; 1 gallon petrol (4*), 35 mins ; Weekly telephone bill, 40 mins ; 1lb rump steak, 58 mins ; Weekly gas bill, 1hr. 7 mins ; Weekly electricity bill, 1hr. 14 mins ; 1cwt coal, 1hr. 31 mins ; Long playing record. 1hr. 41 mins ; 1 bottle whisky, 2hrs. 20 mins ; Colour TV licence. 14hrs. 40 mins ; Car tax. 27hrs. 10 mins ;

MONEY

Women shopping for the household spend £25·73 on food every week and a complete family shop, including food, costs £38·58. Two in ten men have no idea how much of the family income goes on food, even though four out of ten men actually help with the weekly shop. Most don't mind doing it and 17 per cent. positively enjoy it.

Every week households in the middle income group spend about £150, broken down to £56 per person. That's about double the figures for the low-income family with one member out of work. In the high-income group (households where the woman and the man both have jobs) the weekly spend is £200. Throughout the country, food takes the highest percentage of our weekly income.

BODY-TALK

WOMEN generally start dieting when they are 20, though one in four start at 15. Most weigh themselves once a week, but 25 per cent step on the scales daily. Most women think they're overweight and 20 per cent think they are very overweight. Five per cent think they're just right and diet to stay that way.

Women take a bath four times a week, men only three. Both spend about the same time in the bath — women 24 minutes and men 26.

A woman will sleep for eight hours and 20 minutes and doesn't snore : a man sleeps for eight hours and does snore. Both sexes dream, with an average span of 1½ hours in five separate periods. Whatever the interpretation of dreams, they're slimming stuff — women and men lose about 1lb while asleep.

Most women will live until they are 75·6 years old, men to 69. British children born now will do better than their parents. Girls will live until they are well over 80, men to 77.

121

Tax Free

When the government first began levying taxes, wives were regarded as the property of their husbands, anything they brought into the marriage then belonged to the husband and he paid tax on it accordingly. In 1870 married women were granted limited rights over their own property or earnings and throughout the reminder of that century and into the twentieth those rights were extended so that by 1988 wives had a right to their own earnings and savings, and a right to a share in the family property and possessions. What a wife did not have a right to was to be taxed independently of her husband. A husband and wife could elect to be taxed separately but then they did not receive the married couple's allowance.

The system was archaic and patently unfair to women. The Inland Revenue had by 1988 ceased to send to husbands correspondence about, and any tax rebates due on, wives' income but that was about the only concession to women. There was a catalogue of discrimination.

A woman whose husband earned below his threshold for tax could not, if she earned more than him, be given the married allowance so long as her husband was in employment. If her husband was in full-time education she could have both her personal tax allowance and the married allowance. For a husband with a wife in full-time education, or at home with children, her tax allowance was not transferable to him. Women whose husbands fell into the higher-rate tax bracket paid his highest rate of tax on anything they earned over their allowance. The interest on any savings a woman made out of her own income and banked in her own name had to be declared on her husband's income tax return and he was held legally responsible for any tax that might be due.

The Budget of 1988 swept aside all of these anomalies and made way for a complete and long overdue change in the taxation of husbands and wives. From April 1990 wives were to be responsible for their own tax affairs and their incomes were to be taxed independently of their husbands'.

NEW CHARTER FOR WIVES

After years of debating the way husbands and wives are jointly taxed, and bemoaning the fact that couples who live in sin get all the tax breaks, the government has confirmed its commitment to marriage in a major reform of family taxation to come into effect in 1990.

At the same time the Chancellor's shake-up of the system will remove some of the sex inequalities which married women have been complaining about for years.

In future women will be treated as tax payers in their own right instead of merely appendages to their husbands – a relic of the Victorian era when women as well as children knew their place.

Daily Mail, 16 March 1988

Valium—Mother's helper or Mother's ruin?

THE lynx wasn't spitting any longer. The wild cat was acting more like a kitten. The scientists who had come to the San Diego zoo were astonished. They had never seen anything like it. It had been achieved by the injection of a new drug called Librium. They were surprised because the animal was wide awake despite the drug and reacting normally. Yet it was tame. A new type of tranquilliser had been born. That was in 1957 and it signalled the start of a revolution that was to sweep the world. The man behind it was Austrian-born chemist, Leo Sternbach. Two years later he made another drug that was even more remarkable—Valium. As a muscle relaxant it was found to be ten times more effective than Librium.

It was capable of removing the sharp edges of emotional anguish while enabling people to carry on normal lives. That was the way the company behind it, the Swiss-based giant, Hoffman La Roche, sold it. It meant you could suffer acute anxiety and still go to work. It was, they said, a drug of its time—a means of combating the ever increasing stress of the 20th century.

It is now 21 years since the drug came to Britain. An estimated seven million people take Valium and other so called 'minor' tranquillisers each year.

It has been far too freely issued because it is easier for a doctor to scribble a prescription than to listen to a complex problem when his waiting room is full of patients. The fact that it is cheap compared with other NHS drugs also makes it popular.

A course of 100 tablets (5mg) costs only £1·65 and can provide five weeks' treatment. The average cost of an NHS prescription is about £4·50. However, the drug once hailed as 'the housewife's choice' and immortalised by the Rolling Stones as Mother's Little Helper is now subject to a barrage of criticism.

Far from softening the cruelties of 20th-century life, it is claimed, tranquillisers can hook people—especially women.

1980s Postscripts

May 1988: Liberal MP David Alton's Abortion Bill which sought to reduce the time limit for abortion from 28 to 18 weeks' gestation failed when it was 'talked out'.

November 1988: Benazir Bhutto of Pakistan was the first woman ever elected to lead an Islamic country.

September 1989: A majority of magicians in the Magic Circle voted to admit women members but the majority was short of the 75 per cent required to carry the motion so women continued to be excluded. There were six women members of the Magic Circle in 1905 but after they left a rule banning women was introduced in 1909.

October 1989: Following a pilot scheme in 1988, Midland Bank, which had a 56 per cent female workforce and already offered a five-year career break, opened its first crèches for employees' children.

December 1989: The Institute of Directors reported that there were only nine women on the boards of Britain's largest companies and that whereas in 1975 women held ten per cent of the 'top jobs' in business in 1985 that figure had dropped to just over six per cent.

Women and AIDS

In July of 1990 a World Health Organisation report said that AIDS was the most common cause of death for women between the ages of 20 and 40. Ten years before no one had ever heard of AIDS. Suspicion of the existence of the disease was first revealed in 1981 and the AIDS, or HIV, virus was identified in 1984.

The principal ways of contracting the HIV virus are through having sex with an infected person, injecting drugs with a contaminated needle and maternal transmission. A number of haemophiliacs and other patients who received contaminated blood products in the early and mid-1980s also contracted the disease but routine blood screening stopped that route of infection.

There is as yet no cure for AIDS and in the early 1990s there was no treatment for either HIV infection or AIDS, only precautions to be followed. Intravenous drug users were given free sterile needles. The use of condoms also helped reduce infection rates. But for women, using condoms also meant that they could not become pregnant so the issue of safe sex became caught up with the question of fertility.

In the mid-1990s it was estimated that globally there were around 16 million cases of HIV/AIDS, with more than 10 million of those cases in sub-Saharan Africa. Most of the women in Africa were infected through sexual intercourse but illiteracy, limited methods of mass communication, and the isolation of areas made it difficult to distribute information, education and condoms to prevent the further spread of the disease. Additionally, for many years there was a lack of willingness on the part of men in the region to practise safe sex.

The introduction of antiviral therapy in the late 1990s dramatically changed the outlook for sufferers of the disease in the West. The use of antivirals can extend life expectancy by as much as 40 years and yet while victims in developed countries had access to these treatments, drug companies would not reduce the costs of these medicines to enable sufferers in the poorest nations to benefit. It took several years of activism and campaigns to reach an agreement that enabled people in many of the most severely affected countries to have access to antiviral therapy. For women,

antiviral drugs, together with caesarean births and abstaining from breastfeeding mean that maternal transmission to babies is very significantly reduced. Again, in sub-Saharan Africa it is not always possible for women to have access to these treatments and procedures but transmission and death rates are slowing even here.

"THEY'RE AWFULLY FIDDLY TO PUT ON. ISN'T THAT HALF THE FUN?"

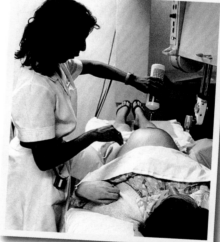

Above: Condom advertisements became much more overt and for the first time targeted women as well as men.

Left: A pregnant woman having an ultrasound scan – a procedure which was rapidly becoming more routine as the use of technology in childbirth increased.

Postscripts 1990s

1990: The 1967 Abortion Act was amended by the Human Fertilisation and Embryology Act, which reduced the original time limit of 28 weeks to 24 weeks for most abortions.

April 1990: King Baudouin of Belgium, an opponent of abortion, stepped down for 24 hours to allow the passage of a bill legalising abortion.

July 1990: Martina Navratilova beat Zena Garrison in the Wimbledon Ladies Final to win a record ninth Wimbledon Singles title.

November 1990: Mary Robinson, pro contraception, women's rights campaigner and an advocate of divorce and abortion in

a state whose constitution denies both, was elected as the first woman President of Eire.

November 1990: Margaret Thatcher was ousted as leader of the Conservative Party and Prime Minister. She was succeeded by John Major who announced a cabinet devoid of women, although women were promoted to many advisory roles.

1990: Independent taxation for women was introduced. For the first time married women were taxed separately from their husbands.

January 1991: The beginning of the Gulf War brought to public attention the issue of women soldiers, especially those who are

mothers, and the question of whether they should be deployed in combatant roles as American women troops had been in the eighties in military actions such as the invasion of Grenada. British women military personnel are still kept from combat even though they may be armed and serve close to the front line.

March 1991: A husband was found guilty of raping his wife and the judge, Lord Lane, said, 'The time has now arrived when the law should declare that a rapist remains a rapist subject to the criminal law, irrespective of his relationship with his victim.'

Top left: New technology had changed office life.

Top centre: Anita Roddick had become a business success when The Body Shop was quoted on the Stock Exchange. Her philosophy of selling body-care products based on natural ingredients in simple bottles without fancy labels or extravagant claims to make the user more beautiful captured the imagination of millions of consumers.

Top right: Bill and Hillary Clinton during the 1992 presidential campaign. During her husband's presidency, Hillary Clinton took on more than the traditional role of the first lady, which was greeted with disapproval by many Americans. In 1993 Bill selected her to head the commission on National Health Care Reform. The appointment was highly controversial and after strong opposition the plan produced by the commission was abandoned in September 1994.

Above left: Helen Sharman became the first Briton in space when she spent two weeks on the Russian Mir Space Station.

Above right: Kate Adie, whose reporting in the Gulf War was one of several assignments from scenes of conflict or strife. She reported from Libya following the US airstrike on Tripoli, from Romania as the Ceausescus fell and from Tiananmen Square.

Left: On 28 November 1990, after more than 11 years as the nation's first female premier, Margaret Thatcher resigned. Here she is pictured at Victory Green in the Falkland Islands in June 1992.

'Blair's Babes'

Despite the demeaning epithet applied to the record number of female Labour MPs elected in 1997, a term which *Guardian* columnist Polly Toynbee dubbed a 'casual misogynist tag', that election marked a watershed in the drive for equal representation for women in Parliament. The 120 female MPs elected represented just over 18 per cent of the House, doubling the 60 women MPs elected in 1992, then the highest ever total. This growth was as result of two factors. Firstly, it was a landslide victory for Labour under Tony Blair and secondly the Labour Party had pursued a policy of all-women shortlists in the run-up to the election.

Although controversial, and despite being overturned by legal challenge in January 1996, the Labour Party had established a large number of female candidates in winnable seats, many of whom would not have been selected by their constituency without an all-women shortlist; of 101 female Labour MPs returned in 1997, 35 had come from constituencies which had selected their candidate in this way. For the 1992 election the Labour Party had introduced a policy whereby each constituency was to have a woman

on its shortlists when selecting a candidate. The impact of this policy was minimal with few women being selected in winnable seats. The successes of the 1997 election and the upward trends seen for several decades were somewhat tarnished when in 2001 there was a slight decrease in the number of women elected. Hence the re-introduction of all-women shortlists for the 2005 election following the Labour Government's passing of the Sex Discrimination (Election Candidates) Act, 2002 which permitted, until the end of 2015, positive discrimination in the selection of candidates.

While the Labour Party can be seen to be the most successful in driving up the numbers of female MPs, the Conservative Party too has been acutely aware of the need to increase the number of women representatives. Unlike Labour, the Conservative party has not used women-only shortlists but the leadership has sought to persuade constituencies to select women candidates in winnable seats. In 2010 David Cameron said he was concerned about the slow pace of change within the Conservative Party

Postscripts 1990s

March 1991: Great controversy was stirred when it was revealed that a woman who had never had sexual intercourse was receiving fertility treatment with a view to being artificially inseminated in order to conceive a baby.

March 1991: Leader of the Bangladeshi National Party, Begum Khaleda Zia, became Bangladesh's first woman Prime Minister following the fall of the military dictatorship against which she had campaigned throughout the 1980s.

April 1991: 'The Condom Crisis' in Ireland broke when the Irish Prime Minister reduced the age at which condoms could be bought from 18 to 16, which was the legal age for marriage, without consulting the Catholic Church. Condoms were only supposed to be sold as a means of preventing the spread of HIV and not as a contraceptive device.

April 1991: The 'abortion pill' which had been used extensively was withdrawn from use in France after a number of women had died after taking it. British trials of a similar method of abortion remained.

April 1991: In the Swiss canton of Apensfal women voted for the first time in local elections.

May 1991: Edith Cresson took office as France's first female Prime Minister.

May 1991: Women workers forced to retire from their jobs at the age of 60 under British law were granted the right to compensation for the loss of earnings up to the age of 65 by the European Court, as Britain had agreed to equal employment laws but had not brought them onto the statute book.

and would not rule out all-women shortlists. The Liberal Democrats also ruled out all-female shortlists for UK Parliamentary elections and has never had more than 12 per cent women MPs. However, the party has operated a 50:50 policy for elections to the European Parliament.

Despite the slight dip in the 2001 election the 21st century has seen significant rises in the proportion of female MPs in the UK parliament: 20 per cent in 2005, to 22 per cent in 2010 and 29 per cent in 2015. The Labour Party has seen the most improvement with 43 per cent in 2015, moving closer to parity of numbers with male MPs. Other mainstream parties have also seen increases, with the Scottish National Party in their landslide election in Scotland in 2015, increasing its female representation to 36 per cent from 17 per cent in 2010 in the wake of the increase from 6 to 56 MPs. With 68 female MPs elected in 2015, the Conservative party increased its proportion of women MPs to 21 per cent in 2015, a 5 per cent rise from 2010. For the Liberal Democrats female representation was cut to zero after the party's disastrous performance in 2015 when it secured only eight seats. In contrast to their representation the Commons, in the House of Lords where women make up 25 per cent of the House, the Liberal Democrat party has the highest proportion of female peers with 34 per cent, as against Labour's 31 per cent and the Conservative group mirroring the 21 per cent of its membership of the Lower House.

While progress has been made, nearly 100 years after women were first allowed to stand for Parliament through legislation which ran parallel to the partial female franchise in 1918, less than a third of MPs in the House of Commons are female. This is the chamber of Parliament where major decisions are made which affect the lives of the 51 per cent of the UK population who are female. It is to be hoped that the gains and progress made since 1997 will rapidly move the country closer to equal representation.

Opposite: 'Blair's Babes' pose with the new Prime Minister on the steps of Church House, Westminster. On 1 May the Labour Party swept to power with a landslide victory. A record number of women MPs were elected, comprising almost one in four of Labour's successful candidates.

Left: Labour stalwart Clare Short.

Right: J.K. Rowling with her first book *Harry Potter and the Philosopher's Stone* in 1997. Publishers decided to use the initials J.K. rather than her name, Joanne, for fear that the fact that the author was a woman would discourage boys from picking up the novel. The book launched a seven-title series that dominated family reading and cinema around the world for years to come, transforming the fortunes of Rowling and her publishers.

Above: A different take on 'Girl Power' – the Spice Girls perform in Istanbul in late 1997. The Spice Girls first exploded onto the pop scene in mid-1996, with their debut single, 'Wannabe', which became the first of six consecutive UK number one singles between 1996 and 1998; they included '2 Become 1' and 'Spice Up Your Life'.

Postscripts 1990s

August 1991: Designed by Tim Berners-Lee, the World Wide Web became publicly available, a technological innovation which would have a major impact on women throughout the world in the coming decades. As a channel for people across the globe to speak about their lives and experiences, it brought new opportunities for women to organise and press for change, from attempts to overturn the driving ban for women in Saudi Arabia to the beginnings of the transformation of attitudes towards rape in India in 2013.

October 1991: Two years after the Scottish High Court of Justiciary abolished the defence that rape could not take place within marriage, the House of Lords upheld the decision of the Appeal Court that: 'in modern times the supposed marital exemption in rape forms no part of the law of England.'

1991: Stella Rimmington became the first woman to head MI5.

1992: Barbara Mills was the first female Director of Public Prosecutions.

1992: Betty Boothroyd, Labour MP for West Bromwich, was elected as first female Speaker of the House of Commons, a role she fulfilled until 2000.

1993: Rebecca Stephens was the first British woman to reach the summit of Everest. (Alison Hargreaves made it to the top without oxygen in 1995, but died on K2 later the same year.)

March 1994: Seven years after the Synod voted overwhelmingly in favour of the ordination of women, Angela Berners-Wilson was the first of 32 women ordained as Church of England vicars in Bristol Cathedral.

Right: For many Madonna's lyrics and performances pushed at the boundaries of acceptability, provoking discussion about female sexuality.

Below: Charles and Diana's separation was announced in December 1992 and their divorce was finalised in 1996. During the decade the Princess continued to work with many charities including the Halo Trust, the mine clearance team. News of her sudden death shocked the world in 1997. Thousands turned out to pay tribute to the 'people's princess', leaving flowers outside her home at Kensington Palace and lining the route of her funeral procession.

Above: Roman Catholic nun Sister Wendy changed many people's preconceptions about nuns during the 1990s when she found fame with a series of books and television documentaries on the history of art.

Postscripts 1990s

1995: Pauline Clare was appointed Chief Constable for Lancashire, the first woman to hold this rank. Only since 1976, when the Sex Discrimination Act came into effect, had women police officers been able to access the same career structure as men. Before this, most Forces had a separate structure for women which did not give access to the higher ranks.

May 1997: 120 female MPs were elected to Parliament, the highest number to date and double the total returned in 1992.

June 1997: J.K. Rowling published the first in a series of seven Harry Potter novels. *Harry Potter and the Goblet of Fire* became the fastest selling book ever. Rowling re-energised children's and young people's reading while going on to become the richest author in the world.

August 1997: Diana, Princess of Wales, was killed in a car crash in Paris. She had become the compassionate face of the Royal Family and despite her divorce from Prince Charles had remained high in the affections of the British public and her death saw an outpouring of grief.

September 1997: Mother Teresa of Kolkata died. The Albanian Catholic nun who had won the Nobel Peace Prize in 1979 for her humanitarian work amongst the poorest and most disadvantaged, was granted a state funeral by the Indian government in gratitude for her services to the poor of all religions in India.

1999: In Britain a new law on parental leave enabled both men and women to take up to 13 weeks off work to care for children under the age of five.

Women's Military Corps Disappear

The early 1990s saw seminal changes in the relationship between the women's military forces, products of the First World War, and the much older, men's military forces when the male and female services were integrated. The first service to be assimilated was the Women's Royal Army Corps (WRAC) with its soldiers being transferred to appropriate units in the British Army in April 1992. The Royal Navy, Britain's oldest military service, was the next to merge when in 1993 the Women's Royal Naval Service (WRNS; popularly known as 'the Wrens') was disbanded. The Women's Royal Air Force followed suit in 1994.

Prior to assimilation, each of the Women's Forces had their own Commanders-in-Chief, though in all of the women's services, the most senior ranks were significantly below that of their male counterparts. For example the highest ranking female in the Women's Royal Army Corps was a Brigadier, three ranks below that of General, a rank available only to men until integration. However, it was nearly twenty years after the absorption into the Navy, Army and Air Force that a woman reached a rank above that available to women before the merger, when Elaine West became an Air Vice-Marshal in the RAF in August 2013. In September 2015, Susan Ridge reached the equivalent in the British Army when she became a Major-General but the Royal Navy lags behind with Captain being the highest rank attained by any female officer, two ranks below their counterparts in the other services. However, the ranks of Air Vice-Marshal and Major-General are the equivalent of 'one star' ranks and women in the British military have some way to go to catch up with the four women who hold, or have held, 'four star' rank in the USA Forces, the first being General Ann Dunwoody, appointed in November 2008 as General of the US Army.

For all of their histories, the roles for servicewomen had been principally in support of their male counterparts. Their roles were key to freeing up men for combat operations and could range from cooks and clerks to mechanics and electricians to wireless operators and radar plotters to piloting transport planes. The move to integrate the services highlighted issues of equality which had been surfacing and there had been moves to open up more roles to women. In 1990 women in the WRNS were allowed to go to sea for the first time and in 1992 Jo Salter became the first woman to qualify as a fast-jet pilot, becoming the first woman operational pilot, flying Tornados protecting the No-Fly Zone over Iraq in the Gulf War.

By the end of the decade many more roles had opened up to women in each of the services, including frontline jobs in the Royal Engineers, Royal Artillery and Royal Electrical and Mechanical Engineers but female military personnel were not allowed to become, among other roles, infantry soldiers, tank crew or until recently submariners. Women made up 8 per cent of the military and each of the services had developed to accommodate female entrants. For example the Army introduced fitness tests designed to be 'gender neutral', enabling the prediction of the capacity to carry out physical tasks rather than meet specific fitness targets. The Navy continued its policy of deploying women at sea so that on around 40 of its ships women made up between 10 per cent and 15 per cent of crew. In the Army and Navy women were able to apply for around a quarter of the available posts. With more than 95 per cent of posts available to female applicants, the RAF provided the most equal opportunities for servicewomen but women are still not permitted to join the RAF Regiment which is a close combat force. None of the services as yet allow women to serve in close combat roles, though the Danish military has had women in infantry roles since 1988.

Below: British troops wait to leave Kandahar in Afghanistan in 2014.

Reaching for the Top

The opening of a new millennium was a pertinent point to evaluate the extent to which equality of opportunity legislation such as the Sex Discrimination Act (1975) had given women access to powerful roles in all areas of work. In the Civil Service structural changes such as the introduction of part-time and flexible working, as well as equal opportunities training to try to address attitudes, alongside challenges to the institution's culture, enabled more women to progress through the ranks. By 2000 the numbers of women reaching the ranks of senior civil servant had almost tripled to just below 18 per cent, though, given that 49 per cent of the Civil Service is female, there is substantial under-representation in roles which can have significant influence over policy and the way in which the country is run.

Within the Criminal Justice system the progress of women into top roles was much slower than in other areas of public life. Although Lady Hazel Cosgrove had been appointed a Law Lord in Scotland in 1996, in England and Wales there was no female Law Lord in 2000 and, apart from a significant increase in female High Court judges where they comprised 9 per cent of the total, every other level of the judiciary had seen only minute increases in the number of women appointed to senior positions. The Judiciary's counterpart in the criminal justice system, the Police Service, saw an increase in senior appointments but from a woefully low base – in 1990 there were no women at the rank of Chief Constable and only around 2 per cent of senior officers were women. By 2000 women accounted for around 7 per cent of all senior ranks, including that of Chief Constable, with Pauline Clare being the first in the role when she was appointed as head of the Lancashire Constabulary in 1995.

One area in the public domain that saw more rapid progress was the BBC where in 2000 the senior management comprised 27 per cent women out of a workforce that was 40 per cent female, an increase of 17 per cent in a decade. As a publicly funded body BBC statistics are visible but in the commercial media, television, radio and print media, it is much less so. Nevertheless, throughout the 1990s there had been a number of women editors of high profile national daily newspapers such as Rosie Boycott, Janet Street-Porter and Eve Pollard and they had made it clear that it was possible for women to successfully take on such powerful and influential roles .

'Opportunity 2000' set up by Business in the Community to improve gender balance saw some successes. Over a third of management staff in businesses that were members of 'Opportunity 2000' were women as opposed to just over 20 per cent in businesses that were not part of the campaign. However, at the highest levels of the most valuable companies – the FTSE 100 – only one company had a female CEO and 42 of the companies had no women at Board level. Of the 58 companies that had female representation, 46 had only one women director. It could be argued that one female member on a company Board is little more than tokenism.

Twenty-five years from the passing of the Sex Discrimination Act many structural and institutional changes had been enacted, such as the introduction of more flexible working practices, particularly in the public sector. These changes eased some of the barriers for women, who still bore the major responsibility of managing day-to-day family life, enabling more to reach powerful and influential positions. Nonetheless, as the new millennium opened, there was far from equal gender representation at the highest levels in Britain's public life and within the business sector. Senior women judges, such as Lady Brenda Hale, who was to become the first female Law Lord, complained that judges' official lodgings were run like gentlemen's clubs where ladies were expected to retire after dinner. Such attitudes make it clear that women are not seen as belonging to the group and women who succeed in the face of such exclusion had to be very strong-minded. In academia, Professor Susan Greenfield pointed out that with a focus on the quantity of published research as a criterion for professorial posts, women were often at a disadvantage if they had career breaks, resulting in fewer publications and consequently less access to funding. She argued more could be done to ring-fence research grants for such women returning to research.

Postscripts 2000s

2001: Clara Furse became chief executive of the 200-year-old London Stock Exchange – the first woman to do so.

2002: Sheila Macdonald was the first woman to become an executive director of a UK high street bank, when she was appointed chief operating officer of the Co-operative Bank.

2003: Brenda Hale was apppointed the first female Law Lord.

2004: Condoleezza Rice was appointed the first female national security adviser to a US president.

2005: Ellen MacArthur became the fastest person to sail single-handed around the world and at 28-years-old, the youngest person to receive a damehood.

2006: St Hilda's, the last all-women college at Oxford University, ended more than a century of tradition by voting to open its doors to men.

2006: Margaret Beckett was appointed Foreign Secretary, becoming the first woman to hold the post.

January 2006: Ellen Johnson-Sirleaf was sworn in as the world's first black female president, and Africa's first elected female leader after winning the Liberian Presidential elections. She was re-elected to the role in 2011.

2007: Nineteen-year-old Private Michelle Norris, an Army medical officer, became the first woman to be awarded the Military Cross, one of the highest honours for gallantry in combat. She braved machine-gun fire from 200 insurgents to save the life of a wounded comrade in Southern Iraq.

2007: Moira Cameron was the first woman to serve as a Beefeater, breaking the 522 year male monopoly at the Tower of London.

2008: Norway brought in legislation that required all companies to have at least 40 per cent women on their boards.

2009: Carol Ann Duffy was selected as the first female Poet Laureate, Britain's most prestigious poetry job, ending 400 years of male domination.

2010: Flight Lieutenant Kirsty Moore joined the Red Arrows team – the first woman pilot to fly with the prestigious troop.

Women Going the Distance

Before the 1980s there were no women's distance races in the Olympic Games. Distance running was considered too physically demanding for female athletes. In the 1980 Moscow Games, the longest race for women was the 1,500 metres, which had been instituted in Munich eight years earlier. Women had been excluded from track and field competition altogether until 1928, when the longest race was the 800 metres. It was at the 1984 Olympic Games in Los Angeles, that Joan Benoit became the first Olympic Marathon champion.

Just under 20 years later, on 13 April 2003, Paula Radcliffe won the London Marathon in 2 hours 15 minutes and 25 seconds. Her time was not only a massive world record, beating her own previous world record of 2:17:18, but it moved her over three minutes ahead of the next fastest female marathoner in the world. Fifty years before setting her world record no man had run the distance faster than 2 hours and 20 minutes. The legendary Jim Peters was the first man to run under the 2:20 landmark, a feat he achieved in 1953 – nearly four minutes slower than Paula Radcliffe's current women's world record.

Above: The women's marathon World Record holder Paula Radcliffe.

Below: Denise Lewis flies through the air in the long jump section of the women's heptathlon in the Sydney Olympics in 2000. Achieving 6584 points overall, Lewis won the gold medal over the Russian Yelena Prokhorova.

Above: In July 2002 Venus Williams won the first Grand Slam singles title of her career at Wimbledon. The Williams sisters emerged in the late 1990s and their athletic, powerful style of play changed the women's game.

Right: Kelly Holmes threw her arms wide with a big smile as she crossed the line in the women's 800 metres at the Athens Olympics, although she said later that she had to see the replay twice to be sure she had won. She also took gold in the 1500 metres, making her the one of the most successful UK athletes of recent years.

The Most Powerful Woman in the World

In November 2005, Angela Merkel, a former research scientist, became the first female Chancellor of Germany. She was one of a growing number of women being elected to Head of State during the opening decade of the millennium. In Ireland, Mary McAleese had made history by becoming the first elected female Head of State to succeed another when she won the Presidency in 1997 after Mary Robinson, Ireland's first female president, stepped down. Across the world, from Finland where Tarja Halonen became the first female Finnish President in 2000, to Michelle Bachelet's election in 2006 as Chile's President, to Ellen Johnson Sirleaf's election as President of Liberia, also in 2006, women were increasingly being seen as credible, electable leaders. In some cases, like that of Benazir Bhutto, twice Prime Minister of Pakistan in the late eighties and nineties, in unstable political situations, they were as susceptible to violence as male politicians and in December 2007 Bhutto was assassinated while on her campaign to return to parliament. Many of these women, such as Ellen Johnson Sirleaf who was the first elected female head of state in Africa, pressed for gender equality. She, together with Leymah Gbowee of Liberia and Tawakel Karman of Yemen, was awarded the Nobel Peace Prize in 2011 for her part in the 'non-violent struggle for the safety of women and for women's rights to full participation in peace-building work'. Her influence in this area has helped to put her on the Forbes list of the 'World's Most Powerful Women'.

Angela Merkel has also made it onto the Forbes list, having been named the most powerful woman in the world for 10 years running since her election as Chancellor. She has also featured in the top 10 list of the World's Most Powerful People since 2010. While she is seen as a powerful figure on the global stage, using her knowledge of Russian in attempts to broker a peace deal between Vladimir Putin and the West over the Ukraine crisis, negotiating solutions to the Greek financial crisis, Merkel is a popular leader at home.

Subsequent to her first election in 2005, she has won two further mandates, each time her CDU (Christian Democratic Union) Party increasing its share of the vote, to make her the European Union's longest serving elected Head of State. Her popularity can be attributed to the way in which she has steered Germany to become the most powerful nation in Europe. In the midst of the global economic crisis which started in 2007, Angela Merkel acted to ensure that German business survived, subsidising firms that had to cut workers hours, while also increasing payments to new parents. At the same time she has also managed to push ahead with increasing the age for retirement in Germany. Her tenure of office has also seen more women in senior public positions and a commitment to steep greenhouse gas cuts in a bid to make Germany more eco-friendly.

Top: Angela Merkel addresses delegates at the Copenhagen Climate Summit.

Centre: Former Pakistani Prime Minister Benazir Bhutto waves to supporters as she arrives at a local court in Larkana in 2007 to submit her nomination papers for the forthcoming Pakistani general election. Bhutto had only recently returned to the country from a self-imposed exile in Dubai. However, in December of the same year she was assassinated as she was leaving a Pakistan People's Party campaign rally in the city of Rawalpindi.

Above: Christine Lagarde, managing director of the International Monetary Fund (IMF), and Angela Merkel attend a news conference.

Below: On 9 September 2015 the Queen became Britain's longest-reigning monarch, passing Queen Victoria's 63 years seven months and two days on the throne.

Below centre: Condoleeza Rice achieved several notable firsts during her political career. In 2005 she was appointed US Secretary of State, becoming the first female African-American to hold the position and only the second woman after Madeleine Albright. Rice was President Bush's National Security Advisor during his first term, making her the first woman to serve in that role.

Above left: Having conceded the Democratic presidential nomination to Obama in 2008, Hillary Clinton was appointed US Secretary of State the following year. Clinton put women's rights and human rights at the forefront of policy initiatives, as well as heading up diplomatic efforts in major world events such as the Arab Spring of 2010.

Left: Secretary Clinton with President Obama and Prime MInister Gordon Brown.

Above: After much speculation, Clinton launched her bid to become the Democratic candidate for the 2016 presidential race. If successful, she will be the first woman to earn the nomination of a major party. Although likely, her nomination is not guaranteed, and her bid for the presidency is not a foregone conclusion. Hillary Clinton is a polarising figure, particularly in the US popular media, where much focus has been on her gender (including her changing hairstyles) and her role as a Washington 'insider', as much as her efforts and successes as one of America's most powerful politicians.

Right: Prince Charles and Camilla Parker Bowles married in 2005. Initially the immense popularity of Princess Diana made it difficult for Camilla Parker Bowles to gain public acceptance. However, as time has passed she has increasingly become involved in the Prince's public life.

Above: Talk show host, actress and philanthropist, Oprah Winfrey has been labelled by many 'the most influential woman in America'.

Above: After 50 years of working as an actor, it's Helen Mirren's appearance that inspires more column inches than her performance.

Above centre: Judy Dench made her stage debut in 1957 but it was not until she was in her 60s that her film career took off, and has not stalled since.

Above right: Lady Gaga brightens up the stage at Glastonbury. Her unique and flamboyant style along with her celebration of individuality and self expression have inspired thousands of young fans whom she calls the 'Little Monsters'.

Far right: Adele surprised many when she put her career on hold after her son was born in 2012.

Right: Taylor Swift has gone from country artist to feminist role model. Her highly autobiographical lyrics and desire to connect with her many fans are two of the reasons for her runaway success.

Postscripts 2010s

August 2012: In the 30th Olympics, held in London, women were represented in every country's team with countries such as Saudi Arabian sending their first ever female athletes. Britain's 'poster girl' promoting the games and the move to get more women involved in sport was Jessica Ennis, who won gold in the heptathlon, one of almost 40 per cent of medals won by the Team GB's women.

July 2013: Announcement from the Bank of England that Jane Austen will feature on the new £10 note after a campaign to ensure that, after the removal of Elizabeth Fry's portrait, a female historical figure would appear on British currency. The campaign's leader, Caroline Criado-Perez, received threats of death and rape via Twitter for her stance and this brought to the attention of a wider

public the threats of physical violence which outspoken women can face on social media.

2014: Nicola Sturgeon became the first female First Minister of Scotland.

2014: After the ban on women serving on submarines was lifted in 2011, Lieutenants Maxine Stiles, Alexandra Olsson and Penny Thackray became the first women submariners when they report for duty on board HMS *Vigilant*

September 2014: Members at the historic home of golf, the Royal and Ancient Golf Club of St Andrews, voted overwhelmingly to admit women members, leaving Royal Troon, Muirfield and St George's as the only clubs in Britain to refuse membership to women.

January 2015: Twenty-one years after the ordination of the first female Anglican priest in Britain, Libby Lane was consecrated as a bishop in the Church of England.

May 2015: Princess Charlotte, daughter of Prince William, is the first female to benefit from the change to the laws governing succession to the crown. In 2013, just prior to the birth of her brother Prince George, an Act of Parliament came into force which meant that male children did not take precedence over female children in the line of succession. Although not applied retrospectively, from 25 April any child born to a member of the Royal Family would take their place in the line of succession, regardless of gender.

Size Zero

In many ways the problems raised by Size Zero can be seen as the result of the meeting of law of unintended consequences with the fashion industry's obsession with thinness. The original impetus for Size Zero came early in the 2000s from a desire in the US to re-size garments to appeal to the vanity of retail customers. With the growing size of the average American – due in part to better nutrition but largely to the mounting rates of obesity, retailers had the idea of changing the labelling of women's clothing, with the effect that a US size 10 (equivalent to a UK size 12) became a size 8, size 8 (UK size 10) became size 6 and so on. Prior to the revision the smallest size in the US was a size 2 which necessarily became size 0. For most customers, the re-sizing flattered them into thinking that they were smaller or thinner than they really were. But for some, the newly created Size Zero became an aspiration. Size 0 varies slightly from brand to brand but the average measurements are 32 inch (81cm) bust, 23 inch (58cm) waist and 34 inch (86cm) hips. The average waist measurement of an eight-year-old child in the UK is 23 inches.

The growth of the publicity about size 0 or 'Size Zero' as it was coined, coincided with the high profile deaths of models in the fashion industry. In 2006 the Brazilian model, Ana Carolina Reston, and the Uruguayan model, Luisel Ramos, died within months of each other from medical complications which were a direct result of the eating disorder anorexia nervosa. Luisel's sister, Eliana, also a model, died the following year, from the same cause. Their deaths sparked a debate about the trend in fashion modelling, and in the media generally, for images of impossibly thin female figures, aspiration to which helped fuel the paradox of burgeoning numbers of women and girls in the modern world developing eating disorders related to the pursuit of thinness, while at the opposite end of the scale many women were suffering the effects of obesity through over-eating.

As a concept Size Zero is an interesting metaphor for the position of women in society. The negation of the body inherent in the idea suggests that women should not be seen. Indeed, tales of fashion models being told they are 'too fat' when they have a body mass index below that which is considered healthy emphasises the fact that for many designers the model in the clothes is not a consideration; the thinner the figure, the better the clothes look and the less of the model's persona is visible. The risks to the long-term health of girls and women, whether in the fashion industry or just those who aspire to achieve 'Size Zero' are well-documented: poor skin and hair condition; cessation of menstruation which can result in fertility problems; loss of immunity to fight off infections; loss of muscle and bone density; excess pressure on the heart which can lead to heart failure.

'Size Zero' highlights the wider issue of the way in which women's bodies are portrayed, in particular in the media, and the messages it sends to girls and young women about how they should look and the deleterious effects it can have on both physical and mental health.

Right: 'Posh and Becks' pictured leaving her parents' home, as the couple headed to Ireland for their wedding at Luttrellstown Castle in 1999. Victoria Beckham has left her singing career behind and is now running her own fashion label, VB. Throughout the years, much press attention has been focused on her appearance, and particularly her weight.

Left: Starting out as part of the hugely successful girl band Destiny's Child, Beyoncé is one of the highest earning solo entertainers of the decade – and famed for her curves.

Breaking the 'Stained Glass Ceiling'

On 22 July 2015 Rachel Treweek and Sarah Mullally were consecrated as bishops in the Church of England. Their consecration brought to four the number of female bishoprics granted since the enabling resolution was passed at the 1988 Lambeth Conference of Bishops. This had followed an overwhelming vote in Synod the previous year to permit the ordination of women as priests. As Bishop of Gloucester, Treweek's consecration made her the most senior female cleric and granted her a seat in the House of Lords. The ceremony in Canterbury Cathedral, led by Archbishop Justin Welby, came just six months after that of Libby Lane's consecration as the first woman to hold such a senior position in the Church. Alison White had been consecrated as Bishop of Hull in July 2015.

It had taken over 25 years since the undertaking by the Church of England that women could become bishops, and 21 years since the first 32 women priests were ordained in March 1994, for the first woman bishop to be appointed. In Britain, as the established church, the Church of England has influence in the country, mainly through the Lords Spiritual, the 26 bishops who sit in the House of Lords and can therefore vote on the legislation being scrutinised by the House. For several years, debate raged as to whether any women could, or would, become a bishop and thus have access to one of these seats. The arguments were much the same as those rehearsed when moving towards the ordination of women but with some also contending, citing the teaching of St Paul, that men could not be governed by women, thus male clergy could not take authority from a female bishop. In 2012, despite the clergy contingent of the Synod voting overwhelmingly in favour of women bishops, the proposal was vetoed by its lay members.

Despite the arguments in Britain, the Anglican Church worldwide had already consecrated a number of women as bishops. The Episcopal Church in the USA was the first to appoint a female in this senior role when Barbara Harris was ordained as Bishop of Massachusetts in 1989, and in 2006, Katharine Jefferts Schori was elected as its Presiding Bishop and Primate, the equivalent of Archbishop in the Church of England. Indeed by 2012 when the idea of women bishops in Britain seemed stalled, countries such as New Zealand, Australia, Canada all had female bishops and in November of that year Ellinah Wamukoya was consecrated as Bishop of Swaziland. With intense lobbying and behind the scenes discussions to find ways of reassuring opponents that their views would be catered for, it would take two more years for the motion to finally pass through the Synod, clearing the way for women clergy to take their place on an equal footing alongside their male counterparts in the Church of England.

Below: Archbishop of Canterbury Justin Welby stands with newly consecrated Rachel Treweek, Bishop of Gloucester, and Sarah Mullally, Bishop of Crediton in 2015.

Above: The Right Reverend Kay Goldsworthy became Australia's first Anglican bishop in 2008.

Aung Sang Suu Kyi —
'an astounding example of the power of the powerless'

For more than twenty-five years Aung San Suu Kyi has been subject to severe restrictions on her movements as a consequence of her commitment and determination to bring freedom and democracy to the people of Burma (Myanmar).

Although the daughter of General Aung San who modernised the Burmese Army and who was assassinated in 1947 by political rivals, Aung San Suu Kyi's early life did not suggest that she would become such an iconic figure for democratic change in the face of repressive regimes. At the age of 19, she left India, where her mother was Burmese ambassador, and travelled to Britain and St Hugh's College, Oxford, where she read Philosophy, Politics and Economics, graduating in 1969. At Oxford she met Michael Aris and they married in 1972. The couple had two sons, Alexander and Kim and Suu Kyi lived quietly in Oxford while raising her young family, returning to study for a Masters degree in the mid-1980s.

1988 was a momentous year for Suu Kyi when she returned home to look after her ailing mother. At that time Burma was in the midst of political upheaval when General Ne Win who had led a military government for over two decades stepped down. Aung San Suu Kyi found herself at the forefront of a movement that wanted democratic reform and free elections. Inspired by leaders such as Ghandi and Martin Luther King who had sought change through peaceful, non-violent protest, as well as her own Buddhist beliefs, Suu Kyi organised rallies and travelled around the country, calling for a peaceful transition to democracy. However, the military responded violently, brutally suppressing the movement and seizing power in September 1988. Soon after, Aung San Suu Kyi was placed under house arrest where she remained during elections in 1990 in which her party, the National League for Democracy (NLD), won an overwhelming majority of the seats. She herself was banned from standing as a result of the constraints put on her by the junta, but it is assumed she would have become Prime Minister. This was not to be as the military government refused to accept the result and Suu Kyi remained under house arrest until 1995.

Meanwhile, in 1991, Aung San Suu Kyi was nominated for and won the Nobel Peace Prize, the citation stating that 'Suu Kyi's struggle is one of the most extraordinary examples of civil courage in Asia in recent decades. She has become an important symbol in the struggle against oppression...'. Despite this and other international recognition and calls for her release, it was not until 1995 that Suu Kyi was freed from house arrest. However, she was banned from leaving Burma and she spent the next five years working inside the country alongside her NLD party, campaigning peacefully for democratic change, until in 2000 she was again placed under house arrest.

Since 2000 Suu Kyi has spent many more years under house arrest, and has been imprisoned at least once. It was only in 2010, after the NLD boycotted the general election, that she was finally released and the government began talks with her to try to bring about reform. But the pace of change has been slow and laws have been put in place which bar anyone who is married to a foreign national or who has foreign children from standing for election.

It is ironic that the woman who gave up a normal family life for her commitment to her country should be barred from holding office in the country for which she has sacrificed so much. Her husband, Michael Aris, had seen her only five times since she was placed under house arrest in 1989 when he died from prostate cancer in 1999. Although the military authorities gave permission for Suu Kyi to visit Britain to see her husband before he died she had to make the difficult decision to stay in Burma for fear that if she left she would not be allowed to return. The other painful loss she has suffered has been the lack of involvement in her children's lives. She had to leave her sons of 15 and 11 behind in England and over the years there have been only a handful of visits. She has acknowledged the difficulties her sons have faced, especially after the death of their father and in her long-delayed Nobel Peace Prize acceptance speech in 2012 Suu Kyi reflected on the six aspects of suffering, or dukkha, in Buddhism, noting that 'to be parted from those one loves' was one that particularly absorbed her. Bearing this suffering with grace and calm for more than quarter of a century more than bears out the statement by Francis Sejested, Nobel Peace Prize Committee Chairman, in 1991 that Aung San Suu Kyi is 'an astounding example of the power of the powerless'.

Left: Aung Sang Suu Kyi speaks at the Global Development Summit in South Korea in 2013.

Below: President Obama meets with Aung Sang Suu Kyi at the White House in 2012 after she received the US Congressional Gold Medal.

Girls' Education Under Attack

In 2000 the United Nations set eight development goals to be achieved by 2015. One aspect of the goal to empower women was to 'Eliminate gender disparity in primary and secondary education, preferably by 2005, and in all levels of education no later than 2015'. By 2005 these goals had not been achieved and there remained disparity between the numbers of girls enrolled in primary school with around 95 girls for every 100 boys. Parity in primary education was much closer in 2015 with more than two thirds of countries in the developing world, where the gap had existed, having equal numbers of girls and boys in primary school. However, as students get older equality of opportunity reduces and there is significant disparity between boys' and girls' access to education in two thirds of developing regions, and a tiny percentage of countries demonstrating parity at tertiary level.

While the UN has shown commitment to gender equality in access to education, there are areas of the world where this commitment faces ideological threats. In parts of Sub-Saharan Africa militant groups such as Boko Haram (translated as 'Western education is forbidden') profess a fundamentalist Islamic belief which curtails the rights of women and girls. Boko Haram has conducted a campaign against western influences in its attempt to establish an Islamic Caliphate in Nigeria and the surrounding countries. Although the group have kidnapped girls for years, one of its most notorious strikes against western education was seen in April 2014 when more than 275 schoolgirls were abducted from Chibok Secondary School in Nigeria. Boko Haram's leader Abubakar Shekau claimed responsibility and said that he would sell the girls as slaves, that the girls should not have been in school and instead should have been married, claiming girls as young as nine are suitable for marriage.

In the second decade of the 21st century girls' education was also under attack in Pakistan where another fundamentalist Islamic group, the Taliban, took control in the Swat Valley, blowing up girls' schools and banning their education. Out of this repression came a girl who was to show great courage and become a significant voice for education. Malala Yousafzai was a schoolgirl caught up in the Taliban's prohibition on girls attending school. Following a request from the BBC Urdu website to her father who ran a school in the area and who is a strong advocate of women's education for a schoolgirl to blog of her experiences, Malala began posting under the pseudonym Gul Makai. Anonymity was thought essential to protect her safety.

In the summer of 2009, a documentary was made about Malala. This lead to an increasing public profile, interviews on television and in newspapers. By the end of 2009 her identity as the blogger on the BBC Urdu website was revealed but she had also gained international recognition for her commitment to girls' education. She was planning to set up a foundation to allow girls from poor families to attend school. The Taliban saw her as a threat to their ideas and in 2012 planned to kill her. An attack on her school bus in which she was asked to identify herself lead to her being shot through the head by a masked gunman.

Severely wounded, Malala was treated for injuries which had caused swelling on the brain and to remove the bullet which had lodged near her spinal column. Later she was moved to the Queen Elizabeth Hospital in Birmingham, which has extensive experience of dealing with military personnel with severe injuries. Here she underwent additional treatment and surgery to reconstruct her face and restore her hearing.

The attack by the Taliban has not cowed Malala; in fact, it has had the opposite effect. She has been vocal in pressing for the rights of education for all young people. Addressing the UN in 2014 she said, 'I'm here to speak up for the right of education for every child. I want education for the sons and daughters of the Taliban and all terrorists and extremists.' In 2014 she became the youngest ever recipient of the Nobel Peace Prize for her commitment to children's rights, particularly the right to an education.

Right: First Minister of Scotland Nicola Sturgeon. With Ruth Davidson as leader of the Scottish Conservative Party and Kezia Dougdale newly elected leader of Scottish Labour, women are making an impact in the Scottish Parliament.

Above: Home Secretary Theresa May has long been regarded as the leading female contender to replace David Cameron when he stands down.

Left: A fixture in the gossip columns, Angelina Jolie is also a Goodwill Ambassador for the UN Refugee Agency, drawing attention to global issues such as sexual violence in military conflict zones. She also made the news in 2013 when she announced that she had undergone a double mastectomy to try to prevent breast cancer in the future.

Top right: A female head of state is no longer a talking point – Argentinian President Cristina Fernandez de Kirchner *(top right)*, Dilma Rousseff, President of Brazil *(above right)* and South Korean President Park Geun-Hye *(right)*.

Below left: There was worldwide condemnation of the kidnap of the Nigerian schoolgirls by Boko Haram. Michelle Obama was one of those who became involved, adding her voice to the protest.

Below right: Kate Middleton has taken over from Princess Diana as the woman the press most want to photograph.

'I think being a woman is like being Irish... Everyone says you're important and nice, but you take second place all the time.'

Iris Murdoch

'Taught from their infancy that beauty is woman's sceptre, the mind shapes itself to the body, and roaming round its gilt cage, only seeks to adorn its prison.'

Mary Wollstonecraft

'My parents, especially my father, discussed the question of my brothers' education as a matter of real importance. My education and that of my sister were scarcely discussed at all.'

Emmeline Pankhurst

'No woman can call herself free who does not control her own body.'

Margaret Sanger

'Men should think twice before making widowhood women's only path to power.'

Gloria Steinem

'Human rights are women's rights, and women's rights are human rights.'

Hillary Clinton

'Men are from Earth, women are from Earth. Deal with it.'

George Carlin

'It seems to me that the fact that I am a woman is a bigger issue than the fact that I'm from the East. For me it isn't really important. I've only ever known myself as a woman.'

Angela Merkel

'You can have it all, just not all at the same time.'

Betty Friedan

'The education and empowerment of women throughout the world cannot fail to result in a more caring, tolerant, just and peaceful life for all.'

Aung Sang Suu Kyi

'Whisky, gambling and Ferraris are better than housework.'

Françoise Sagan

'We cannot succeed when half of us are held back.'

Malala Yousafzai

'I don't think a female running a house is a problem, a broken family. It's perceived as one because of the notion that a head is a man.'

Toni Morrison

'When girls are educated, their countries become stronger and more prosperous. No country can ever truly flourish if it stifles the potential of its women and deprives itself of the contributions of half of its citizens.'

Michelle Obama

'I've yet to be on a campus where most women weren't worrying about some aspect of combining marriage, children, and a career. I've yet to find one where many men were worrying about the same thing.'

Gloria Steinem

Milestones

1903: The Women's Social and Political Union is founded in Manchester by Emmeline Pankhurst, her daughters Christabel and Sylvia, and a small group of like-minded women.

December 1903: Marie Curie became the first woman to win a Nobel Prize when, together with her husband Pierre and Henri Becquerel, she was awarded the prize for Physics.

October 1905: Christabel Pankhurst, oldest of Emmeline's five children, and Annie Kenney were the first suffragettes to be imprisoned when they refused to pay the fines imposed for assaulting a policeman at a political meeting.

May 1908: Following the passing of the Qualification of Women Act in 1907, which enabled women to stand for county and borough councils and to be elected Mayor, Elizabeth Garrett Anderson, Britain's first female doctor, became Britain's first woman Mayor in her home town of Aldeburgh.

June 1908: The largest suffragette rally to date took place – 200,000 women and men gathered in Hyde Park. Chartered trains brought suffragettes from all over Britain to London.

November 1910: 'Black Friday' the 18th, when 119 suffragettes were arrested attempting to rush the House of Commons. The following day Home Secretary Winston Churchill ordered that charges against 100 women be dropped. Mrs Mary Clarke, sister of Emmeline Pankhurst, and Cecilia Wolseley Haig both died as a result of 'Black Friday'.

1912: The 'Cat and Mouse' Act is enacted in Britain, allowing the government to temporarily discharge women prisoners hunger striking for the vote – until they were fit enough to be imprisoned again.

January 1913: The first sickness and maternity payments were made under the new National Insurance Act. However, the act only guaranteed the family of an insured worker an income if he was off sick, but while her husband had access to free or assisted medical care, a wife and her children did not. There was not even medical care during pregnancy and childbirth.

June 1913: Emily Davison, a member of the WSPU, died as a result of injuries sustained when she stepped out in front of the King's horse in the Derby to draw attention to the cause of female suffrage.

June 1913: Emily Dawson was appointed the first woman magistrate in Britain.

August 1914: The outbreak of the First World War put on hold all claims and possibilities of women's suffrage.

1915: The first Women's Institute in Britain was founded at Llanfairpwll in North Wales.

October 1916: Ethyl Byrne and Margaret Sanger opened the first birth-control clinic in the USA. They were later arrested and convicted for running the clinic.

1918: The Maternal and Child Welfare Act was passed enabling local authorities to provide services such as welfare clinics and health visitors.

February 1918: Women over the age of 30 are granted the right to vote subject to some property qualifications.

July 1918: Marie Stopes published her controversial book *Married Love*, which suggested that sex could and should be a pleasure for both men and women.

November 1918: The House of Commons passed the Parliament (Qualification of Women) Act to allow women over 27 to stand as Parliamentary candidates.

December 1918: The first General Election in which women could vote and stand as candidates took place on the 28th. Of the 1,600 candidates, only 17 were women and only one was elected. She was Constance Markiewicz ,who stood for Sinn Fein and refused to take her seat in the House of Commons.

December 1919: Nancy Astor became the first woman to sit in the House of Commons.

January 1921: The first women undertook jury service in a Divorce Court.

1922: Rose Witcop, a socialist and women's rights campaigner, was prosecuted and found guilty of producing an obscene work when she published US birth control pioneer Margaret Sanger's *Family Limitation*.

August 1922: A one-day Olympiad for women athletes was held in Paris.

February 1923: A bill was passed making married women responsible for any crimes they committed in their husbands' presence. Previously husbands were deemed responsible for offences their wives might commit in their presence on the assumption that the wife was coerced by her husband into acting criminally.

May 1929: The first General Election in which women had an equal franchise returned 13 women MPs.

June1929: Labour Prime Minister Ramsay MacDonald named Margaret Bondfield as Minister of Labour. She was the first woman member of a British Cabinet.

July 1936: The Midwives Act was passed. This instructed local authorities to provide a service of trained midwives available to every expectant mother, whatever her circumstances.

December 1941: Parliament passed a second National Service Act which widened the scope of conscription by making all unmarried women and all childless widows between the ages of 20 and 30 liable to call-up.

1948: A new Nationality Act allowed a woman marrying an 'alien' to keep her nationality unless she took steps to change it.

5 July 1948: The introduction of the National Health Service gave everyone free access to healthcare.

February 1952: Princess Elizabeth is proclaimed Queen following the death of her father, King George VI.

1956: Women civil servants, teachers and local government workers were awarded equal rates of pay with their male colleagues.

April 1958: The Church of England gave its blessing to the use of artificial methods of birth control, accepting the idea of planning the number of children and frequency of their birth as a moral one.

1958: The Life Peerages Act entitles women to sit in the House of Lords for the first time. Baroness Swanborough, Lady Reading and Baroness Barbara Wooton were the first to take their seats. Women who inherited peerages could not sit in the Lords.

June 1963: Lieutenant Valentina Tereshkova, a Russian cosmonaut, became the first woman in space when she orbited the earth in a spaceship.

July 1964: The first Brook Advisory Clinic opened giving birth-control advice to unmarried couples.

1967: MP David Steel sponsored an Abortion Law Reform Bill, which became the Abortion Act. Technically the law did not legalise abortions but provided a legal defence for those carrying them out under certain conditions.

1968: Epidural pain relief was first introduced for women during childbirth.

February 1970: The House of Commons gave an unopposed second reading to the Equal Pay Bill which said that women and men doing the same job would have to be given the same rates of pay by January 1976.

1972: Erin Pizzey set up the first women's refuge in Chiswick.

1974: Contraception became available through the National Health Service.

1975: The Sex Discrimination Act made it illegal to discriminate against women in work, education and training.

1975: The Employment Protection Act was passed giving women the right to maternity leave with some pay and for their job to be held open for 29 weeks after the birth.

February 1975: Margaret Thatcher, described as the wife of a wealthy businessman and mother of twins, was elected leader of the Conservative Party.

1976: The Equal Opportunities Commission came into effect to oversee the Equal Pay Act and Sex Discrimination Act.

1977: The first rape crisis centre opens in London.

June 1978: The Inland Revenue announced that future correspondence about wives' tax affairs and any rebates owed to them would be sent to them and not their husbands.

May 1979: Margaret Thatcher, MP for Finchley, became the first woman Prime Minister of Britain when the Conservatives won the General Election.

1980: Women can apply for credit or loans in their own name without the signature of their husbands.

1981: The House of Lords had its first woman leader when Baroness Young was appointed.

November 1981: The Church of England Synod voted overwhelmingly in favour of admitting women to Holy Orders as deacons, enabling them to conduct weddings, funerals and baptisms but not to give Holy Communion.

1982: Thousands of women gathered at Greenham Common to protest against American missiles sited there. The camp would remain open for 19 years.

August 1984: The first Women's Olympic Marathon was run at the Los Angeles Games.

1985: The Equal Pay (Amendment) Act is passed, entitling women to be paid the same as men for work of equal value.

1990: Independent taxation for women is introduced. For the first time married women are taxed separately from their husbands.

1990: The 1967 Abortion Act was amended by the Human Fertilisation and Embryology Act, which reduced the original time limit of 28 weeks to 24 weeks for most abortions

November 1990: Margaret Thatcher was ousted as leader of the Conservative Party and Prime Minister. She was succeeded by John Major who announced a cabinet devoid of women although women were promoted to many advisory roles.

March 1991: A husband was found guilty of raping his wife and the judge, Lord Lane, said, 'The time has now arrived when the law should declare that a rapist remains a rapist subject to the criminal law, irrespective of his relationship with his victim.'

May 1991: Women workers forced to retire from their jobs at the age of 60 under British law were granted the right to compensation for the loss of earnings up to the age of 65 by the European Court, as Britain had agreed to equal employment laws but had not brought them onto the statute book.

1991: MI5 appointed Stella Rimmington as its first female head.

1992: Betty Boothroyd, Labour MP for West Bromwich, is elected as first female Speaker of the House of Commons, a role she fulfilled until 2000.

March 1994: Seven years after the Synod voted overwhelmingly in favour of the ordination of women, Angela Berners-Wilson was first of 32 women ordained as Church of England vicars.

1995: Pauline Clare was appointed Chief Constable for Lancashire, the first woman to hold this rank.

May 1997: 120 female MPs were elected to Parliament, the highest number to date and double the total returned in 1992.

2003: Brenda Hale became Britain's first female law lord and in 2009 tranferred to the Supreme Court.

2013: An act of Parliament came into force which meant that male children did not take precedence over female children in the royal line of succession.

2014: Nicola Sturgeon became the first female First Minister of Scotland.

January 2015: Twenty-one years after the ordination of the first female Anglican priest in Britain, Libby Lane was consecrated as a bishop in the Church of England.

Published by Atlantic Publishing 2015

Atlantic Publishing
38 Copthorne Road
Croxley Green, Hertfordshire, WD3 4AQ

© Atlantic Publishing

Photographs © Associated Newspapers Archive except the following:
9; 13; 29; 127 left and centre; 129; 132 top and bottom; 133; 134 top left, top centre, bottom
right and left; 136 top and bottom; 137; 138; 139, 140 (except top left) © Getty Images
Main front cover image © Conde Nast Archive/Corbis

A catalogue record for this book is available from the British Library.

ISBN 978-1-909242-18-0

Printed and bound in the UK

Acknowledgements:
The photographs in this book are from the archives of the Daily Mail.
Particular thanks to: Steve Torrington, Dave Sheppard, Brian Jackson, Alan Pinnock and all the staff.